Understanding Research in the Social Sciences

A practical guide to understanding social and behavioral research

CURTIS HARDYCK
University of California, Berkeley

LEWIS F. PETRINOVICH
University of California, Riverside

1975
W. B. SAUNDERS COMPANY
Philadelphia • London • Toronto

W. B. Saunders Company: West Washington Square
Philadelphia, PA   19105

12 Dyott Street
London, WC1A   1DB

833 Oxford Street
Toronto, Ontario M8Z 5T9, Canada

Library of Congress Cataloging in Publication Data

Hardyck, Curtis D

Understanding research in the social sciences.

(Saunders books in psychology)

Includes index.

1. Social science research.   2. Sociological research.
   I. Petrinovich, Lewis F., joint author.   II. Title.

H62.H2563   300'.7'2   74–6685

ISBN 0–7216–4518–6

Understanding Research in the Social Sciences   ISBN   0-7216-4518-6

Last digit is the print number: 9   8   7   6   5   4   3   2   1

To

HENRY AND HELEN HARDYCK

and

JOHN AND OLLIE KATE PETRINOVICH

preface

A great many people contribute to the writing of a book; some knowingly, some not. The idea for this book originated with the first author one winter afternoon while listening to a colleague tell him at great length about how she had been mistreated by the university administration. The connection between her narrative and the germination of this book was unanalyzeable then and remains so now. This colleague is certainly deserving of thanks, although, given the circumstances, she would probably prefer to remain anonymous, as she will.

Of equal importance and anonymity are two of the five reviewers of the first manuscript submitted to the publisher. Two of the reviews were mildly favorable, one was petulantly opposed, and one was so devastating in its detailed criticism as to provoke homicidal thoughts in both authors. However, after a cooling-off period, that reviewer's comments stimulated a drastic and extensive revision, resulting in a greatly improved manuscript. A fifth review, following the drastic revision, resulted in still more changes and modifications. We owe much to these two constructively critical reviewers.

Not all influences are positive. Much of the first draft of this book was written in the summer of 1971 in the village of Lindos, Rhodes, Greece, where an especially hot summer made typing after 11 A.M. as much an exercise in not dripping sweat into the typewriter as in composing. Among negative influences, the Island customs authorities deserve special mention for impounding needed reference books—statistics texts—for five weeks while examining them for possible subversive content. Other influences (divorce, foreign travels, and similar vagaries of modern life) conspired to delay the completion of this work until the present date.

Fortunately, many contributions are positive and can be identified. Baxter Venable, Psychology Editor for the W. B. Saunders Company, was both encouraging and supportive. Professor Robert Singer, the consulting editor, deserves thanks for his help on numerous occasions.

We would like to thank Professors Ramon J. Rhine, Sarah J. Hill, Susan E. Wandruff, Leonard A. Marascuilo, Kathleen Penfield, David L. Rosenhan, William D. Rohwer, Jr., Steve Lynch, Alan S. Kaufman, and Nadeen L. Kaufman for permitting us to reprint from their published work and comment on it. We are grateful to the trustees of *Biometrika,* who permitted us to paraphrase a 1930 publication by "Student."

Professors William Rohwer and Leonard Marascuilo also assisted the authors by abridging their articles and by reviewing our commentary. Professor Henry Kaiser reviewed our chapter on factor analysis and Professor Roy Goldman our chapter on multivariate analysis, and we would like to express our gratitude. A special note of thanks is due Professor Marida Hollos, who, in addition to permitting us to quote from her field studies of Norway, reviewed the chapter on field observational methods and allowed us to use her research data for the majority of examples in our chapter on multivariate statistical methods.

Typing a book containing symbols is a constant battle against error. For producing an error-free manuscript and also for spotting errors we overlooked, we are most appreciative of Edith Lavin's help.

Usually a preface has something to say about the purpose of the book. However, we are firmly committed to the belief that no one ever reads a preface. The purpose of this book will be made clear in Chapter 1.

CURTIS HARDYCK
LEWIS PETRINOVICH

Carthage, Tunisia
Estridge Estate, Mount Misery, St. Kitts, British West Indies

contents

chapter one

on understanding research publications

© 1967 United Features Syndicate, Inc.

Today, research on human behavior is of interest to individuals in a large number of diverse fields. The undergraduate may want to read psychology or anthropology research reports before he has had formal training in research methods. The classroom teacher is interested in research that will aid in the improvement of teaching methods. Social workers and public health workers actively seek information that will help them to carry out their jobs more effectively. Research on mental health problems is of use to psychiatric technicians and nurses as well as psychotherapists and physicians.

Similarly, individuals with formal research training may seek information from other disciplines. The anthropologist may want to know whether or not phenomena he has noted in certain cultures have been studied using experimental methods. The political scientist with knowledge of survey techniques may wish to understand conclusions based on experimental studies of social movements.

While such information is readily available in professional journals and books, it may be quite difficult to understand the manner in which the information is reported. Experiments require controls and measurement, and the results of experimental studies are usually reported in terms of inferences based on statistical calculations.

Although the social scientists' professional colleagues may benefit from the publication of new insights into human behavior and social movements, the professional in related fields who is concerned with applying the results of experimental and survey findings to his own professional field is often left out in the cold. The political scientist who sees the relevance of survey material to his field is faced with the problem of learning an exhaustive amount about survey design and sampling techniques in order to understand the material as it is usually reported. The nursery school teacher, the pediatric public health worker, or the nurse interested in research in child development soon finds that much potentially interesting and useful information is presented in terms of a complex experimental design, hedged about with statistics of a complexity not even hinted at in an introductory statistics course.

The individual whose experience with statistics is nonexistent, or whose knowledge is limited to an introductory course taken some years ago, frequently finds the statistical presentation of research findings to be beyond his understanding and gives up in disgust or apathy. He may well conclude that the information would be of use to him, but that he has neither the time nor the inclination to acquire the skills that would allow him to understand technical research material.

An intermediate level of proficiency *is* possible, however. Very few individuals could design and build an internal combustion engine, a radio, or an electrical appliance. However, most individuals do know how to use these devices, and with some study could develop a reasonable grasp of the theoretical principles underlying their operation. Similarly, it is possible to understand the logic of statistics and experimental design without being able to carry out calculations or to design experiments.

Before beginning this book, you should be clear on what may be accomplished by studying it. This book is *not* written for the individual who wishes to learn how to design and carry out research. Numerous texts for this purpose already exist.[1] In addition to studying texts, one can best learn to do research by engaging in an active apprenticeship with qualified research workers and by carrying out research work and submitting it for the commentary and criticism of others.

This book will attempt to provide you with the knowledge necessary to become an intelligent and critical reader of research in the social and behavioral sciences. Hopefully, after finishing it you will be able to read much of the research literature in the social and behavioral sciences with some understanding of what is being communicated in the technical shorthand that social scientists use to describe experiments. You will not know much more about how to calculate statistics than you did before you began, and it is doubtful that you will have any great skill in designing experiments as a result of the discussions presented here. However, you should know more about how to interpret statistics as they are presented in the majority of social science publications and should understand the principles an experimenter or a survey research worker adheres to in designing his studies. This will allow you, within limits, to reach an independent decision concerning the validity of the statements made by a research worker about the meaning of his findings.

Reading this book will not enable you to understand every variety of research report you may encounter. The number and variety of statistical techniques is constantly increasing, and a comprehensive account, particularly at a beginning level, is an impossible task. We have chosen to limit our presentation to the logic underlying the most commonly used methods in the social sciences.

Undoubtedly some teachers of research methods will object to our approach as being oversimplified and will argue that we are ignoring many aspects they find to be important. Our opinion is that individuals not intend-

ing to do research are much better off with a good overview of the basic principles applicable to understanding a variety of research as reported than with
detailed knowledge of statistical models or calculation methods. The effect of
social sciences research on our society is potentially as far-reaching as that of
any discoveries in the physical sciences, and much of this effect will be
brought about by individuals who attempt to apply the results of research to
problems plaguing society. Our social progress will be much more satisfactory
if these individuals are prepared to critically understand social science research.

FOOTNOTES

[1]In our opinion, one of the best of many such texts is *Foundations of Behavioral
Research* (2nd ed.), by F. N. Kerlinger. (New York, Holt, Rinehart & Winston, 1973.)

chapter two

evaluating an experiment: a first example

"Apple fall thirty-two feet per second per second."
Drawing by Robt. Day. © 1973 The New Yorker Magazine, Inc.

Perhaps the simplest definition of an experiment is that it is a question asked under controlled conditions. In an experiment you have a set of conditions that enable the researcher to discover the effects of some change he has introduced on a particular phenomenon. The object is to try and specify a cause and effect relationship as precisely as possible under a known set of conditions.

As an illustration, look at the converse situation — an inquiry under everyday, uncontrolled circumstances. Townsend, in his book on research methods,[1] illustrates this point with the example of a man being killed in an automobile accident. Inquiry after the accident reveals the following facts:

1. The accident happened on a night when it was raining heavily.
2. The driver of the car had been drinking heavily for some hours prior to the accident.
3. The driver of the car had been arguing with his wife and appeared to observers to be in a towering rage.
4. The automobile was in poor mechanical condition, with tires that were worn smooth and faulty brakes.

What was the cause of this accident? The inclement weather? Impaired judgment and reactions due to alcohol? Extreme emotional tension affecting judgments? The faulty mechanical condition of the automobile? Clearly, under the existing circumstances, it is impossible to specify one cause of the accident.

This somewhat gruesome example illustrates the conditions that are to be avoided in an experiment. Ideally in an experiment, all the conditions are known and are under the control of the experimenter, so that a definite cause and effect relationship can be established. Although this state of affairs is difficult to attain, especially in studying human behavior, it still represents an ideal standard for performing an experiment, even though it may not be the only or the best way to understand complex behavior.

Before proceeding, a few terms that are commonly used in discussions of experiments should be explained. We have already mentioned *controls* in our opening discussion. Controls in an experiment refer to those precautions an experimenter takes to insure that conditions that may affect his results are minimized. For example, someone interested in the effects of a particular drug on the learning ability of animals might collect three dogs, four cats, five white rats, and a duck, all of unknown age, background, and health, and set about to determine whether injecting them with the drug improves their ability to learn. The results obtained could not be taken very seriously. Under such circumstances, nothing could be concluded, except perhaps that the research worker did not understand how to do experiments.

Assuming that such factors as age, prior experience, health, species, amount of the drug, diet, and the task to be learned all have potential effects on the subject under study, an experimenter should take the following precautions to control for these factors:

1. Select animals of a given species.
2. Select animals that vary as little as possible in age and that have been raised under known conditions of health and diet and have not been used in any other experiment.
3. Select a learning task appropriate to the animals' capacities.
4. Carry out preliminary tests to determine the amount of the drug to administer or, even better, use several groups of animals, giving each group a different amount of the drug.
5. Assign the animals to the various groups to be studied on a completely chance basis so that any animal may be put in any group. (This is known as *random assignment* and will be discussed in more detail in later chapters.)
6. One group of animals should be given no drug but should be subjected to exactly the same procedures as the animals in the group given the drugs. For example, if the drug is injected into the animals by means of a hypodermic, the group of animals given no drug should also receive injections of some substance known to have no effect, for example, distilled water. Such a group is known as a *control group,* and its purpose is simply to control for the effects of the experimental procedure itself.

In the terminology used in experimental design, the administering of the drug is known as the *experimental treatment*; if several different amounts of a drug are given to different groups of animals, it is known as *levels of experimental treatment.* The group actually given the experimental treatment is known as the *experimental group.* If there are several *levels of experimental treatment,* there will be several *experimental groups.*

Three other concepts need to be introduced and defined before proceeding:

1. Variables (dependent, independent, and extraneous)
2. Hypothesis
3. Experimental validity (internal and external)

In experimental terminology, *variables* refer to the attributes under study, specifically, those qualities that may show change as a result of the experimental treatment. In the example given earlier of the effects of drugs on learning, the primary variables are the drug and the learning. The drug is known as the *independent* variable. In an experiment, the independent variable (here, the amount of the drug) is what is varied by the experimenter. The effect (the amount learned by the animal), however measured, is known as the *dependent* variable. *Extraneous* variables are those which might affect the determination of the relationship between the drug and the measurement of learning. Some extraneous variables, such as age, health, and prior experiences, were mentioned earlier when the concept of control was introduced. In a well-designed experiment, control of extraneous variables is at a maximum, allowing as precise a specification of the relationship between independent and dependent variables as possible.

A *hypothesis* is a prediction of what will happen in an experiment and how the results will come out. For example, the experimenter doing the drug study may hypothesize that animals given the experimental drug will learn a given task in fewer trials, or require less time than the control animals. An additional hypothesis could be that the speed of learning will continue to increase as larger amounts of the drug are given, up to some amount above which there is no increase in learning speed.

There is a wide range within which the term "hypothesis" is useable. A hypothesis may be no more than the experimenter's best guess as to what will happen, especially if the area under study is a new field of inquiry, or it may represent a carefully reasoned and elaborately specified prediction based on a long series of previous experiments and a detailed theory. However, regardless of what it represents in terms of precision, a hypothesis is what is tested in an experiment.

Experimental validity refers to the meaningfulness of the experiment. To ask the extent to which an experiment has *internal validity* is to ask whether the results—the effects of the experimental treatment—are due to the treatment rather than to some extraneous variables. For example, if you are puzzled by the results of an experiment, it is perfectly appropriate to entertain questions about the meaningfulness of the experimental treatment and procedure. In other words, does it seem reasonable to you that (1) the experimenter's treatments resulted in the difference he found and (2) that this difference occurred for the reasons he claims? If not, perhaps other factors of which the experimenter was unaware may have affected his results. In most instances it would be necessary to repeat the experiment to find out if you were right, but such speculations and doubts on your part are perfectly appropriate, as is your right to suggest other hypotheses which might explain the experimental findings.

The *external validity* of an experiment refers to whether the findings can be generalized beyond a specific experimental situation. For example, in an experiment it might be found that the sexes differ on the dependent variable as a result of the experimental treatment. As an illustration, suppose that a medical research group found that a drug developed to reduce high blood pressure was more effective on the women studied than on the men. Does this suggest a general sex difference in the area of study? Or is the result such that it has no meaning outside the specific group being studied? If you were to read an experiment carried out on mental hospital patients in which the experimenter discusses his findings as though they applied to all mankind, you might justifiably raise the question of external validity. While the experimental findings may be true for the group studied, their validity when applied to all people must be established by further experimentation.

As the next step in learning to evaluate experiments, you are asked to read the following research report. Reprinted as originally published in *Child Development* in 1967 it was selected because (1) it is on a topic of general interest to almost everyone, (2) the presentation is reasonably straightforward, and (3) some knowledge of experimental design and statistical methods is necessary to fully understand the article. Interpretive comments explaining the general format as well as specific points of the report are inserted throughout. The article and our accompanying commentary are intended to serve as an introduction to some of the problems you will face in seeking to understand social sciences research. The comments are necessarily brief, and most of the items commented on will be discussed in more detail in the chapters to follow.

Perhaps one word of caution should be added. This research report is fairly straightforward and clearly written. You may not always be so fortunate in other studies you may encounter. Many published accounts of experiments require considerable background reading if one is to understand the conceptual basis of the research. This preparation may be necessary to understand the relationship of the original questions posed, the experimental manipulations used, and the final inference drawn from the obtained results. Also, if a research report is turgid, obscure, excessively pedantic, or presented in an idiosyncratic fashion, no book can help you to follow it. You will have to decide for yourself whether the material communicated is worth the effort required to dig it out.

Evaluative Responses of Preschool Children

RAMON J. RHINE, SARAH J. HILL, and SUSAN E. WANDRUFF, University of California, Riverside

The abstract concepts good and bad are loaded with evaluative meaning. Evaluation is important as an ingredient of attitude learning, and the child's understanding of good and bad is also significant in early personality development. 50 children, aged 2–6 were shown 12 sets of multiple-choice pictures. Each set of 4 alternatives contained 1 good activity, or 1 bad activity, or all neutral activities. The growth in the ability of the child to select the loaded pictures is a regular curve starting at chance near age 2 and approaching

The cooperation of Mrs. Marian Fedri and Mrs. Shirley Brooks of the March Air Force Children's Nursery is gratefully acknowledged. This research received partial support from an intramural grant from the University of California, Riverside. Author Rhine's address: Psychology Department, University of California, Riverside, California 92502.

the point of all correct near age 6. Bad pictures are more readily identified than good at all ages beyond 2 years, 5 months. The results are discussed in relation to the children's language capacity. It is suggested that bad is acquired before good because early socialization provides a concept-formation environment more fitting to the learning of bad.

Most research reports begin with a short abstract, written by the authors, giving a capsule statement of hypotheses, procedures, results, and interpretation. Occasionally the initial abstract is replaced by a summary at the end of the article.

The growth of evaluative behavior is important in attitude and personality theories. It is often assumed that much of the basic framework of personality is laid down before the child reaches the age of 6. The theory of superego development rests on the assumption that the young child can discriminate good (via rewards) from bad (via punishments). Acquisition of the concepts *good* and *bad* is implicit in the idea of a developed conscience that enables a child to regulate his own behavior without outside agents.

Most research reports begin by briefly stating the general area of interest with which the research is concerned. References to theories relevant to the problem might also be included in the introductory remarks.

This research examines the growth of the concepts *good* and *bad* during the critical ages of 2–6. These concepts were chosen to represent evaluative response for two reasons. First, they probably reflect evaluation as well as any other concepts in American culture. The good-bad scale of the semantic differential is highly correlated with a general evaluative factor (Jenkins, Russell, & Suci, 1958; Osgood & Suci, 1955). Second, *good* and *bad*, probably to a greater degree than other highly evaluative concepts like *kind-cruel* or *beautiful-ugly*, are concepts with which quite young children are repeatedly bombarded. Hence, *good* and *bad* are probably among the evaluative concepts earliest understood by children.

The next section of the paper delineates and outlines the particular aspect of the problem on which the research is focused. In this study, the ability of pre-school children to apply the concepts "good" and "bad" to specific behavior situations is examined in relation to the age of the children.

The words *good* and *bad* are considered verbal concepts when their meaning is understood, regardless of whether or not these words exist in the child's spoken vocabulary. Verbal concepts are of particular significance. Verbalized concepts represent mediational processes which make possible wide generalization. Once a concept like *good* is verbalized, previously unexperienced objects can receive a modicum of understanding the moment they are labeled with the concept name. Perhaps nonverbal learning provides the earliest rudiments of evaluation. The child acquires affective responses and approach and avoidance behavior prior to language. Nevertheless, the growth of verbal evaluative concepts is important in its own right.

The experimenters take pains here to define what they mean by the term "verbal concepts." This is a standard procedure whenever terms that may have a wide range of interpretation are used. It is the responsibility of the experimenter to provide explanations and definitions of any terms that he wishes understood in a specific or limited way.

METHOD

Subjects and Materials

The subjects were 25 boys and 25 girls attending an Air Force nursery school. They ranged in age from 26 months to 70 months. The boys' average age was 50.04 months and the girls' was 48.96 months.

> *It is customary in research reports to describe the sample in enough detail so that anyone reading the article will have a clear idea of what kind of people participated as subjects. In this respect, this article is not as specific as might be desired. We learn later in the article that the fathers are both officers and enlisted men, but no other information, such as average education of the parents, is provided. Exactly how important such information is in evaluating the results is largely a function of the problem under study. However, a research report that provides little information about the sample of subjects studied should be scrutinized carefully. As an illustration, in the present report, no mention is made of how the subjects were selected; it might be important to know whether or not all children in the school were included in the study, whether or not the children volunteered, and so forth.*

The children were shown line drawings on plain 6 × 9-inch cards.* Among these cards were eight pictures of children engaging in activities commonly considered bad, eight of good activities, and forty of neutral activities which were neither obviously good nor bad. Activities represented in loaded pictures were modeled after situations which children commonly experience, and their final design was determined on the basis of information obtained in a preliminary study. Preliminary pictures were modified or replaced if they elicited ambiguous evaluative responses, contained activities that were not understood, or failed to elicit evaluative responses.

> *This section describes the materials used. Such descriptions should be succinct, but with enough detail so that the reader has a clear picture of what was done. One rule of thumb is that the descriptions of materials and procedures should be detailed enough for another investigator to repeat the study in its essential procedures.*
> *Although ideally a research report should contain all the information necessary for another research worker to repeat the study, the cost of publishing such detailed accounts usually is prohibitive. These authors have deposited copies of their experimental materials with the American Documentation Institute (ADI), thus allowing any research worker who wishes to examine their research material in detail to write and obtain photocopies. (See footnote, below.)*

As each picture was shown to the child it was described briefly. Each description started with the words, "This little boy (girl) is . . ." The standard descriptions indicate the

---

*Material supplementary to this article has been deposited as Document No. 9621 with the ADI Auxiliary Publications Project, Photoduplication Service, Library of Congress, Washington, D.C. 20540. A copy may be secured by citing the document number and by remitting $2.50 for photoprints, or $1.75 for 35 mm. microfilm. Advance payment is required. Make checks or money orders payable to: Chief, Photoduplication Service, Library of Congress.

content of the pictures. The remainder of the sentences describing good pictures are as follows: *(a)* cleaning up her room, *(b)* helping his mommy feed the baby, *(c)* getting dressed by himself, *(d)* hugging his sister because her teddy bear is torn, *(e)* hugging his mommy, *(f)* holding the door open for her mommy, *(g)* going to the bathroom in the toilet, not in his pants, and *(h)* helping mommy sweep. The remainder of the sentences describing bad pictures are as follows:*(a)* kicking his dog, *(b)* scribbling on the wall, *(c)* tearing up his book, *(d)* won't go to bed ("won't" replaces "is"), *(e)* chasing his ball into the street, *(f)* taking a toy away from his baby sister, *(g)* messing up the bathroom, and *(h)* trying to take the teddy bear away from a friend. Examples of phrases completing descriptions of neutral pictures are as follows: *(a)* looking out the window, *(b)* standing in the front yard, *(c)* coming through a door, *(d)* walking, *(e)* looking at a butterfly, *(f)* playing tea party, *(g)* eating a banana, and *(h)* sitting in a chair.

Two sets of pictures were constructed. Set A contained four good and four bad pictures chosen randomly from among the eight good and eight bad pictures and also all forty neutral pictures. Set B contained the remaining four good and four bad pictures and the same forty neutral pictures. In set A, each child saw 48 pictures, four at a time. Twelve subsets of four each contained either one good picture and three neutrals, or one bad picture and three neutrals, or four neutrals. Three groups of subsets were devised with different randomly determined positions of good and bad pictures within a subset. The three groups of subsets were used approximately equally often. The order of presentation of the 12 subsets was determined randomly, and was the same for all three groups of subsets. Twenty-five separate random orders were obtained for the forty neutral pictures. When the order of the sets and the position of the good and bad pictures within subsets were determined, an individual random order of neutral pictures was assigned to the remaining forty positions within the 12 subsets.

A parallel ordering was carried out for set B, with all new random orders, except that the same 25 orders for neutral pictures were used again. The 25 orders of set A were randomly assigned, one each to 12 girls and 13 boys, and those of set B to 13 girls and 12 boys.

In the introductory section of this chapter, the concepts of control and extraneous variables were discussed. The procedure described in this section illustrates how one kind of extraneous variable that might affect the results is controlled.

Suppose that all the children were shown the pictures in exactly the same order. Also, since 4 pictures are shown to a child at a time, suppose that the "good" or "bad" picture was always the third picture in a row of 4. Would this make any difference in how the children evaluated the pictures? Perhaps not, but there is the possibility that the order in which the pictures are shown might affect the answers, and thus this variable should be controlled. In this study, control was accomplished by the randomization procedure just described. Such a procedure varies the order in which children see the pictures, eliminating the possibility that the order of presentation might affect the results.

Randomization is one of the most effective procedures an experimenter can use to minimize extraneous variation. In the experiment discussed here, the authors have gone through an exceedingly careful procedure to insure that no effects due to the order of presentation exist. As an illustration of how randomization is done, let us consider the procedure described here in more detail. For example, set A consisted of 48 pictures — 4 good, 4 bad, and 40 neutral. These were further divided into 12 subsets of 4 pictures each, con-

taining either 1 good and 3 neutral pictures; 1 bad and 3 neutral; or 4 neutral. The first step in the randomization process was to assign the position of the good and bad pictures within a subset. A given subset might be represented in the following manner:

		Picture Position			
		I	II	III	IV
Subset No.	1	☐	☐	☐	☐
	2	☐	☐	☐	☐
	3	☐	☐	☐	☐
	4	☐	☐	☐	☐
	5	☐	☐	☐	☐
	6	☐	☐	☐	☐
	7	☐	☐	☐	☐
	8	☐	☐	☐	☐
	9	☐	☐	☐	☐
	10	☐	☐	☐	☐
	11	☐	☐	☐	☐
	12	☐	☐	☐	☐

The first task to be accomplished is the assignment of the 4 good and 4 bad pictures within these 12 rows and 4 positions within each row. The actual mechanics of doing this will not be discussed here. However, random assignment means that every picture has an equal chance of being assigned to a given row and position. There are some restrictions of course. Once a good or bad picture has been placed in a given row, the remaining 3 positions in that row must be filled by neutral pictures. When the procedure of randomization is complete, the results might look like this:

G = "good" picture
B = "bad" picture
N = "neutral" picture

		Picture Position			
		I	II	III	IV
Subset No.	1	N	N	N	N
	2	G	N	N	N
	3	N	N	G	N
	4	N	N	G	N
	5	N	B	N	N
	6	N	N	N	N
	7	N	N	N	N
	8	N	B	N	N
	9	B	N	N	N
	10	N	N	B	N
	11	N	G	N	N
	12	N	N	N	N

Note that in this ordering, no good or bad picture ever ended up in Position IV. This is not surprising, given actual random assignment. In the randomizing of the good and bad pictures in the next subset, it is possible, though not likely, that all eight pictures could end up in Position IV. Sometimes restrictions are placed on randomization, and an experimenter might specify, in this instance, that the "good" and "bad" pictures must appear equally often in each position. Such specifications are permissible since the intent is to attain adequate control of extraneous variables (see Chapter 2, p. 7), and randomization is only one way to attain this end.

Once the positions of the good and bad pictures were fixed, the experimenters then randomized the order in which the 12 rows were presented. As a final step, 25 different random orders of the neutral pictures were determined and the neutral pictures then assigned to the remaining 40 positions.

The net result of this process is as follows: Of the 50 children, only 2 see the same order of presentation of the neutral pictures. Of the subgroup of 25 children seeing the good and bad pictures of set A, no more than 9 children see the good and bad pictures in the same location, and no child sees these pictures in relation to the same neutral pictures. The same is true of the children seeing the good and bad pictures of set B.

This may seem to be a tremendous amount of work to remove what might be a minimal amount of interference and other possible position effects. However, unless such precautions are carried out, the possibility exists that some of the results are simply a function of the order in which the pictures were shown. For example, there might be a tendency to rate a bad picture more if it followed several good pictures. By using the randomization process, the experimenters have eliminated this possibility.

All children were given form L-M of the picture vocabulary test from the Stanford-Binet (Terman & Merrill, 1960) intelligence test. The picture vocabulary test appears at age levels 2, 2 years and 6 months, 3, and 4. It was used as a rough index of verbal capacity.

The use of an item from the Stanford-Binet intelligence test serves as a check on the verbal levels of the children by providing independent evidence that the children possess the verbal skills adequate for the task. If they did not, the results could be meaningless, since there would be no evidence that they really understood the task.

Another consideration in evaluating research of this kind is the manner in which tests are used. It is the responsibility of the researcher to show that the test he uses is appropriate and valid. The test used here is part of a well-known intelligence test for children and seems entirely appropriate for the purposes of the experiment.

Procedure

Each child was tested individually by two female experimenters working together. One experimenter tested the child, while the other recorded his responses and took notes. Each child was asked to come with the experimenter to play a new game. After a brief warmup, the experimenter gave the following standard instructions: "Let's play our game now. I am going to show you some pictures of little boys and little girls. I want you to show me the one who is doing something very good or very bad. Let's begin. In these pictures, somebody is doing something very good (or bad if the set contained a bad picture). Point to the one who is doing something very good (bad)." At this point the first subset of four pictures was laid on the table in front of the child, one at a time, and the standard description of each picture was given. The experimenter said again, "Now point to the one who is doing something very good (bad)." Then the child made his selection. If the child could not arrive at a choice, he was encouraged to guess. The same procedure was repeated for all 12 subsets in a set. For the four subsets of all neutral pictures, the child was told to find the bad picture in two cases and the good picture in the remaining two cases. Whether good or bad was requested was determined randomly. Following the picture choices, the Stanford-Binet (Terman & Merrill, 1960) picture vocabulary test was administered. The whole procedure took approximately one-half hour per child.

> *In reporting research, it is necessary that the procedure used to collect the data be specified in enough detail to allow another experimenter to repeat the experiment with the same procedure.*

RESULTS

Several preliminary analyses were done. Girls correctly identified a mean of 5.24 good and bad pictures, and the boys had a mean of 4.72, a difference producing a $t = 1.03$, $df = 48$, $p > .10$. The mean number of correct choices on sets A and B, respectively, were 5.16 and 4.80 ($t < 1$, $df = 48$, $p > .10$). Whether a child's father was an enlisted man or an officer was taken as a rough index of socioeconomic status. There were 44 children whose father's military rank was known. Officers' children got a mean number of correct choices of 4.93 and enlisted men's a mean of 5.07 ($t < 1$, $df = 42$, $p > .10$). The boys' mean on the picture vocabulary test of 13.04 did not differ significantly from the girls' mean of 12.36 ($t < 1$, $df = 48$, $p > .10$). The picture vocabulary scores indicate that the average mental age of the 23 children up to and including age 48 months (this is the latest age at which the test appears in the Stanford-Binet) was 3.00, and the average chronological age was 3.24, giving a very rough average IQ of 93. Of the 27 children older than 48 months, 14 exceeded the 4-year norm of 14 correct, three equaled the four-year norm, six received scores of 12 or 13, and the remaining four scored between 9 and 11. Although a single Stanford-Binet item is not a very reliable measure of the children's intelligence, there is nothing to indicate that their verbal ability is outside the normal range.

A two-factor analysis was performed with 6-month age intervals as one factor and good or bad pictures as the second. An unweighted means procedure (Winer, 1962, pp. 374–378) was used to take unequal N's into account. The criterion measure was the number of correct responses to the pictures. The difference between age levels is significant ($F = 5, 33$, $df = 7, 42$, $p < .001$). The bad pictures were identified more readily than good at well beyond the .001 level ($F = 21.50$, $df = 1, 42$). There was no significant age by good-bad interaction ($F = 1.16$, $df = 7, 42$, $p > .10$).

> *At this point in the article, some technical knowledge is called for. The term "mean" in this context always refers to the arithmetic mean, a quantity calculated by dividing the sum of a set of values by the number of values. The mean of three scores such as 3, 4, and 5 is found by adding the scores and dividing by the number of scores. The terms t, F, df, p, >, and .10 are all a type of statistical shorthand. The terms t and F refer to particular kinds of statistical tests (the former to the student's t ratio, the latter to the F ratio in analysis of*

variance) used to determine whether the means of 2 or more groups can be considered to differ on a variable. The letters df are shorthand for "degrees of freedom," which, for the t statistic, is 2 less than the number of scores involved. (The t statistic is discussed in greater detail in Chapter 7, p. 104; the F ratio is discussed in Chapter 8, p. 117.) The letter p stands for probability; the sign ">" is the mathematical symbol for "greater than"; "<" is the mathematical symbol for "less than"; and ".10" is the numerical value of the probability. The probability of an event is simply the number of times it is expected to occur relative to the total number of possible events. Probability may range from .00 (zero probability — the event never occurs) to 1.00 (the event always occurs). In the present context, probability is evaluated relative to what could be expected on the basis of random chance occurrence. The statement "t = 1.03, df = 48, p > .10" translates to: the value of the t statistic as calculated is 1.03 with 48 degrees of freedom. The probability of obtaining this value of t by sheer chance alone is greater than .10. This means that if this experiment were to be repeated 100 times, we would expect a calculated value of the t statistic at least this large more than 10 times out of 100 by chance alone. Since the agreed upon convention usually used by statisticians is that a difference should be expected to occur by chance alone with a probability of no more than .05, this difference between boys and girls is not a meaningful one — it is too likely to have occurred by chance rather than as a function of the variable under consideration.

By now, especially if you have no training at all in statistics, you may be quite confused. However, don't give up yet. The background necessary to interpret these statements and discussion of the specific types of statistical measures you may encounter are given in the chapters to follow.

As a preliminary exercise, try interpreting the underlined statement in the second paragraph of the "Results" section. Leaving aside the question of the nature of the statistic represented by the letter F, try interpreting the probability statement. If you come to the conclusion that the value of an F this large or larger is one that would occur less than 1 time out of 1000 by chance, and that this difference is then accepted as a real one, you are on the right track.

The relation between age and correct responses is depicted in Figure 1. The lines in the figure were fitted to the regularly rising points. The points for identification of bad pictures start near chance (one out of four) and progress to completely correct responses at the upper end. The points for identifying good pictures also start near chance and progress upward. Except for the youngest age, more identifications of bad than good occurred throughout the range of ages studied. At the highest level good was still not as easily identified as bad, but the children averaged over three out of four correct responses. For each point in Figure 1, individual *t* tests were made of the hypothesis that more identifications occurred than would be expected by chance. For good, all points from and including 48–53 months or greater are significant beyond the .05 level, whereas the points for earlier ages are not. For bad, all points except the youngest age group are significant beyond the .01 level.

It is common practice to depict the results of an experiment by using numerical tables or graphs. These present the results in an interest-

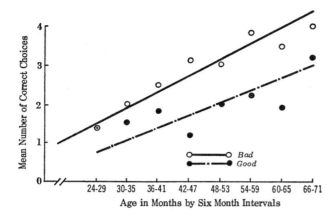

ing form that can be grasped with a minimum amount of effort by the reader.

The regression equation for good predicts a chance result at 31.86 months, and the equation for bad predicts a similar result at 18.32 months.

Regression (prediction) equations are discussed in Chapter 9, pp. 150–151.

The extent to which there were more bad identifications than good is striking, as may be seen from Table 1. There were more correct responses to any bad picture compared with any good one. The results for all bad pictures are significant beyond the .001 level and also for good pictures a, b, e, and h. Good pictures d and f show significant results beyond .02, and c beyond .05. Only one good picture, g, fails to reach the .05 level.

Pictures g and c were correctly identified least often, and they have an interesting similarity. These are the only pictures in which a child is shown partially undressed (genitals not shown). It is possible that the sexual content creates a conflict such that the activity is less likely to be seen as good despite the description. If so, the occurrence of more bad identifications than good might rest entirely on the sexual aspect of these two pictures. Therefore, we obtained individual average scores for good and bad pictures, with pictures c and g omitted, and then found the difference between the average good and bad scores for each child. Eliminating ties, bad pictures were more readily identified than good for 30 out of 37 children, a figure significant beyond the .01 level by a two-tailed sign test.

One and two-tailed tests are discussed in Chapter 8, p. 117. The sign test is discussed in Chapter 8, p. 143.

Table 1 indicates that the good and bad pictures do indeed contain material seen by children as good or bad. These results may be compared to responses to the forty neutral

TABLE 1   Correct and Incorrect Choices by Individual Pictures*

SCORE	GOOD PICTURES								BAD PICTURES							
	a	b	c	d	e	f	g	h	a	b	c	d	e	f	g	h
Correct	15	13	10	11	15	11	6	14	17	19	18	22	21	21	20	16
Incorrect	10	12	15	14	10	14	19	11	8	6	7	3	4	4	5	9

*Letters identifying pictures correspond to the letters for picture descriptions given under "Method."

pictures when used in the four subsets with exclusively neutral pictures. Four-fold tables were constructed with "chosen" and "not chosen" as columns, and the experimenter's request of the child, "asking for good" or "asking for bad," as rows. Fisher's exact test was applied for each picture separately to determine if a given neutral picture was chosen more or less often when a good picture was requested than when a bad one was requested. Of the forty tests, one picture reached the .05 level and one the .025 level, indicating that the neutral pictures as a whole, unlike the loaded pictures, were neither obviously good nor bad.

> *Fisher's exact test is another test used to evaluate the probability of obtaining a given difference on the basis of chance alone. This test is discussed in Chapter 8, p. 141. Different statistical tests are used in different situations because the data to be compared are often in different forms. In one situation we may have changes in magnitude, such as differing scores on a test. In another situation, we may have measurements of frequency, such as the number of people who answer "yes" to a question. The form of the data determines the type of permissible statistical analyses that can be used. Also, different statistical tests are required according to the nature of the questions we are asking of the data.*

DISCUSSION

There are two main findings. First, understanding of the verbal concept *bad* appears to come into cognitive focus around the age of 2, or possibly earlier, and to be well acquired by 6. The concept *good* is understood during the ages of 3 and 4 years and is well acquired by 6. Intuitively, the third and fourth years may seem surprisingly late for the occurrence of the concept, but it should be remembered that we are dealing with a verbal concept. Approach and avoidance responses, which no doubt appear earlier, might give the mistaken impression that the concept is also acquired.

It is possible that the steady growth of the concepts is due to a difference in the capacity of children of various ages to understand the instructions and picture descriptions. The children were not required to talk at all. They had only to understand the instructions and descriptions and point to one of four pictures. The instructions and picture descriptions were not very complex. They may be compared to those at the 2-year level of the Stanford-Binet (Terman & Merrill, 1960) which include the following: "now put them back into their holes"; "put your finger on the dog"; and, "look, I'm going to hide the kitty and then see if you can find it again."

Even the youngest children must have understood at least part of the instructions, for they had no difficulty in understanding they were to point to one of the four pictures. If differences in the capacity of children to understand the instructions produce the curves in Figure 1, then it is likely that these curves reflect at the same time differences in the understanding of good and bad. The basic instruction was "point to the one who is doing something very good (bad)." "Point" was understood, and it is difficult to see how differential understanding of the remainder of the words, *without good (bad)*, would produce the curves.

A second possibility is that the growth curve merely represents increasing experience with the activities depicted. The children at all age levels tested may have acquired the concepts *good* and *bad,* and they may have understood the instructions and descriptions, but the younger children might not recognize the pictures as specific instances of the concepts. Perhaps this is true to some extent, but the pictures represent activities common in the experience of middle-class American children. They were constructed on the basis of preliminary tests of a variety of children's activities. It is particularly unlikely that the growth from age 3 forward is attributable solely to lack of experience with the situations depicted.

The second main finding is that the concept *bad* appears to be acquired earlier than *good*. This is seen from the analysis of the growth curves. Kohlberg (1963) has postulated six stages of moral development, the first being punishment and obedience orientation and the third being good-boy morality. Recognition of bad activities before good is in line with Kohlberg's views, for punishment and demands for obedience are major sources from which the concept *bad* is derived.

Although our data do not permit us to pinpoint the reason for more identifications of bad than good, it seems probable that feedback will occur for a higher proportion of instances of the concept *bad* than *good*. The activities continuously drawn to the child's attention, often with the accompaniment of considerable affect, are the behaviors of which his elders disapprove. It would drive an adult to distraction if he tried to tell the child everything that was not bad. Consequently, the concept *bad* should be more firmly acquired at an early age than the concept *good*.

Finally, the meaning of the obtained results is discussed in terms of the original question posed in the introduction. Alternative explanations of the findings are also considered and, in this case, argued against.

REFERENCES

Jenkins, J. J., Russell, W. A., & Suci, G. J. An atlas of semantic profiles for 360 words. *American Journal of Psychology*, 1958, **71**, 688–699.
Kohlberg, L. The development of children's orientations toward a moral order: I: Sequence in the development of moral thought. *Vita Humana*, 1963, **6**, 11–33.
Osgood, C. E., & Suci, G. J. Factor analysis of meaning. *Journal of Experimental Psychology*, 1955, **50**, 325–338.
Terman, L. M., & Merrill, M. A. *Stanford-Binet intelligence test*. Boston: Houghton Mifflin, 1960.
Winer, B. J. *Statistical principles in experimental design*. New York: McGraw-Hill, 1962.

THE EVALUATION OF RESULTS

At this point, after reading the research report and accompanying commentary, it is appropriate to ask: How good is this work? Do the conclusions seem justified from the results? Are the procedures and materials used appropriate to the problem as stated? Is the sample of subjects and the methods by which they were selected appropriate to the problem under study? These and other questions enter into the evaluation of an experiment.

There is no one ideal sequence for evaluating a research report of an experiment—different approaches call for different sequences of evaluation. However, we have had an opportunity to become familiar with the procedure, methods, and analysis as described by these authors. Now let us look at the report in terms of three main criteria: control of extraneous variables, experimental validity, and adequacy of research design.

Control of Extraneous Variables

What sorts of factors might affect the results of this experiment? Such things as inappropriate test materials, effects produced by specific experimental procedure, a biased selection of subjects, and a particular order of presentation of the testing materials could all seriously affect any results. By examining each of these in turn, we might conclude the following:

Test Materials.   The authors report extensive pre-testing of the test materials used, to determine that the concepts they wished to portray were correctly seen by children in the age group studied. It seems safe to say that the test materials here were appropriate.

Effects Produced by the Experimental Procedure.   The authors specify their procedure in detail and there seems to be little about it that would bias the results.

Selection of Subjects.   This is an area in which it would be helpful to have more information about the subjects than the authors provide in the article. We can assume that the subjects used are reasonably homogeneous, but in the absence of specific data, we cannot be sure. How many of these children were children of enlisted men and how many of officers? How many children are within each 6-months age group? Questions such as these are directly relevant to the external validity of the experiment and will be mentioned again in discussion of that topic.

At this point it is necessary to introduce two new terms; *population* and *sample*. These concepts are of fundamental importance in understanding both research methods and statistical techniques.

POPULATION.   A population is defined as all of the members of a given class or set of events. Populations can be defined in a variety of ways and can range from a very small to an extremely large number of things or people. For example, a population of interest to a research worker may be all the students enrolled in a given college course—a relatively small population. A larger population would be all children between the ages of 3 and 5 living within the geographical limits of the city of Stockholm, Sweden. Another population could be all automobile owners in the United States—a large population. At the extreme, our population of interest could be all living human beings on Earth.

Only in the first and second examples just listed would it be feasible to measure some characteristic of all of the members of the population; the latter two populations are simply too large to make such a measurement practical. If we want to know something about a large population, we face the problem of never being able to make the appropriate measurements on everyone. The costs in time and money clearly make this impossible. What must be done is to select members of the population in such a way that they represent that population and will allow us to make the best decision possible about the characteristics of everyone in the population. Such a selection procedure is called *sampling*.

SAMPLE.   A sample is defined as those members of a population on whom measurements of some characteristics have actually been made. If we are to use only a few individuals to find out what we think is true of a very large number of people, *then we want to be as certain as possible that the individuals we select are representative of the population.*

There are a variety of ways to select samples from populations, and we will discuss this problem in more detail in Chapter 7. For the moment it will do to keep the relationship of the sample to the population in mind as a possible source of extraneous variation. For example, if we wanted our results to be applicable to all children in the United States, we would have to show that our sample was obtained in such a manner as to be representative of that population. Rhine and coworkers have specified the nature of their sample and have made no direct claims that the results should apply to children other than to groups similar to those in their study. In the discussion, however, the meaning of the results is presented in such a way that would lead one to believe that they do apply to the population at large.

Order of Presentation of the Testing Materials.   We have seen earlier what elaborate precautions were taken to insure that no bias would be introduced by order of presentation, and thus it seems quite safe to conclude that the order did not influence the results.

Overall, the control of extraneous variation in this experiment seems to have been quite well done.

Experimental Validity

Earlier, the topics of internal and external validity were briefly discussed. If you have forgotten these topics, you should go back and review pp. 7–8 before continuing. In examining the internal validity of this experiment, we should ask: Are there conditions or factors present which would account for the results in ways other than those noted by the experimenters? In this research, the evidence for internal validity in terms of controlling extraneous variation and establishing suitability of experimental materials and procedure is quite good.

The question of external validity is not as easy to answer. To what larger population of people can the obtained results be generalized? Here is where more information about the subjects would have been helpful. One factor suggesting that the results are applicable to children in general is that the situations the children are asked to evaluate here are not particularly controversial. If the children had been asked about the "goodness" or "badness" of situations about which adults might hold drastically differing views, the experiment might have produced results that would have much less generality. However, given the nature of the situations studied, external validity would seem to be adequate.

Adequacy of Research Design

Is there a better way to study this problem than the one used? Is there a design that could improve on the approach used by the experimenters? The answer offered here may seem paradoxical: There is probably no better way to study this problem; however, there are some limits on what can be concluded from this study, because of the type of research design used.

In an "ideal" experiment, the experimenter has control of the independent variable and can change it and vary it under controlled conditions. For instance, in the example of the drug study discussed earlier, the independent variable—the drug—was under the control of the experimenter. The experimenter in the drug study could randomly assign animals to treatment groups and thus eliminate the possibility that the groups differed in any way before the experimental treatment was introduced. In the study by Rhine and coworkers, the independent variable is age, and clearly, age is not something that can be randomly assigned to a subject by an experimenter. The children were assigned to groups and the analysis was done on the basis of age. Thus, there always remained the possibility that some other factor was present that might have affected the results, such as changes in child-rearing practices over the years which exposed the children in different age groups to changing standards of "good" and "bad." As a result, the conclusions can never be as firm as those established under conditions where the experimenter has the ability to manipulate the independent variable.

This may seem like hairsplitting, and for many situations it may be. However, consider another situation which has been studied using exactly the same design: the relationship between smoking and lung cancer. This is an identical situation in that the independent variable—smoking—is not under the control of the experimenter. The people studied made their own decision as to whether to smoke or not and how much tobacco to consume. Consequently, the advocates of smoking can always claim that there might be some other factor present in the smoking group that accounts for the increase in incidence of lung cancer. Despite the overwhelming evidence showing the relationship between smoking and lung cancer, the possibility of another causative factor cannot be dismissed entirely. The only way to accomplish such a thing would be clearly unethical: to randomly assign individuals to smoking and non-smoking groups and study the incidence of lung cancer in the two groups. Only by such a procedure could the possibility of another causative factor be eliminated.

In general, we can conclude that the experiment evaluated in this chapter was well planned, well executed, and adequately controlled. In later chapters, there will be a more detailed account of some of the points discussed here and the development of a set of general criteria for the evaluation of experiments. First, let us examine and evaluate a second experiment.

FOOTNOTES

[1]J. C. Townsend, *Introduction to experimental method.* New York: McGraw-Hill, 1953.

chapter three

evaluating an experiment: a second example

"I'll give you something that four out of five doctors recommend, and we'll see what happens."
Drawing by O'Brian. © 1973 The New Yorker Magazine, Inc.

The experiment we have just finished discussing was presented exactly as it was published in a professional journal. The next research report to be evaluated differs considerably from the previous example. It is not so much a report of a research study as a critique and set of suggestions for repeating an experiment.

The experiment itself was carried out in 1930 in Lanarkshire, England, for the purpose of assessing the relative merits of feeding raw versus pasteurized milk to school children. The critique, which contains a description of the experiment, was done in 1931 by the famous statistician W. S. Gossett, who wrote under the pseudonym "Student"[1] Gossett's original account was written in a prose style that is somewhat difficult to follow, and therefore we have taken the liberty of rephrasing the original account.

The Lanarkshire Milk Experiment

"STUDENT"

In the spring of 1930 a large scale nutritional experiment was carried out in the schools of Lanarkshire (England).

For four months, 10,000 school children received three fourths of a pint of Grade A

This article is revised, with permission, from one which originally appeared in *Biometrika*, 23:398–406, 1931.

milk per day. Five thousand of these children were fed raw milk, 5000 were fed pasteurized milk, and another 10,000 children were selected as controls. Each of the 20,000 children was weighed and his height measured at the beginning and at the end of the experiment.

This review is presented not so much in criticism of what was done as it is in the hope that any further work will take full advantage of the best possible methods to use in studies of this type.

The 20,000 children were chosen from 67 schools, with not more than 400 or fewer than 200 being chosen from any one school. Of the number chosen from each school, half were assigned to be fed milk and half were control subjects who were given no milk. Some of the schools were provided with raw milk and the others were given pasteurized milk. In view of the administrative difficulties involved in assuring that each child received the proper kind of milk, no school received both raw and pasteurized milk. Unfortunately this procedure introduces the possibility that the groups of children receiving raw milk and those receiving pasteurized milk were not strictly comparable. Secondly, the selection of the children was left to the Head Teacher of each school, who was instructed that both control children and children to be given milk should be representative of the average children between 5 and 12 years of age. Since the actual method of selection is quite important, a quote from the original report of the experiment is instructive. "The teachers selected the two classes of pupils, those getting milk and those acting as control subjects in two different ways. In certain cases they selected them by ballot and in others on an alphabetical system." So far so good, but after selecting randomly in this fashion they unfortunately wavered, since they go on to state: "In any particular school where there was any group which, by the earlier selection methods, had an undue proportion of well fed or ill-nourished children, others were substituted in order to obtain a more level selection." This is just the sort of afterthought that most of us have now and again and which can spoil the most systematic and best laid-out plans. In the above situation, it effectively served to ruin the experiment since, as the original report pointed out, the control children were definitely superior in both height and weight to the children to be fed milk by an amount equivalent to about 4 months' growth in height and 3 months' growth in weight.

Presumably this discrimination in height and weight was not made deliberately but was due to the fact that the teachers were responding to the very human feeling that the poorer children needed the milk more than the children from comparatively well-to-do families. They, therefore, included too many ill-nourished children in the group to receive milk and too few in the control group.

Still another source of error is present in the measurement procedure. It was clearly impossible to weigh such large numbers of children without their clothes. Consequently, they were weighed in their indoor clothing in February when the study began. Consequently, the difference in weight between their February clothing and their June clothing (when they were weighed and measured at the end of the experiment) is going to be subtracted from their actual increase in weight between the beginning and the end of the experiment. If the selection of control children and children receiving milk had been a random one, the difference in clothing weight would not have mattered since we could then assume that both groups would have been equally affected. However, since the selection seems to have been affected by considerations of poverty, it is reasonable to assume that the children fed milk, being from poorer families, would tend to have a smaller variety of clothing available than would the economically better off control children. We would expect both that the control children would have heavier and warmer clothing during the winter and that the poorer children would be more likely to wear the same clothing the year around. With these constant sources of error present, it was not at all surprising to find that the gain in weight of the more ill-nourished children fed milk was much more marked. How much of this is due to the removal of heavy winter clothing by the better-off control children is impossible to state.

Still another source of error is present in the fact that the controls from those schools which were given raw milk were combined with those from the schools which were given pasteurized milk.

With 67 schools participating, the best division possible would be 33 against 34. In school districts which are so heterogeneous both racially and socio-economically, it is quite possible that there was a difference between the average height and weight of the pupils in the 33 schools and the corresponding averages of the pupils at the other 34 schools, both in terms of the original composition of the groups and in the rate of growth during the experiment. If such is the case, the average control subject could not be used appropriately to compare with either the group fed raw milk or the group fed pasteurized milk. This possibility is enhanced by the method of selecting control children which was clearly not carried out in a uniform manner in the different schools.

> *In summary, what "Student" has pointed out is that a failure to use random selection in establishing the groups for the experiment has effectively eliminated any possibility of directly comparing the groups, since they differed before the experiment began. In addition, it should be pointed out, as McNemar has done,[2] that since the purpose of the experiment was to compare the relative merits of pasteurized vs. raw milk, the 10,000 control children served no effective purpose. Recognition of this fact could have eliminated half of the effort and expense involved in this experiment. Now, consider "Student's" suggestions for repeating the experiment.*

If it is considered necessary to do further work on this subject, I suggest the following:

1. If the experiment is to be repeated on the same grand scale,

a. The control subjects and subjects to be fed milk should be chosen by the teachers in pairs of the same age group and sex so that they are as similar in height, weight, and state of nutrition as possible. These pairs should be divided into control and milk fed children by tossing a coin for each pair and in this way assigning a child to one of the conditions. Each pair should then be considered to be a unit, and the gain in height and weight by the child receiving milk over his paired control could be used to determine the chance variation in height and weight. In this way the error will almost certainly be smaller than if calculated from the means of children receiving milk and controls.

If, in addition, the socio-economic status of each pair is noted, further useful information would be available for comparison.

If this procedure is found to be too difficult, a perfectly good comparison can be made by adhering to the plan of the original experiment and drawing lots to decide which should be controls and which are fed milk (this is preferable to an alphabetical arrangement), but the error of the comparison is likely to be larger than in the plan outlined above.

b. If it is at all possible, each school should supply an equal number of children to be given raw and pasteurized milk, again selecting one member of a pair by coin tossing.

c. Some effort should be made to estimate the weight of the clothing worn by the children, both at the beginning and at the end of the experiment; possibly the time of year could be chosen so that there would be little change in the type of clothing worn.

2. If, as seems obvious, it is decided that milk is a useful addition to a child's diet and that the difference between raw and pasteurized milk is the central problem of interest, it would be possible to obtain much greater certainty for only 1 to 2 per cent of the cost of the original experiment (the Lanarkshire experiment cost about $38,000 in 1930!) and less than 5 per cent of the effort. This could be accomplished, since among 20,000 children there should be at least 160 pairs of twins. Since there are more children in the Lanarkshire schools than were used in the experiment, there might be as many as 200–300 pairs of twins available for such a study. Of 200 pairs, about 50 would be identical

and half of the remainder would be non-identical twins of the same sex. The errors of comparison using identical twins may be relied upon to be so small that 50 pairs would provide more reliable results than the 20,000 children with whom we have been dealing.

My suggestion is to experiment on all pairs of twins of the same sex. One of each pair should be fed raw milk and the other pasteurized milk, deciding in each case by the toss of a coin. Weekly measurements should be made and the children weighed without clothes.

With such comparatively small numbers of children required for the experiment, further information about the dietetic habits and socio-economic position of the children could be collected and would allow other valuable comparisons to be made.

To sum up: The Lanarkshire experiment was devised to discover the value of giving a regular supply of milk to school children, was planned on a grand scale, organized in a thorough manner, and carried out with the dedicated assistance of a large team of teachers, nurses, and doctors. It failed, however, to produce a valid estimate of the advantages of giving milk to children or of the relative value of raw vs. pasteurized milk. This was because of an attempt to improve on a random selection of the subjects which in fact ended up selecting control children who were on the average taller and heavier than the children selected for milk feeding. It is likely that this was the result of the teachers' tendency to assign the needier children to the groups receiving milk since they would be most likely to benefit from a dietary supplement.

In the second section of his paper, "Student" pointed out that the same experiment could be repeated at a fraction of the original cost (a possible saving of $75,000 in today's currency) by using a subpopulation of identical twins that would be present in the original sample of 20,000 children. This is made possible through the use of statistical methods to control variability and thereby to gain maximum information from the available subjects.

The criticisms of this experiment have been limited to those made by "Student" in his original paper. Now let us examine the research in terms of some of the criteria discussed in Chapter 1 and some additional criteria introduced here.

CONTROL OF EXTRANEOUS VARIABLES

Campbell, in his discussion of "Factors Relevant to the Validity of Experiments in Social Settings,"[3] defines seven types of extraneous variables that must be controlled if an experiment is to have any internal validity. Let us see how well the Lanarkshire milk experiment fares when evaluated against these criteria. Keep in mind that we are evaluating an experiment in which a measurement was taken at a given time, an experimental treatment introduced, and a second measurement taken to measure the effect of the experimental treatment.

1. History. During the time span between the two measurements, in addition to the experimental treatment, a great many things can happen that may have an effect on the later measurement. "Student" has pointed out one such problem in the Lanarkshire milk experiment: the effect of a change from winter to summer clothing. This in itself would not have been serious if the children had been randomly assigned to the groups. However, the assignment of the less well-nourished children to the groups receiving milk does introduce a contaminating effect. As "Student" noted, the less well-nourished children are almost certainly from poorer families and, consequently, are much more likely to wear the same clothing year-round than the children from more prosperous families.

Given the long period between measurements, a great many contaminating factors could occur. For example, suppose the economic conditions within the Lanarkshire area had suddenly improved, providing increased employment. Such a change would almost certainly benefit the poorer families more, and one consequence of increased income would be a better diet and consequent weight gain. Given the biased assignment of subjects to groups, such an effect would be substantial.

2. Maturation. Maturation refers to effects which are specific to the passage of time and are not a function of specific events, as in history. For the Lanarkshire milk experiment, maturation would not seem to be a source of extraneous variation, since we can assume that the maturation rates of all the children in the study were about the same.

However, there is one possibility of maturational variation. Suppose that rate of maturation was hindered by an inadequate diet. If the milk feeding were to compensate for this in any way, the effect might be a larger increase in weight gain than could be attributed to the milk alone. Again, this would have made no difference if the children had been randomly assigned to the conditions.

3. Testing. There are many kinds of experiments, particularly in psychology, in which the experience of being tested results in a change in the measurement being taken. For example, a person given the same intelligence test twice will almost certainly show a higher score on the second testing. Campbell defines the distinction between *reactive* measures — measures that change the thing one is studying — and *non-reactive* measures — those which have no effect. For the present experiment, it seems safe to conclude that measuring the weight of English schoolchildren will not have any reactive effect on their weight.[4]

4. Instrument Decay. This type of variation refers to a change in the measuring apparatus. For example, if the scales used to measure the children developed a defect between the first and second measurements, another source of error would be added. Whatever the type of measurement apparatus — scales, rulers, ratings by judges — it is important to have some way to detect possible changes in the apparatus itself. For the Lanarkshire milk experiment we have no evidence of instrument decay, but we also have no evidence in the research report that there was none.

5. Statistical Regression. Regression refers to the tendency for individuals having extreme scores (either high or low) on the variable being measured the first time to have scores closer to the average of the groups on a second measurement. For measurements such as IQ, this can be a serious source of extraneous variation. However, for the measurements taken in the present study, the effects of regression would seem to be minimal.

6. Biased Selection.   "Student" has already discussed the effects of bias in terms of assignments to groups in some detail. One way of looking at the experiment in view of these multiple sources of extraneous variation is to consider how many sources of extraneous variation were present as a result of the biased sampling. The aforementioned problems relating to history and maturation are sources of error that would not have existed if the selection had been unbiased.

7. Mortality.   Campbell uses this term to refer to the loss of subjects in the sample being studied from the time of the first measurement to the second. In the present study, it seems safe to disregard mortality as a meaningful source of variation, unless there had been a large exodus of people from the area between the time of the first test and the second. This could be serious if the exodus was produced by factors that would affect selectively either the very poor or the well-to-do children.

Internal Validity.   Does the Lanarkshire milk experiment have any internal validity? As "Student" has shown, clearly not, since the variation in weight gain can easily be accounted for by factors not controlled in the experiment and by biased selection and assignment. Since the experiment lacks internal validity, the question of external validity is, by definition, nonexistent. There exists no population to which an invalid result can be generalized.

It is just as important to evaluate critically experiments that appear in the latest issues of journals—newness is no criterion of excellence. It was not at all necessary for us to go back to 1930 to find an experiment with major flaws.[5] It did, however, enable us to avoid certain problems of tact in dealing with contemporaries.

The next chapter will deal with some general principles and considerations in the evaluation of experiments, and will review and summarize much of the material discussed to this point.

FOOTNOTES

[1]Gossett was employed as a statistician by the Guiness Brewery. This firm had a rule forbidding employees to publish the results of any of their research. However, since Gossett's work contained no secrets of importance to the brewing industry, he was allowed to publish his work under a pseudonym—"Student."

[2]Q. McNemar, *Psychological statistics.* (3rd ed.) New York: John Wiley & Sons, 1962, p. 386.

[3]D. T. Campbell, Factors Relevant to the Validity of Experiments in Social Settings. *Psychological Bulletin*, 1959, **54**, 297–312.

[4]However, this might not be true for other groups. In his article, Campbell suggests that weight measurement on adult American women would almost certainly be reactive, resulting in attempts to lose weight.

[5]For example, an extensive, elaborate, and rather costly study of the effectiveness of psychotherapeutic methods conducted a few years ago is useless for almost exactly the same reasons as the Lanarkshire milk experiment. Only the overall complexity of the therapy study prevented us from selecting it as an example of faulty design.

chapter four

the evaluation of experiments

". . . weather permitting, of course."
Copyright © 1974. Reprinted by permission of Saturday
Review/World and Bill Hoest.

AN "IDEAL" EXPERIMENT

Perhaps the simplest way to review the major considerations in evaluating an experiment is to indicate one ideal experiment that illustrates the concerns and goals of general experimental research strategy. The simplest example is what is known as the classical single-factor experiment. Such an experiment can be represented in a block diagram as shown in Figure 4–1.

In this "ideal" experiment, a sample of subjects is chosen randomly from a population. These subjects are then assigned on a random basis to one of two conditions, condition A or condition B. The experimenter then exposes Group A to his experimental treatment. The situation is identical for Group B, except that the group is not exposed to the experimental treatment. Under ideal conditions, Groups A and B are identical at the outset, and remain so, except for the exposure to the treatment. Following the experimental treatment, measurements are taken on that variable in which the experimenter is interested and which he expects to change as a result of his experimental treatment. After the measurements are completed, some summary descriptive statistics based on the individual measurements (such as means and standard deviations) are calculated for each group, and the probability that the groups now differ is evaluated by some statistic such as the *t* test. If the mean values of the groups differ significantly more than would be expected by chance, the experimenter concludes that his experimental condition has had a significant effect on the variable measured by him.

Such an experiment meets the following criteria:

1. The experimenter can safely assume that his groups are identical on the variable he is interested in before he begins his study.

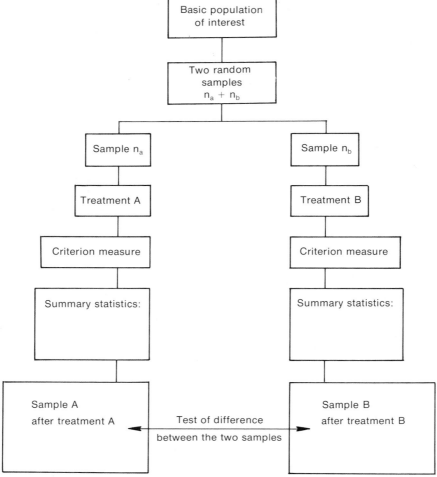

Figure 4–1   Outline of steps in an experiment. (Adapted from Winer, B. J. *Statistical principles in experimental design.* (2nd ed.) New York: McGraw-Hill, 1971.)

2. All conditions except the one under study are unchanged by the exper-imental setting—in experimental terminology, all conditions except the one under study are "held constant."

3. The experimenter introduces the treatment in which he is interested under circumstances which he has specified and in amounts that he has deter-mined.

4. Changes in the variable in which he is interested are measured by ap-propriate procedures and at appropriate times.

5. The procedures used to measure the variable under study meet satis-factory criteria of reliability and validity. (See Footnote 1 for definitions of these terms.)

6. Since all conditions have been controlled, it is possible to estimate

with some precision the effect of the experimental treatment on the variable studied.

These ideal criteria are difficult to satisfy when one is studying living organisms; probably there are very few experiments in the social sciences that satisfy all of the criteria. However, they are useful in providing some standards for the evaluation of experimental research, since the more closely an experiment satisfies these six criteria, the more confidence we can place in the results.

It is because of practical limitations that we can only approximate this ideal in actuality. For one thing, in many kinds of research work, randomization of subjects in experimental groups is not possible. For example, in comparing a sample of smokers with one of non-smokers, we can obtain a random sample from populations within each grouping, but we cannot be sure that the two groups do not differ systematically on other variables. Often it is almost impossible to obtain experimental groups that are the same on all variables except the one under study. The research worker then has to settle for a sample in which the variable he is interested in is related to other variables that will also have an effect on the variable being studied. All he can do in such circumstances is to describe his sample in terms of such relevant variables and acknowledge the possible influence on his results.

Other practical problems are (1) the experimenter may not always be able to introduce the experimental treatment when he wishes and in the degree he wishes; (2) he may be severely limited as to when and how he can make his measurements on the response variable in which he is interested; and (3) he may have to use measuring instruments of marginal reliability and validity.

In reading experiments subject to any or all of the above difficulties, is it appropriate to reject the research because it does not meet ideal experimental criteria? Of course not, since the measurements may be the best obtainable given the conditions under which the experimenter had to collect his data. Such results should be examined for all that can possibly be learned from them. However, the findings of an experiment that has some of the above limitations should not be given equal weight with those of an experiment that comes closer to the ideal. The greater the degree to which an experiment fails to meet the six criteria we have presented, the greater the possibility of misleading results, and thus the greater the likelihood that the results would be different if the experiment were repeated.

In evaluating an experiment, it is important to consider what effects not satisfying the outlined criteria may have had on the results. An experiment that follows the path of least effort in controlling extraneous variation seldom produces results that imbue one with confidence. If subjects could have been randomly assigned to conditions and the experimenter chose instead to use two intact groups, such as two school classes, then the results are correspondingly less trustworthy. Assuming that two intact groups of people are going to be enough alike to use as equivalent groups in an experiment suggests at best a lack of concern with equating the groups to be studied. If a research study could have been carried out with one experimenter testing all subjects, and 20 experimenters were used instead, then there will be increased extraneous variability as the result of such factors as the different experimenters' placing different emphases on instructions and having different qualities of interpersonal interactions with the subjects. As a contrast, note the concern expressed by Rhine, Hill, and Wandruff about the possibility of effects due to order of presentation, and the careful procedures they followed to eliminate this possibility (Chapter 2, pp. 11–13).

CONTROL OF VARIATION

As Kerlinger[2] has pointed out in his excellent work on the subject, research design has two basic purposes: (1) to provide answers to research questions, and (2) to control variation.

Variation, as you know from the discussions in Chapters 2 and 3, can be caused by many things. A good research design for a particular problem is one which helps the investigator to answer his questions while controlling sources of variation related to his experiment. The ideal research design is one that allows the investigator to answer his research questions economically, accurately, and objectively, and to arrive at valid conclusions. Any time there are factors present that may affect the validity of measurements on the variable being studied, there is the problem of extraneous variation. Kerlinger discusses four methods that may be used to control extraneous variation.

1. *Eliminating the extraneous variation.* This is analogous to the earlier discussion of holding variables "constant." If we are concerned about the possible contaminating effects of income on the relationship of attitudes to educational level, the effect of varying amounts of income can be eliminated by selecting subjects whose income level is the same. If sex differences are a source of extraneous variation, this could be controlled by using subjects of only one sex. However, while this is certainly the most effective way, it also limits the extent to which our results can be generalized. If the extraneous variable of sex is eliminated, then our results are interpretable only in reference to the sex studied.

2. *Randomization.* You have already become acquainted with randomization procedures, by which the effects of extraneous variables should be nullified, since the presence of the variable should be at the same level in all groups involved in the experiment.

3. *Inclusion of the extraneous variable in the research design.* In this approach, the possibility of an extraneous variable is dealt with by including it within the design, so that any effects due to it can be systematically examined. For example, if sex differences are thought to be a source of extraneous variation, sex can be included as a variable in the experiment, and differences due to sex can be examined and compared with other differences.

4. *Matching.* Still a fourth way to control extraneous variation is to match subjects on the variable thought to be a source of extraneous variation. If we are concerned about the effect of IQ on a measure, we can control this effect by matching the IQ's of the subjects in the groups to be studied, so that a person of high IQ in one group is matched with persons of high IQ in the other groups.[3]

TYPES OF RESEARCH DESIGNS

To illustrate some of the points just discussed, we will outline a few types of research designs and comment on their adequacy. It should be noted that this list is far from complete. Research design is a complex subject, and a detailed treatment of it would require a volume in itself.

Bad Designs

In a strict sense, some of the designs discussed in this section do not deserve to be called "research designs," since in many instances the degree to which a question is answered using such approaches is little better than no answer at all. Consider what can be called the "unevaluated event." With such a "design," a new event is simply introduced into a situation and no attempt is made to evaluate it. For example, suppose a school system were to change its techniques of teaching arithmetic and simply assume that the new methods are better. If we use the notation of Popham,[4] where T stands for a treatment (or event) and M for a measurement, then this design would be represented as:

$$T$$

Such a design, if it can be called that, informs you of absolutely nothing. In such a procedure, you have no idea whether or not any change or improvement has taken place as a function of your treatment.

A variation on this type of design is the single event measurement, in which a new treatment is introduced and a measurement is taken after the treatment. Such a design would be diagrammed as follows:

$$T \qquad M$$

All you will learn from such a design is how well (in an absolute sense) your subjects performed. You have no way to compare any change with other groups not exposed to this treatment, since no comparable data exist. Although such an approach may be preferable to complete ignorance, it is only a slight improvement.

Still another variant on this approach is the design in which one group is pre-tested, a treatment is introduced, and then an additional measurement is taken after the introduction of the treatment. This would be represented as follows:

$$M \qquad T \qquad M$$

This approach is in many ways a more dangerous one than the first two approaches, since there is the possibility that you will conclude that you have learned something of importance. A concrete illustration of the $M-T-M$ design may be helpful. Suppose that a group of people suffering from severe arthritis are given a new drug that is purported to drastically reduce arthritic swelling and pain. If a sizeable percentage of the patients treated in this manner were to show improvement, the conclusion would very likely be drawn that the drug is effective. However, such a conclusion is totally unjustified on the basis of the evidence—it might well be that the subjects improved spontaneously, and that the drug had nothing to do with it. The critical point is that there is no way to tell in such a design.

A design that represents a slight improvement is one in which a control group is measured in the same way as the treatment group, but the treatment is omitted. Such a design would be diagrammed as follows:

Experimental	M	T	M
Control	M		M

For this design to be useful, however, it is essential that the subjects in the control group be well matched with those in the treatment group. You have already been exposed to one experiment based on this design, in which the control groups were clearly *not* equivalent to the treatment groups (the Lanarkshire Milk Experiment in Chapter 3), and have seen the sort of erroneous conclusions that can be drawn from such data.

Good Designs

We began this chapter with an illustration of the "ideal" experiment, outlined in some detail. If we were to diagram that experiment using Popham's notation, it would look as follows:

Experimental	T	M
R		
Control		M

Randomization. Note that there is one new symbol—R—entered prior to the introduction of the experimental treatment. The R stands for the *randomization* of subjects between the experimental and control groups, and this randomization constitutes the single most powerful factor in making this a good design.

The advantages of randomization have been discussed at length earlier and will not be repeated here. The Lanarkshire Milk Experiment with randomization would be diagrammed as follows:

Experimental	M	T	M
R			
Control	M		M

Eliminating the Effects of Pre-measurement. While the design just shown is a good one, there is always the possibility that pre-measurement will have some unknown effect on the group being studied. This was not a consideration in the Lanarkshire study, but in many other areas of study, particularly in psychological research, the very act of testing people in itself may produce a change in the attribute being measured. To control for such problems, the following design is one of the most powerful that can be used. To illustrate it, we will have to make a slight change in the notation we have been using to describe designs.

	Experimental treatment	No experimental treatment
Pre-measurement	experimental group	control group
No Pre-measurement	control group	control group

The above arrangement shows how all possible combinations of effects on measurement and experimental treatment can be evaluated. A design such as this is known as a *factorial* design and will be discussed in more detail in Chapter 8.

UNTANGLING RESEARCH DESIGNS

As was mentioned earlier, the topic of research design is an extensive one, and a detailed treatment would occupy a book in itself. Some suggestions for additional reading are given in the Appendix, but these selections are not easy reading and will require considerable effort. A useful procedure when reading an article in which the design becomes difficult to follow is to diagram it as we have done here in illustrating the organization of good and bad designs.

Pre-Selection of Samples

In Chapter 2, p. 21, we discussed some of the problems that arise when groups have to be constituted on the basis of a pre-existing difference, such as whether or not they smoke cigarettes. While some excellent research has been done and some kinds of comparisons can only be done on such a basis, there are numerous circumstances where the nature of the pre-selection can invalidate the entire procedure. Three examples will serve to illustrate:

1. A research worker was interested in the effects that different college living situations have on social attitudes. He proposed to study the changes in attitudes toward societal control over decisions involving individual morality that occurred over a 3-year period in residents of fraternity houses as compared to residents of college dormitories. At the end of this period, the two groups would be compared to see what changes in regard to moral decisions the different living arrangements had brought about.

A moment's reflection should convince anyone that such a research program is meaningless from the start. People make their own decisions as to whether they live in fraternities or dormitories, and the factors entering into this choice—social class, income, education of parents, and so forth—are simply too numerous for even the most optimistic researcher to consider the groups comparable at the beginning of the study. If it were possible to randomly assign male college freshmen to either dormitory or fraternity living groups, such a study would be feasible. Given the existing conditions, however, the best that could be done would be to attempt to match subjects on the relevant variables.

2. A project was initiated to develop a test of true-or-false items that would detect tendencies toward sexual deviancy. The test items were administered to all individuals arrested for sexually deviant activities in a large western city during a 6-month period. As a comparison group, students

in a graduate School of Education were given the same test items and the responses were compared to see which items, if any, differentiated the two groups. A set of items was then selected on which a high score would indicate a tendency toward sexual deviancy.

Apart from the dubious validity of letting an arrest serve as a criterion of sexual deviancy, the deficiencies of such a procedure should be obvious. The two groups as defined are different in so many ways (probable differences would include education, income, background of parents, attitudes toward police, social class, age) that comparing them on almost any conceivable psychological or sociological measure would probably result in large differences. The test as constructed is a measure of the differences between two extremely different groups and is thus useless for the purpose for which it is intended. For example, the ability of such a test to differentiate between persons arrested for sexual crimes from a larger group of persons arrested for a variety of crimes would probably be zero.

3. A research group was interested in developing new psychological tests to detect the presence of brain damage in hospital patients. To do this, a sample of patients with a diagnosis of brain damage were tested with the new tests and compared with a sample of non–brain-damaged patients hospitalized for other reasons. The new tests were found to be highly effective in distinguishing between the two groups.

Again, such a finding would hardly be surprising, since finding measures that differentiate between patients with clear-cut diagnoses of brain damage and those with normal brain functioning should not be difficult. If a person is to be examined for signs of organic brain damage, he probably displays certain behavior patterns or neurological symptoms that would lead a physician to suspect the possibility of brain damage. Thus, the test is detecting only those patients who both display a symptom pattern and have subsequently been found to have brain damage. A test that would be useful in these circumstances would be one that detects instances of actual brain damage from the population of all individuals displaying the behavior patterns or neurological signs that lead a physician to suspect this possibility. An appropriate group to examine in such a situation is all persons initially suspected of brain damage. The technique must then be evaluated on its effectiveness to separate individuals found to have brain damage from individuals initially suspected of brain damage who are found to have no such problem.

Sampling of Experimental Objects

If you were to read a research report in which the experimenter says he has studied the ability of individuals to identify emotions from facial cues in photographs and then says that he used two photographs of the same person, one showing the person laughing and the other showing him crying, you might justifiably feel that this experimenter has little basis on which to make his claim. Yet many research reports indicate just this sort of inadequate sampling of the material used as the experimental variable.

A similar sort of inadequate object sampling can occur in tests of more complex situations. Suppose a Public Health administrator is interested in comparing two types of infant clinic procedures used by community health teams. To do this, he uses two teams, each consisting of a physician, a nurse, and a medical technician, to try out the two approaches. The neighborhoods served by these teams are matched on appropriate variables, such as income level, number of infants, and so forth. The criterion of success is the number of return visits by mothers using the service. Such a procedure is very likely to produce a misleading result simply because of the lack of object samples. The situation is analogous to judging the difference between two photographs. In the clinic example, the procedures cannot be separated from the personalities of the individuals in each team. One procedure may be more effective in a general sense, but since only two samples were used, the direction could be completely reversed by an irascible physician or an unpleasant nurse. To properly evaluate such procedures would require several such clinic teams, equally divided as to approaches, so that individual differences in personalities would cancel out. It is often as important to take a representative sample of situations and of stimuli as it is to take a representative sample of subjects—a point that is often neglected in social science research.

Subtle Biases in Experiments

Until now, the discussion has been concerned with specifiable sources of extraneous variation—problems which can be easily identified and, if not controlled, at least observed.

However, other possibilities for bias exist which are much more difficult to identify. To illustrate this problem, we will present brief accounts of two studies in the field of psychology.

The first is an experiment by Bruner and Goodman[5] attempting to show how personal need and wishes might affect how people see things. To study this, they constructed a device that projected a circle of light on a screen. By turning a dial, the circle of light could be made smaller or larger. Subjects in the experiment were (1) children enrolled in an expensive private school, serving upper income and professional people, and (2) children in a settlement house whose parents were unable to provide for their care. The experimenter would show a child various coins such as a dime, nickel, quarter, and half dollar, and ask the child to adjust the circle of light so that it was the same size as the coin. When the data were analyzed, they found that the children from the settlement house had consistently made the circle of light larger than the children from the private school. They concluded from this that the much greater importance of the coins to the poor children led them to overestimate their size as compared to the children of well-to-do parents.

Other research workers became curious about the findings and repeated this study. The first repetition failed to find any difference between two groups of children similar in background to the groups tested by Bruner and Goodman. This particular study was repeated a total of 11 times, each time by different investigators, and the original results were never duplicated.

Should we conclude from this that the original investigators were in some way dishonest? Definitely not—the original researchers took every precaution to insure objective measurements and to avoid bias. When their results could not be repeated, they urged other investigators to repeat the study to further test the possibility of bias, and attempted and failed to achieve their original result when they repeated the experiment themselves. It is still difficult to explain the reason they obtained the results they did in the first experiment. Perhaps the experimenters managed in some way unknown to themselves to give the children some cue as to how they hoped the experiment would come out—some subtle signal to which the children responded. While this may seem far-fetched, the next experiment, by Rosenthal and Fode[6] provides a graphic illustration of how such subtle biases can affect the result of an experiment.

In contrast to the Bruner and Goodman experiment, the Rosenthal and Fode study was specifically designed to study the effects of possible experimenter bias on the results obtained in a research study.

Rosenthal's subjects in his experiment were 13 students enrolled in his course in experimental psychology. Twelve of the students were actually subjects in the experiment—the thirteenth student knew that the students were being used in an experiment and acted as a "spy," checking on what the students did.

The students were told that as part of their training in experimental psychology, they should become familiar with the procedures used to do experiments with albino rats, of the type often used in psychology experiments. Six students were told that they had been given "maze-bright" rats and the other six students were told that their rats were "maze-dull" rats. The rats were run in a simple T-maze with white and black arms, and were to be trained to go to the black for reward. An illustration of the maze is shown in Figure 4–2.

The terms "maze-bright" and "maze-dull" refer to strains of rats that have been bred for many generations to improve a particular ability. "Maze-bright" rats are literally rats that are genetically superior at learning to find their way through mazes (interestingly enough, the rat is not necessarily better at other tasks). "Maze-dull" rats, as you have probably guessed, are rats who are remarkably poor at finding their way through mazes. They are developed by the same process used to produce the "maze-bright" rats.

The students were randomly assigned to run either "bright" or "dull" rats. The task of each student was to have his rat learn a maze to a criterion of two consecutive error-free passages through the maze from beginning to end.

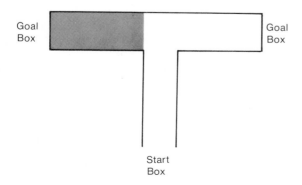

Figure 4–2 T-maze.

The student was to conduct the number of trials necessary for the rat to reach the criterion.

As you may have suspected, the rats used were ordinary laboratory rats with no special talent or deficiency in maze learning. They were selected at random from a laboratory colony of rats all of a certain age (within a few days).

The students were allowed to carry out the procedures without supervision. However, the thirteenth student, who acted as a "spy" on the other students, reported that she had observed every one of the other 12 students carrying out the trials and that she did not observe any of the students doing anything to bias the results or to falsify them in any way.

There should have been no differences in the maze performance between the rats of the six students who thought they had bright rats and the six students who thought they had dull rats. However, Rosenthal found that the rats of the six students who thought they had "maze-bright" rats made significantly fewer errors than did the rats of the students who thought they had "maze-dull" rats. The difference was statistically significant. When the students were asked to fill out rating scales describing some characteristics of their animals, the "bright" rats were described as brighter, more pleasant, and more likeable.

It seems quite likely that the students who were assigned "bright" rats took more interest and were more eager to see their animal perform well than the students with "dull" rats who perhaps saw themselves as faced with a long, tedious, and repetitive task: getting a stupid animal to learn this procedure. Apparently the experimenter's outlook can bias what should be a thoroughly objective procedure.

It is quite possible for an experimenter to bias his research work without his even being aware of it and even though he is carrying out what appears to be a thoroughly objective procedure. In evaluating a report of an experiment, it is entirely appropriate to consider the possibility of bias if the procedure as reported is such that the experimenter could have "led" his subjects to respond in one direction or another. Numerous possibilities for bias exist, and we should be alert to them in considering our interpretations of research findings.

Interpreting (and Misinterpreting) Experimental Results

In their excellent text on psychological research,[7] Scott and Wertheimer tell the story of a man doing research on fleas. He trained a flea to jump over a pencil on spoken command. After the flea was trained, the man removed two of the animal's six legs and commanded: "Jump." The flea jumped as commanded, and the man removed two more legs and again told the flea to jump. The flea still managed to jump and the man then removed the last two legs and commanded the animal to jump. This time the flea did not move. The man wrote his conclusion to his work: "When a flea has all six legs removed, it becomes deaf."

While the misinterpretation of results is rather easy to understand in this story, equally unlikely interpretations may occur in published research articles and may not be so easy to uncover. It is quite possible for an experimenter to become so entangled in the intricacies of a complex experiment that he ends up losing sight of his original goal, and inadvertently carries out a series of operations that do not really provide information about the specific question he was asking. In reading the published account of an experiment, it is entirely appropriate to question whether the procedures and the results really say anything about the question originally asked.

The Problem of Outlook

It is difficult to suggest what your overall frame of reference should be when reading research papers. To reject summarily any research that does not meet all the criteria presented earlier is foolishly limiting and certainly unrealistic. At the opposite extreme, it does no good to offer tolerant acceptance to poorly planned, incompletely thought out, and sloppily executed research. Such work tells you nothing and can be dangerously misleading, as we have tried to show in some earlier sections of this chapter. Perhaps the best outlook is one of tolerant (but not too tolerant) skepticism, asking yourself, in consideration of the conditions under which the research was done, how much trust you can put in the conclusions.

FOOTNOTES

[1]The topics of reliability and validity are of considerable importance in research and are discussed at some length in Chapter 9, pp. 154–156. For the moment, we will provide some capsule definitions of these topics.

Reliability refers to the accuracy with which something can be measured. Measuring the distance between two points with a standard ruler laid between the points should produce the same answer no matter how many times you do it if you follow the same procedure. This is spoken of as a reliable measurement. However, if you were to put your thumb and forefinger on the two points and then walk across the room to a ruler while attempting to keep your hand from moving, you might find a good deal of variation over several measurements. This is called an unreliable measurement.

Validity refers to the meaningfulness of your measure—the evidence that you are measuring what you claim to be measuring. In the Rhine et al. experiment in Chapter 2, the authors have what can be called a face-valid measure for their study of "good" and "bad" concepts. If they had claimed their measure to be an indicator of emotional stability, for example, they would have had to provide evidence that their measure was valid for this claim—that it was a meaningful measure of emotional stability.

[2]F. N. Kerlinger, *Foundations of research in the behavioral sciences.* (2nd ed.) New York: Holt, Rinehart & Winston, 1973.

[3]It should be mentioned that matching is not without its dangers. Subjects can be matched on a number of factors such as age, IQ, income, education, and so forth, and still differ drastically on attributes that could affect the measure in question. Having subjects matched on a number of measures is no guarantee that all the variation relative to the attribute being studied is under control.

[4]James W. Popham, *Simplified designs for school research.* Inglewood, California: Southwest Regional Laboratory for Educational Research and Development, 11300 La Cienega Blvd., 1967.

[5]J. S. Bruner and C. C. Goodman, Value and need as organizing factors in perception. *Journal of Abnormal and Social Psychology,* 1947, **42**, 33–44.

[6]R. Rosenthal and K. Fode, The effects of experimenter bias on the performance of the albino rat. *Behavioral Science,* 1963, **8**, 183–189.

[7]W. A. Scott and M. Wertheimer, *Introduction to psychological research.* New York: John Wiley & Sons, 1962.

chapter five

evaluating survey research studies

"And you may tell the Gallup people that, as an American citizen, there is nothing I will not tolerate."

Drawing by Handelsman. © 1973 The New Yorker Magazine, Inc.

Up to now, we have focused primarily on research questions answered by experimental methods and on evaluating experimental data. However, there are many research questions that can only be answered by the process of systematic data collection on the basis of drawing samples from the population and interviewing, or administering questionnaires to the individuals in the samples. Studies done in this manner are usually called surveys or sample surveys.

Surveys are usually carried out (1) when the information necessary to answer certain questions is not known, or (2) when the information needed is not available more easily or more cheaply from other sources. For example, a survey of attitudes toward a proposed change in a community education system can only be obtained by some form of direct contact with the members of the community. If a school board is concerned about the attitudes of parents in a community, its only means of obtaining the information needed would be to conduct some sampling of opinion within the population of parents with children in the school system.

A similar situation occurs when the information needed cannot be obtained in any other fashion. As Campbell and Katona point out,[1] there would be little sense in conducting a survey to determine the number of automobiles in the United States. Since automobiles must be registered, a much simpler and cheaper approach would be to go to the state licensing bureaus to get the information. However, if one wants to find out about attitudes toward new programs such as new safety requirements for cars, in relation to the type and age of automobile owned, then the sample survey is the only way to proceed. In other words, a sample survey attempts to determine the *interrelations* between social variables, such as income, age, and education, and psychological variables, such as attitudes and beliefs.

In order to develop skill at understanding and evaluating survey data, it is necessary to have some knowledge of how a survey is planned and carried out. Campbell and Katona have developed an excellent "flow chart" to indicate the sequence of the tasks involved in carrying out a survey, which we have summarized as follows:

1. General Objectives. This is a statement of why the survey is necessary and what is to be accomplished by it, stated in very general terms to indicate the scope of the study.

2. Specific Objectives. The specific type of data to be collected and the hypotheses to be investigated and tested are outlined at this stage.

3. The Sample. In this stage of development, the population to be sampled is defined and the method of determining the sample is precisely specified. How the sample is to be taken is determined in relation to the questions that are to be answered. For example, a survey in which the population to be sampled consists of all the members of a community of voting age would probably use what is known as an *unweighted cross-section* sample. In this method, all individuals of voting age have an equal chance of being selected into the sample that will be interviewed or sent questionnaires. Alternatively, a method such as the *weighted cross-section* deliberately samples heavily in particular subgroups of a population which have special relevance to the objectives of the survey. For example, a survey on a proposed public transport system deliberately sampled more heavily from subgroups who were most likely to use a new public transportation system, in order to obtain the maximum amount of useful information in planning the transportation routes.

These methods represent only a small fraction of the many types of sampling methods used in surveys. The many ways of taking samples represent almost a separate branch of survey methodology, and to discuss all the varieties used would require a separate volume in itself.

4. Data Collection Method. Once the method of selecting the sample is determined, the manner in which the subjects will be contacted is decided and the questionnaire developed. The way in which subjects are approached is extremely important, in that the questions asked and how they are phrased can seriously affect the nature of the responses. For example, in a survey about attitudes toward the government, the question "Do you think the President has support for the domestic policies he is advocating? Yes _____ No _____ Not Sure _____" would be answered somewhat differently from the question "Do you think it is right for the President to advocate such drastic changes in domestic policy? Yes _____ No _____ Not Sure _____." Questionnaire items have to be developed carefully, to insure that they (1) do not introduce a bias; (2) are intelligible to the respondent; and (3) ask for appropriate information. Usually, a questionnaire is extensively pre-tested and revised prior to the actual collection of data.

5. Field Work. This involves the preparation of interview schedules and the training of interviewers if personal interviews are to be included in the survey.

Such preparation and training are of paramount importance, since bias on the part of interviewers has been shown to markedly influence respondents' answers to even the most innocuous questions. Other sources of bias which must be taken into consideration are such things as the sex and race of the interviewers. For example, there are certain topics regarding aspects of personal sexual behavior about which an interviewer of a different sex from the respondent would have difficulty obtaining information if, indeed, he or she could obtain any cooperation at all. Similarly, members of minority racial groups asked about racial discrimination have been shown to be quite hesitant in discussing their true beliefs with a white interviewer.

6. Content Analysis. Although the data collected in the survey may have been arranged so as to be easily quantifiable, there are usually responses that can only be analyzed by the process of coding and tabulating.

This involves constructing a coding system for the different answers and assigning the answers to the proper coding categories. Such a procedure is often necessary when the original interview categories were not adequate to organize the responses and the interviewers had to quote many of the replies directly. "Coding" as the term is used here is simply the process of developing either a numerical or a content category system for classifying responses. Coding systems can be very simple, as in a situation where responses are classified as either positive or negative, or they can be quite complex in order to represent a variety of diverse views given by respondents.

7. Plan of the Analysis. In the analysis plan, the decisions are made as to what answers will be tabulated against what other answers. For example, a survey may collect data on age, sex, and income in relation to the specific objectives of the survey. There may be considerable interest in a cross-tabulation of age in relation to one of the survey questions and sex of respondent in relation to the same questions, but no interest in the relation between age and sex in the sample.

8. Tabulations. The actual data analysis is usually done by computer, especially for large sample surveys.

9. Analysis and Reporting. This final stage is the preparation of the research report, which analyzes and interprets the findings in relation to the specific objectives defined earlier, as well as discussing additional findings not anticipated in the early stages of the survey.

The problems of determining the reliability and validity of survey data remain to be discussed. However, before proceeding with these topics, you are asked to read a research report of a survey as originally published in *The School Review* in 1966. As with the Rhine, Hill, and Wandruff article in Chapter 2, our own commentary has been inserted throughout the report, organized in terms of the 9 point sequence discussed in this chapter.

A Northern Urban Community's Attitudes Toward Racial Imbalances in Schools and Classrooms*†

LEONARD A. MARASCUILO and
KATHLEEN PENFIELD

INTRODUCTION

The current civil rights movement, augmented by the wave of lower-class Negroes migrating from the rural South, has compelled northern urban communities to study the function and organization of their school systems. In essence, the 1954 Supreme Court decision maintained that "separate but equal" schools for Negro and white children were inherently unequal and contrary to the very purpose of education. It emphasized that:

Today, education is perhaps the most important function of state and local governments. . . . It is the very foundation of good citizenship. Today it is the principal instrument in awakening the child to cultural values, in preparing him for later professional training, and in helping him to adjust normally to his environment.‡

By calling upon the schools to assist in the assimilation of Negro children into contemporary American society, the social significance of the school has been emphasized. In essence, this emphasis states that the function of the schools should not be confined to the academic sphere; as a consequence, the value of education as an instrument of social evolution and enrichment should be carefully examined.

*Reprinted from *The School Review*, 74, 4 (Winter 1966) with the permission of the publisher and authors. Published by the University of Chicago Press for the Department of Education of the University of Chicago. Copyright 1966 by the University of Chicago.

†The research reported herein was performed pursuant to a contract with the U.S. Office of Education, Department of Health, Education, and Welfare, Project No. 5-8005-2-12-1. The authors would like to thank Mr. Seong Soo Lee and Mr. Joel Levin for their assistance in preparation of the final statistics.

‡*Brown vs. Board of Education*, 347 U. S. 483 (1954), as quoted by Kenneth B. Clark, "Educational Stimulation of Racially Disadvantaged Children," *Education in Depressed Areas*, ed. A. Harry Passow (New York: Teacher's College, Columbia University, 1963), p. 142.

In response to the challenge entailed by this emphasis, communities throughout the nation are meeting to analyze the problem. While most would agree that the academic quality of Negro education would be elevated by school integration, the question of its concomitant effect upon previously segregated schools has been the subject of heated controversy.§ Furthermore, there is considerable debate concerning the preferable methods of execution and the desired breadth and depth of such programs among those groups in accord with the theory of school integration.

§For a more complete discussion of the reasons why de facto segregated schools are not conducive to good education, see Passow, *ibid*. In particular, see the articles by Mel Ravitz, "The Role of the School in the Urban Setting," and Kenneth B. Clark, *op. cit.*

In northern communities, where segregation is primarily de facto in nature, two distinct problems exist and are considered in this study. These are: (1) the changing of school boundaries within districts to promote school-wide integration, and (2) the modification of ability groupings or curriculum tracks to promote individual classroom integration.

This study is based on a recent mail survey directed by the author. The results of this survey indicate that, while the public is aware of the "school boundaries" issue, it is virtually unaware of the fact that many "apparently integrated" schools prove to be highly segregated when their individual classroom composition is studied. In these schools, the practice of ability grouping or curriculum tracking generally serves to perpetuate segregated education.

Significantly, while most respondents to the survey indicated that they would support administrative programs to correct racial imbalances within the school district, few indicated concern about the correction of racial imbalances within the classroom. This apparent inconsistency in behavior and some of the variables related to its expression are examined in this report.

> *The opening section of the report outlines the general and specific objectives of the survey, giving the reasons for conducting the survey and explaining the type of survey done.*

THE SURVEY DESIGN

As a statistical convenience, the city was stratified by census tracts. Within each census tract, a 2 per cent sample of adults was selected. The sampling procedure used within a census tract was as follows: (1) On the basis of the 1960 census reports, a city block was chosen at random with probabilities proportional to block size. (2) Within a selected block, a simple random sample of six households was made. (3) A second block was then chosen and a simple random sample of six households was taken. (4) This process was repeated until the number of adults in the sample was estimated to equal 2 per cent of the 1960 census tract adult population. This sampling procedure was repeated for each of the twenty-eight census tracts in Berkeley. Since the population magnitude varied across census tracts, the sample sizes over census tracts ranged from twenty-five to eighty-six adults. Since some of the questionnaires were mailed to empty households or wrong addresses, the actual sampling fraction was reduced to 1.88 per cent. Thus, the initial sample consisted of 1,392 adults.

> *Note in this section how precisely the authors define their sampling methods. Note also how carefully the sampling was followed so that the exact proportion of the population sampled can be determined. (See Footnote 2 at the end of this chapter.)*

The survey was begun on April 15, 1964, with the mailing of letters and questionnaires to the 742 randomly selected households in the community. On April 29, follow-up letters were mailed to all non-respondents. Between May 11 and 19, a random sample of the remaining non-respondents was interviewed by trained female personnel from the Survey Research Center of the University of California.* Information was ultimately obtained from 971 adults of the originally selected sample. The survey was terminated on May 19, the evening the Board of Education was to announce its decisions to the community.

> *One of the essential specifications in any survey research is to supply what is known as the* response rate — *the number of individuals returning the questionnaire or consenting to be interviewed. In any survey it is essential to know how many people did not respond or cooperate. A survey which does not indicate its response rate is of little worth since we cannot determine the representativeness of*

---

*The responses to the original questionnaire, the follow-up letter, and the interviews will not be compared in this report because the response patterns were essentially the same across these three response groups.

the survey replies. For example, if only 10% of the sample responded, we would suspect that some strong selective biases operated to lead people to not respond.

COMPOSITION OF THE QUESTIONNAIRE

The questionnaire was designed to obtain data about the personal background of the respondent and his attitudes toward school integration in Berkeley. Specifically, in the first section, informants were asked to respond to thirteen items relating to the socio-economic variables of homeownership status, voter-registration status, educational preparation, and community background, as well as the demographic variables of sex, age group, and race membership. The second section, composed of nine items, dealt with explicit attitudes toward several recommendations proposed by the Citizen's Committee in their report on *De Facto Segregation in the Berkeley Public Schools.*

Of the nine items in the second section, only the two concerning the "Reduction of Racial Imbalances in Neighborhood Schools by Changing School Boundaries" and the "Reduction of Racial Imbalances in the Classrooms by Changing Ability Grouping Procedures" are examined in this report. Responses to these questions are respectively interpreted in terms of: *(a)* individual demographic and socio-economic data obtained from respondents in the first section of the questionnaire, and *(b)* public data from the 1960 census reports and recent census tract voting records in Berkeley.

Here some information about the questionnaire is given. However, there is no mention of pre-testing, so we must assume that the authors did not pre-test their data-gathering instrument—a factor which could lead to serious errors in data collection.

RESULTS

Two separate statistical analyses were conducted to determine the relationship between the aforementioned demographic and socio-economic variables and the kinds of responses to those items dealing with redistricting and modified ability grouping. Both analyses use non-parametric methods. In addition, all statistical tests were conducted with a probability of a type one error equal to .01

This section provides information about the kinds of cross-tabulations that the authors plan to carry out—the sorts of comparisons that will be made between social and psychological items on the questionnaire.
Non-parametric methods are discussed in Chapters 8 and 9.

SPECIFIC ANALYSES

The Reduction of Racial Imbalances in Neighborhood Schools by Changing School Boundaries

The item related to the correction of racial imbalances in the neighborhood elementary schools read as follows:

For some grade schools, the committee suggested that lines be changed so that the percentage of non-white and white children in these schools would be more like the percentage for the entire school system.
I agree _____ I disagree _____ I am not sure _____

Excluding the "I am not sure" category, an unbiased estimate of the proportion of adults in the community supporting the recommendation was 64 per cent.* Due to significant differentials in race and socio-economic levels throughout segments of the community, this percentage notably varies across the twenty-eight census tracts used as strata in the sampling. In the tract representing the highest socio-economic level in the community, the proportion agreeing to the proposition was only 13.3 per cent. At the other extreme, in the tract with the lowest socio-economic status (SES) indexes, the proportion agreeing with the proposition was 100 per cent.

1. Demographic and Socio-economic Analysis Based upon Data Obtained from the Respondents. The responses made by the informants are summarized in Table 1. For this analysis, the informants were classified strictly on the basis of responses made on the questionnaire, and the percentages of agreement for each of these classifications were tested by simple χ^2 methods.

As the figures of Table 1 indicate, sex and educational background (the latter having been determined on the basis of college attendance or non-attendance) have no over-all

---

*If the "I am not sure" responses are classified with the "I disagree" responses, then the percentage is reduced to 51 per cent.

TABLE 1.   Per Cent Agreement with the Recommendations To Change
School Boundaries and To Reduce the Number of Ability Groupings by Two
Levels of Some Variables Reported on in the Survey Questionnaire

VARIABLE AND LEVEL	AMOUNT OF AGREEMENT SHOWN TO THE CHANGING OF SCHOOL BOUNDARIES			AMOUNT OF AGREEMENT SHOWN TO THE REDUCTION OF NUMBER OF ABILITY GROUPS		
	Percent-age	*Sample Size*	*Value of χ^2*	*Percent-age*	*Sample Size*	*Value of χ^2*
Sex:						
Male	57.1	354	.8	35.0	357	1.8
Female	60.0	408		40.0	408	
Education:						
No college	58.4	231	.1	53.0	234	34.3[a]
Some college	59.6	523		30.5	524	
Relatives in schools:						
Yes	53.5	243	3.6	42.8	238	4.4
No	60.9	527		35.2	534	
Race:						
White	51.1	577	89.6[a]	25.4	582	190.7[a]
Non-white	83.8	179		76.6	171	
Homeowner status:						
Renter	74.1	355	74.8[a]	35.9	365	.6
Owner	44.6	395		38.7	398	
Registered voter:						
Yes	54.4	629	23.8[a]	36.6	629	.9
No	76.4	144		41.1	146	
Length of time lived in community						
Under 6 years	78.8	274	89.8[a]	37.8	275	.1
6 years or more	47.1	488		36.9	488	
Education in community:						
Yes	42.6	122	16.2[a]	34.4	119	.2
No	61.8	628		36.4	625	

[a]Differences are statistically significant at $p < .01$. The 99th percentile of χ^2 with 1 d.f. is 6.64.

effect upon an individual's position regarding the school boundary issue. Agreement with the recommendation also appears to be independent of whether or not one has relatives who are employees or students in the school district. On the other hand, race, homeowner status, and voter-registration status are clearly related to the type of responses given. In addition, the length of time lived in Berkeley and whether the respondent was educated in the community's schools have a decided bearing upon his position. An analysis of these findings suggests that newcomers to the community generally favor the integration proposal. Carrying the analysis one step further, it is significant to point out that most of the community's newcomers are either Negroes, students, and/or young people employed by the University of California.

In the general analysis of the survey results, a large number of two-variable contingency tables were examined. From this analysis (not reported here), it was concluded that race was the most important variable related to attitudes to change school boundaries.* Next to race, the variable that showed the strongest association with attitudes to change school boundaries was the age of the informants. In Table 2 the interaction of age with race, education, and homeownership is shown. The low χ^2 values for the interaction test of age with education and homeownership status suggest that these variables do not interact with age. However, age and race show a significant interaction. Young white persons (ages 21–30) supported the recommendation to the same extent as the non-whites of the same age. As age increases, the two races dissociate with respect to their attitudes toward this recommendation, such that for ages over fifty only 29.8 per cent of the whites supported the recommendation, while 83.8 per cent of the non-whites supported it.

Two variable classifications were also conducted to determine if attitudes interacted with some of the other demographic and socio-economic variables. For this classification, census tracts were combined into three groups. The nine census tracts having the lowest measure on a given variable were ranked as low, the next ten as medium, and the last nine as high. Since separate classifications were used for each of nine variables, a census tract categorized as low in education need not be included in the low level for the other

---

*Interested readers may refer to the final report, Project No. 5-8005-2-12-1, submitted to the U. S. Office of Education, Department of Health, Education, and Welfare.

TABLE 2. Per Cent Agreement to Changing School Boundaries with Respect to Race, Education, and Homeowner Status of the Informants by Adult Ages

VARIABLE	SAMPLE SIZE FOR AGE GROUP			PERCENTAGE OF AGREEMENT FOR AGE GROUP			VALUE OF χ^2
	21–30	31–49	50 and up	21–30	31–49	50 and up	
Age	216	294	246	78.2	60.2	40.2	81.8[a]
Race by age:							
White	169	210	198	79.3	48.6	29.8	41.6[a]
Non-white	47	84	48	74.5	89.3	83.8	
Education by age:							
Some college	190	205	128	74.4	60.0	32.8	5.6
No college	26	92	113	84.6	58.7	52.2	
Homeowner status by age:							
Renter	181	116	58	80.7	75.0	51.7	1.7
Owner	32	178	185	62.5	48.9	37.3	

[a]Differences are statistically significant at $p < .01$. The 99th percentile of χ^2 with 2 d.f. is 9.2.

variables. Thus, while the total sample size of 770 remains constant for each variable, the number in a given level is subject to some fluctuation.[7]

As the figures of Table 3 indicate, considerable support for the recommendation to change the elementary school boundaries came from those census tracts with a high per-

---

[7]The sample size for this analysis is not 971, the total number of respondents, because the "I am not sure" category on this item has been excluded.

TABLE 3. Per Cent Agreement with the Recommendations To Change School Boundaries and To Reduce the Number of Ability Groupings by Three Levels of Some Variables Reported in the Survey Questionnaire

VARIABLE	AMOUNT OF AGREEMENT SHOWN TO THE CHANGING OF SCHOOL BOUNDARIES			AMOUNT OF AGREEMENT SHOWN TO THE REDUCTION OF NUMBER OF ABILITY GROUPS		
Level and Median Value	Percent-age	Sample Size	Value of χ^2	Percent-age	Sample Size	Value of χ^2
Schooled outside Berkeley (per cent):						
Low (76.3)	57.5	228		44.4	225	
Medium (84.1)	52.3	306	17.66[a]	34.7	314	5.64
High (92.0)	69.9	236		36.5	233	
With relations in school district (per cent):						
Low (12.0)	63.9	241		27.6	243	
Medium (30.3)	48.1	310	28.42[a]	34.1	323	44.21[a]
High (45.5)	69.9	219		56.8	206	
Registered to vote 1960 (per cent):						
Low (71.4)	69.9	246		37.2	242	
Medium (82.8)	54.6	291	17.19[a]	37.1	308	.80
High (93.9)	53.6	233		40.5	222	
Vote in 1960 (per cent):						
Low (63.8)	67.8	227		32.9	228	
Medium (75.6)	63.9	291	27.79[a]	44.0	293	7.52
High (93.6)	46.0	252		35.9	251	
Vote in 1963 (per cent):						
Low (48.1)	68.0	247		32.5	246	
Medium (62.4)	59.6	287	17.15[a]	40.6	293	4.73
High (80.0)	49.6	236		40.8	233	
College (per cent):						
Low (37.1)	80.6	211		69.7	201	
Medium (75.2)	43.5	317	72.48[a]	31.7	319	121.58[a]
High (90.0)	61.2	242		21.0	252	
Homeowners (per cent):						
Low (16.2)	67.8	227		28.2	234	
Medium (50.7)	66.6	290	40.73[a]	49.5	285	26.83[a]
High (86.1)	43.1	253		34.4	253	
Median age (years):						
Low (30.0)	73.1	216		34.6	211	
Medium (41.3)	61.7	287	39.42[a]	46.8	293	15.60[a]
High (47.5)	45.3	267		31.3	268	
White (per cent):						
Low (15.2)	80.6	211		69.7	201	
Medium (92.5)	47.6	315	58.60[a]	27.6	326	114.97[a]
High (100.0)	55.7	244		26.1	245	

[a]Differences are statistically significant at $p < .01$. The 99th percentile of χ^2 with 2 d.f. is 9.2.

centage of respondents schooled outside of the community, as well as those tracts in which a high percentage of respondents have relatives who are either employees or students in the school district. However, the percentage of respondents supporting the recommendation is considerably less in those tracts containing a high percentage of registered voters, a high percentage of voters in the 1960 and 1963 elections, a medium percentage of college-educated individuals, and a high percentage of homeowners. An analysis of the demographic variables of median age and per cent white discloses that in those census tracts with the highest median age and greatest percentage of white residents there was also considerably less support for the recommendation. Finally, it can be concluded, on the basis of census tract classification alone, that the tracts in which the greatest percentage of respondents (80.6) favored the recommendation were those with the least number of college-trained individuals and the smallest percentage of white residents. Considerable support (73.1 per cent) was also expressed by informants from those tracts with the lowest median age.

> *In the preceding section, the specific analyses of items are discussed. Note that the authors are careful to specify how the analysis is done and whether or not a category such as "I am not sure" is excluded.*
>
> *χ^2 (chi-square) is a statistical technique for the comparison of frequencies, such as the number of persons answering "agree" or "disagree." As an illustration, examine Table 1 in the article. The first comparison made relates sex to strength of agreement to the changing of school boundaries. The percentage of males agreeing with Item 1 in the questionnaire is 57.1 per cent; that of females, 60.0 per cent (note that the authors include the numbers on which these percentages were calculated). The χ^2 value of this comparison is 0.8, indicating that there is little difference between men and women on this item. However, when homeowners and renters are compared on the same item, 74.1 per cent of renters agree and 44.6 per cent of homeowners agree. The χ^2 value for this comparison is 74.8, indicating that the difference in rate of agreement between these two groups is much greater than would be expected by chance.*
>
> *A discussion of the χ^2 method is given in Chapter 8, p. 139.*

2. Analysis Based upon 1960 Census Reports and Recent Census Tract Voting Records. Whereas the previous discussion was dependent upon demographic and socioeconomic data obtained from the respondents to the questionnaire itself, the following is a supplementary analysis based upon a collation of 1960 census and voting data with the responses to the survey item concerning the recommendation to promote integration by changing local school boundaries. For this investigation, the same procedures were employed as in the previous analysis. The twenty-eight census tracts were ranked on the basis of 1960 census data and recent local voting records. The nine census tracts having the lowest measure on the particular variable of interest were classified as low, the next ten as medium, and the last nine as high. Separate classifications were used for each of the seven variables, as shown in Table 4.

This analysis of the data disclosed that the proportion of the respondents agreeing to changes in the neighborhood elementary school boundaries to reduce the racial imbalances decreased as the educational level of their census tract increased. This is of even greater import when one considers the unusual educational and university orientation of the community.* In the tracts in which fewer than 50 per cent of the adults had completed

---

*As the figures in Table 4 indicate, Berkeley is an unusual community in certain respects. In addition to being the home of a large university, its members tend to be highly educated and to have above-average wealth. The community's 13.6-year median level of education is unusually high, and its median family income in 1960 ($6,420) was considerably above that of the nation as a whole.

TABLE 4. Per Cent Agreement with the Recommendations To Change School Boundaries and To Reduce the Number of Ability Groupings by Three Levels of Some Variables Reported in the 1960 Census Reports and Recent Census Tract Voting Records

VARIABLE	AMOUNT OF AGREEMENT SHOWN TO THE CHANGING OF SCHOOL BOUNDARIES			AMOUNT OF AGREEMENT SHOWN TO THE REDUCTION OF NUMBER OF ABILITY GROUPS		
Level and Median Value	Percent-age	Sample Size	Value of χ^2	Percent-age	Sample Size	Value of χ^2
Education (years):						
Low (11.0)	77.8	216		67.8	205	
Medium (13.6)	55.8	310	46.6[a]	31.5	321	110.4[a]
High (16.5)	47.1	244		22.0	246	
Family income:						
Low ($5,130)	81.9	215		59.5	200	
Medium ($6,420)	59.0	300	95.0[a]	35.1	313	59.2[a]
High ($9,730)	40.4	255		25.1	259	
Voting for sale of elementary school bonds (per cent):						
Low (58.0)	58.1	217		48.4	217	
Medium (66.0)	62.1	293	1.6	40.6	286	23.4[a]
High (75.0)	56.9	260		27.1	269	
Voting for passage of fair-housing law (per cent):						
Low (33)	47.6	267		33.0	264	
Medium (43)	58.8	257	32.2[a]	29.2	264	35.0[a]
High (67)	72.4	246		53.3	244	

[a]Differences are statistically significant at $p < .01$. The 99th percentile of χ^2 with 2 d.f. is 9.2.

high school, 77.8 per cent of the informants favored changing the school boundaries to bring about integration; while in the census tracts in which over 50 per cent of the adults had completed college, only 47.1 per cent favored the recommendation.

As Table 4 indicates, the proportion of the respondents agreeing with the recommendation also decreased as the median family income in the tracts increased. Even though the SES variables measuring the educational level and the median family income level of the individual tracts are confounded, it is feasible to generalize that high SES census tracts were primarily opposed to the recommendation. Therefore, it is apparent that support for changing school boundaries to reduce racial imbalances was centered in the low- and medium-level SES tracts.

It appears that the voting pattern in a recent election to approve an elementary school bond issue had little relationship to attitudes regarding the change of school boundaries.* This result suggests that attitudes relating to financial support of schools are independent of attitudes to integrate schools. However, the analysis of the vote on the community fair-housing law produced more explicit information. As the proportion of respondents voting in favor of the fair-housing law increased, the percentage agreeing with the changing of the school boundaries to promote integration also increased.

In conclusion, the tracts in which the respondents demonstrated the greatest support for the recommendation were those tracts characterized by a population having low me-

*Chi-square equals 1.6.

dian years of education, low median family incomes, and a high percentage of voters who supported the fair-housing law. For the most part, these are the Negro areas of the community.

> *The availability of relatively recent census data allows the authors to run a separate analysis using census data and voting records—a clever way of establishing the validity of the survey findings using an independent method of classification. If the two methods had given results which did not agree, this would have cast doubt on the generality of the conclusions.*

The Reduction of Racial Imbalances in the Classrooms by Changing Ability-Grouping Procedures

The questionnaire item related to the integration of classrooms read as follows:

Now Berkeley schools divide children into classes on the basis of how well they did in earlier classes. This sometimes leads to racial segregation in the classrooms. The committee suggests fewer "ability groupings" be used. This would cut down on segregation and would produce classes with children who have a large range of ability.

I agree _____ I disagree _____ I am not sure _____

Only 47 per cent of the respondents favored the proposition.* Just as with the recommendation concerning the changing of elementary school boundaries, these percentages showed wide variability across the twenty-eight census tracts. The range was 3.4–98.2 per cent.

1. Demographic and Socio-economic Analysis Based upon Data Obtained from the Respondents. The results of this analysis are summarized in Tables 1, 3, and 5. As may be seen by examining the figures in Table 1, it follows that the respondent's sex, homeownership status, voter-registration status, length of time lived in the community, and education in the community's schools showed little or no relationship to positions concerning this recommendation. While informants with relatives in the schools showed a slight preference in favor of the recommendation, this difference is not statistically significant. The race of the respondent was the characteristic most related to support for this recommendation. Within the non-white population, 76.6 per cent favored the reduction in the number of ability groupings, as compared with only 25.4 per cent within the white population. Informants with some college education were, for the most part, against the proposition, while those with no college education were about equally divided in their attitudes. As the figures of Table 3 indicate, support for the reduction in the number of ability groupings was centered in those census tracts in which the members have a high proportion of relatives associated with the school system. Those tracts having a low proportion of college-trained adults and a low proportion of white citizens also supported the recommendation. Essentially, these represent the Negro areas of the community.

Table 5 presents an analysis of the interaction of age with race, education, and homeownership. Although the interaction between race and age is not significant at $p = .01$, it does suggest that young non-white persons support the recommendation less than do their elders. However, white residents and college-trained individuals were generally against the recommendation at all age levels. The significant interaction of age with homeownership status can be partially explained by the composition of the young renters, who are predominantly members of the graduate-student population of Berkeley in atten-

---

*This is based upon an exclusion of the "I am not sure" responses. If one classifies the "I am not sure" responses with the "I disagree" responses, this percentage is reduced to 38 per cent.

TABLE 5.   Per Cent Agreement to Reducing the Number of Ability Groups with Respect to Race, Education, and Homeowner Status of the Informants by Adult Age

VARIABLE	SAMPLE SIZES FOR AGE GROUP			PERCENTAGE OF AGREEMENT FOR AGE GROUP			VALUE OF χ^2
	21–30	31–49	50 and up	21–30	31–49	50 and up	
Age	218	294	253	30.7	44.5	34.8	11.1[a]
Race by age:							
White	179	204	203	25.1	28.4	25.2	7.2
Non-white	39	86	50	56.4	82.6	82.0	
Education by age:							
Some college	194	197	124	26.8	36.5	29.8	1.6
No college	25	92	115	60.0	60.9	46.1	
Homeowner status by age:							
Renter	186	110	67	26.9	50.0	38.8	11.4[a]
Owner	29	175	190	55.2	40.6	32.6	

[a]Differences are statistically significant at $p < .01$. The 99th percentile of χ^2 with 2 d.f. is 9.2.

dance at the University of California. This group of young renters demonstrated significant opposition to the proposed reduction of ability groupings in the schools.

2. *Analysis Based upon 1960 Census Reports and Recent Census Tract Voting Records.* The results of this analysis followed a pattern similar to that noted for the recommendation to change elementary school boundaries except that the percentages are at a much lower level (see Table 4). The tracts that supported the recommendations were low in education, low in median family income, and high in the percentage of voters favoring the fair-housing law. Since most Negroes are members of these groups, it seems that the Negro population was the principal source of support for the recommendation.

A Comparison and Summary of the Responses to the Two Recommendations Based upon the Preceding Data Analysis

In terms of census tract classifications, respondents who were opposed to the changing of school boundaries and the reduction of ability groupings were centered in those census tracts which were classified as high with respect to median years of education and family income. In terms of the questionnaire information, opposition to the changing of school boundaries was expressed primarily by white residents, homeowners, registered voters, persons educated in the community's schools, and by those who have resided in the community for over six years.* Combining the inferences drawn from these two sets of analyses, it is reasonable to conclude that opposition to the recommendations to improve racial imbalances in the school district is centered among the established, older, upper-class white residents of the community.

Support for the recommendation to change school boundaries so as to promote school integration was centered in those census tracts which were classified as low or medium with respect to median years of education and median family income. They also had favorable votes for the passage of the fair-housing law. In terms of questionnaire infor-

---

*Since white adults at all socio-economic levels were in favor of ability grouping, it is evident that this is a unique issue, and it will be studied in more depth in the discussion that follows.

mation, support for the reduction of ability grouping was expressed by non-white residents and those with no college education. Combining these two sets of information, it is evident that the primary support for the reduction of ability grouping to promote classroom integration was localized within the Negro population of the community.

DISCUSSION

One implication of this study is that northern school boards in districts similar to Berkeley can expect to have the general backing of the community for correcting racial imbalances in the schools, but they need not expect the backing of the community for eliminating or reducing the number of ability groupings to correct racial imbalances in the classrooms. If school boards move in this direction, they should be prepared for criticism, and they should be prepared to answer this criticism.

From this study, it appears that most of the opposition to desegregate schools was concentrated among the older, upper-class white members of the community and, in particular, among the adults who had been educated in the community's schools and who had continued to live in the community. In this community, the opposition was localized in the census tracts representing the highest SES levels of the community. Support for desegregation to correct racial imbalances was centered among Negroes, young adults, new residents of the community, and adults who had been educated outside of the community. The major support for the reduction or elimination of ability groupings came from the Negro citizens of the community. White adults at all socio-economic levels appear to be convinced that ability grouping is desirable for educating children, and therefore its "good" characteristics are not worth losing simply to bring about better racial balances in the classrooms.

The following comments, made by respondents on the questionnaire, are indicative of the reasons given by the white public for opposing the recommendation to reduce the number of ability groupings.*

1. Brighter children should not be brought down to the level of achievement of less bright children.

2. The school's *only* problem is education. You have no choice but to provide instruction to develop each student to the maximum of his ability. If this produces segregation, then segregation is mandatory.

3. Fewer ability groupings would, no doubt, cut down on segregation, but might also intimidate the best students and make it difficult to give the poorest students the special attention they need.

4. I am very much in favor of ability groupings. Eliminating those would neither benefit the slow nor the more advanced student. The latter would be left without challenge and the slow would have a very hard time to follow. Give special teaching to all children who need extra help—the integration will follow in time.

5. I do not believe that talented students should be limited in classwork by having to contend with slower students of less ability. I realize that because of existing segregation, many Negro students have a shaky scholastic background, and as a result of ability groupings, classes might tend to become segregated. This poses a dilemma.

6. I strongly suggest that you forget about *fewer* "ability groupings." If our standards of education are based upon excellence and the furthering of those gifted children who can move faster than the pace set by our mediocre school systems, then let that be unaffected by race, creed, or religion. You do not help the cause of any group by lowering standards for them. At first the "whites" may be predominant in these special groupings, but since ability is irrespective of race, soon there would be a mixed group in any special ability . . . which reflects the relative percentage of races *within the school system*.

7. I am all for ability groupings. If this sometimes leads to racial segregation, I regret this fact.

---

*Each questionnaire contained two blank pages with an invitation to the respondents to make any additional comments they would like to have conveyed to the Board of Education. Many people took advantage of this opportunity to express their points of view.

In the earlier discussion, the provision for content analysis of the responses was mentioned. This is not a content analysis per se, but a sampling of content responses to illustrate the reasons given by the respondents for agreeing or disagreeing with a given item.

Implicit in these comments is the uncontested assumption by each respondent that ability grouping is the paragon of modern education. However, ability grouping has its disadvantages and, for the most part, these disadvantages have real meaning for the culturally deprived student. Kenneth B. Clark, in his article on "Educational Stimulation for Racially Disadvantaged Children," describes the web in which the culturally deprived child is caught from the time he is first assigned to a particular ability group:

When a child from a deprived background is treated as if he is uneducable, he becomes uneducable and the low test score is thereby reinforced. If a child scores low on an intelligence test because he cannot read and then is not taught to read because he has a low score, then such a child is being imprisoned in an iron circle and becomes the victim of an educational self-fulfilling prophecy.*

Many other educators have demonstrated concern about its damaging psychological, social, and cultural effects upon the child.†

EVALUATION OF THE SURVEY

Having examined the data presented by Marascuilo and Penfield, we can now ask how the reliability and validity of this survey can be assessed.

In general, the reliability of survey data is determined by the same method used to assess the reliability of any set of measurements — i.e., by a remeasurement. Marascuilo and Penfield do not devote a specific section of their article to the reliability of their survey. However, in describing their sampling procedure, they note that a random sample of the non-respondents were interviewed by trained survey research workers and that the response patterns were essentially the same as for the group returning the mail questionnaires. If this group had responded differently, the reliability of the procedure would have been questionable, and it is doubtful that the conclusions reached would have been warranted without a second survey on a new sample to compare with the first sampling.

Validity is frequently difficult to establish for survey data, since the determination of validity requires an outside criterion. Such a criterion is often unavailable in survey data, especially when the survey represents the first attempt made to learn about a particular problem area. The Marascuilo and Penfield study deals with the problem of validity in an ingenious way, by showing that the distribution of voting responses by census tracts in relation to other census data is exactly what would have been expected from the results of the survey.

---

*Clark, *op. cit.*, p. 150.

†Some helpful reviews of the research on ability grouping are: Maurice J. Eash, "Grouping: What Have We Learned?" *Educational Leadership* (April, 1961), pp. 429–34; Ruth B. Ekstrom, "Experimental Studies of Homogeneous Grouping: A Critical Review," *School Review* (Summer, 1961), pp. 216–26; Harry A. Passow, "The Maze of Research on Ability Grouping," *Educational Forum* (March, 1962), pp. 281–88.

Overall, the Marascuilo and Penfield study is an excellent example of survey work, its only limitation being the lack of evidence of any pre-testing of the questionnaire used. However, as a model of how survey work should be conducted, it has few faults.

FOOTNOTES

[1]A. Campbell and G. Katona, The sample survey: a technique for social science research. In L. Festinger and D. Katz (Eds.), *Research methods in the behavioral sciences*. New York: Dryden Press, 1953.

[2]As an illustration of surveys where the sampling is concealed, you have undoubtedly seen television commercials saying things such as "Out of all dentists surveyed, 75 per cent recommended brushing with *Sludge* toothpaste." How many dentists were surveyed? You can obtain a response rate of 75 per cent by surveying four dentists, three of whom work for the *Sludge* company.

chapter six

field observational studies

"Take no notice of Milton. He's doing some research for that damn book of his."

Drawing by Mahood. © 1973 The New Yorker Magazine, Inc.

In the example of survey research methods given in the last chapter, we can see how a survey can be used to study aspects of a community's attitudes and outlooks in relation to economic and social factors. Such a portrait of a community is meant to have a wide scope and to be representative of the group studied on the problem of interest to the survey workers. The field investigation also attempts to produce a portrait of a community or group, but with two essential differences from the survey approach.

First, the field study is seldom as concerned with representativeness in its sampling as is the survey. The emphasis is usually more on obtaining a detailed picture of the processes and interactions of a given group of individuals, without being overly concerned about generalizing the results to a larger population.

Secondly, the field study is oriented toward the processes of interaction as they occur, attempting to provide a natural picture of interrelationships. By contrast, the knowledge of interaction gained from a survey is basically a result arrived at by statistical analysis.

There are several types of field studies, but the method has had its widest use by anthropologists studying other societies in an attempt to understand the processes by which individuals function and relate to others within the framework of the society. Such an approach often requires that the research worker live within the community he is studying and, as far as is possible, become accepted into the community. It is necessary for him to develop social relationships with individuals in the community and establish contacts that will allow him to gather information about the patterns of social life he observes. As an illustration of the time and effort involved in carrying out such field studies, consider the following summary of the field work carried out by Hollos in her study of a Norwegian community.[1]

. . . Research for the study was carried out in the county of Trysil in Eastern Norway. I selected this particular area after travelling extensively in Norway during the summer of 1966 and investigating settlement patterns of both Western and Eastern parts of the country. I was searching for a farming area with evenly dispersed homesteads, which were spatially isolated from each other but yet maintained community ties and networks of relations. In such an area, for the purpose of comparison, I also hoped to find a nucleated settlement with relatively high population density and possibly a town or marketing center with a somewhat more complex social structure.

The dispersed settlement pattern is the norm in most of Eastern Norway, but Trysil had the additional advantage of being off the major north–south thoroughfare, without railroads and until recently without paved roads. The county is considered underdeveloped and isolated, communications with the outside are minimal, and as yet there are no signs of the general urbanization and industrialization process which is becoming typical in most of the rest of Norway. The location was suggested to me by Dr. Fredrik Barth of the University of Bergen and Helge Kleivan of the University of Oslo. The latter contacted the Trysil county agronomist, Mr. Bjarne Vaage, who received me and travelled with me to different parts of the county. His assistance was invaluable since he was familiar not only with the local economy and problems but with most of the farmers in the area, many of whom have never yet encountered a foreigner. I finally decided to work in the community of Slettås, a former school district in northwest Trysil.

Slettås is a dispersed farm area with a population of almost 300. The total land area included within the community is about 150 km², most of which consists of pine forest, tundra, bogs or mountain pastures. The farms are located off the main road, within the forested regions.

I lived for sixteen months in Slettås as the guest of several farms. I stayed in three neighborhoods at different ends of the community to observe community life and social relations from various points of view. Each of the three families I lived with had three children, of ages ranging from 2 to 8. In addition to observing family interaction and child behavior within the families, I visited all the farms in the Slettås area and interviewed the majority of the people. I also participated in all the community affairs and voluntary associations. I spent two days per week in the school to which Slettås children are now being bussed, observing first and second graders in the classroom and during intermissions. During the summer of 1968 I organized a kindergarten in Slettås to which I transported all the children between the ages of 2 and 8. I also gave a standardized questionnaire regarding child rearing practices to 15 mothers.

During May and June of 1968 I tested 90 children with cognitive developmental tests, 45 in the centralized village and county center of Innbygda and 45 in Slettås. The children were 6, 7 and 8 years of age. Each child was tested on two groups of tests, social cognitive and non-social cognitive.

After preliminary scoring of the tests in Berkeley during the spring of 1969 I decided to return to Norway to test an additional group of children from a somewhat more complex social milieu. During the summer of 1969 I tested 45 children of the same ages in the town of Elverum. During this time I lived in Elverum and in Innbygda and collected observational data on the families and behavior of children at these locations.

I also administered the children's Sigel Sorting Task to mothers of ten of the isolated preschool children in order to gain more specific data regarding mothers' teaching style.

I am grateful to the officials of Trysil county who granted me permission to stay in the county, to study the schools and to test the school children. Above all, I have a deep gratitude to the people of Slettås who accepted me into their homes and into their lives . . .

Clearly, studies of this sort, involving as they do spending long periods of time in a new community, the frequent necessity of learning a new language, and the process of constant observation and recording, are not entered into lightly. As an indicator of the types of questions dealt with in such a study, the following additional excerpt from Hollos' description of her study offers a good example of how a functionally oriented field investigator formulates a problem for study.

I observed child behavior, interaction between adults and children and children of different ages and learning in its natural setting. The dispersed farm environment provided a chance to map out the child's entire social and physical universe.

Families were studied in detail in terms of role performance, interaction and communication. I also investigated the dispersed community through family, neighborhood, and friendship networks as well as through family members' participation in a variety of community organizations.

Regarding the child's social environment and development I was interested in the following questions:

1. To what extent does such a dispersed community function as a social unit and through what mechanisms is this unity maintained?

2. Through what channels and in what manner is social control maintained and norms enforced?

3. What is the quality of social relations in a community where face-to-face interaction is relatively infrequent?

4. How much independence does the family as a system have from the rest of the community and how much do community norms influence the internal arrangement of roles?

5. What are the expected roles, rules of communication and of everyday interaction of family members, and how does spatial isolation from others influence this?

6. Who are the agents of child raising and what role does the child have in the family?

7. What is the preschool and young schoolchild's social universe? With whom is he in contact and what type of interactions does he engage in?

8. How do children spend their day on the farm? What types of activities occupy them most?

9. What are the mechanisms, channels and situations of learning?

The psychological testing was done by a combination of non-social and social cognitive measures, developed by Piaget, Flavell and Smedslund. I tested three groups of children in each of the three locations: Slettås, Innbygda and Elverum. The children were 6, 7 and 8 years of age. I chose these ages since Norwegian children begin school at the age of 7 and thus I had the opportunity to test for another social-interactional variable, namely, the school experience.

Thus, the research is comprised of essentially three different but closely related problems: a sociological investigation of community structure; a study of family roles and interaction with child raising as its focus, and a comparative study of cognitive development in children based on the psychological tests.

Katz, in his comprehensive account of field methodology,[2] suggests a list of the ways in which the field worker should be ready to gather informal information. The following list is adapted from his account.

A. The investigator should not limit his range of contacts to a narrow segment of informants. It is important to develop some contact with at least one person from every segment and subgroup of the society or group you are observing. The field worker has to be particularly careful not to limit his contacts to people similar to himself in background, social outlook, and economic position.

B. The field worker should make an effort to meet informants who themselves have a wide range of contacts in the society. People who are at the center of or are an important part of communications networks in a community are particularly useful.

C. It is extremely useful to make contact with persons in positions of informal as well as formal leadership positions.

D. The field worker should be on the alert for discrepancies in the accounts of his various informants. If a field worker hears the same account from all of his informants, he is probably restricting himself too much in his contacts with people.

E. The field worker should assess the information he receives from his various informants in relation to their social roles, their group memberships, and their personal activities. Consequently, it is important to learn as much about your informants as you can.

F. There is no substitute for participant observation. Even though a field worker may have a wide variety of informants, this information needs to be supplemented by living in the community, participating in activities, and seeing what the people actually do in specific situations.

G. It is useful to collect information about personal and private beliefs as well as the socially approved outlook of the community. It is particularly important to know the extent to which personal and private beliefs differ from the socially approved position.

H. It is absolutely necessary for the field worker to keep complete notes and to record them promptly. Memory, particularly when one is studying situations that are very similar, can be extremely unreliable.

I. It is important to keep track of impressions and global judgments. In a field study, overall impressions are frequently as valuable as detailed documentation.

J. The field worker should make use of all available records and secondary sources and study the procedures by which the records were compiled.

As an illustration of how particular problems can be studied through field methods, you are asked to read the following account of some field observational work in a rather unusual setting.

On Being Sane in Insane Places*

†D. L. ROSENHAN

If sanity and insanity exist, how shall we know them?

*This article originally appeared in *Science, 179*:250–258, 19 January, 1973, and is reprinted with permission. Copyright 1973 by the American Association for the Advancement of Science.

†The author is professor of psychology and law at Stanford University, Stanford, California 94305. Portions of these data were presented to colloquiums of the psychology departments at the University of California at Berkeley and at Santa Barbara; University of Arizona, Tucson; and Harvard University, Cambridge, Massachusetts.

The question is neither capricious nor itself insane. However much we may be personally convinced that we can tell the normal from the abnormal, the evidence is simply not compelling. It is commonplace, for example, to read about murder trials wherein eminent psychiatrists for the defense are contradicted by equally eminent psychiatrists for the prosecution on the matter of the defendant's sanity. More generally, there are a great deal of conflicting data on the reliability, utility, and meaning of such terms as "sanity," "insanity," "mental illness," and "schizophrenia" (1). Finally, as early as 1934, Benedict suggested that normality and abnormality are not universal (2). What is viewed as normal in one culture may be seen as quite aberrant in another. Thus, notions of normality and abnormality may not be quite as accurate as people believe they are.

To raise questions regarding normality and abnormality is in no way to question the fact that some behaviors are deviant or odd. Murder is deviant. So, too, are hallucinations. Nor does raising such questions deny the existence of the personal anguish that is often associated with "mental illness." Anxiety and depression exist. Psychological suffering exists. But normality and abnormality, sanity and insanity, and the diagnoses that flow from them may be less substantive than many believe them to be.

At its heart, the question of whether the sane can be distinguished from the insane (and whether degrees of insanity can be distinguished from each other) is a simple matter: do the salient characteristics that lead to diagnoses reside in the patients themselves or in the environments and contexts in which observers find them? From Bleuler, through Kretchmer, through the formulators of the recently revised *Diagnostic and Statistical Manual* of the American Psychiatric Association, the belief has been strong that patients present symptoms, that those symptoms can be categorized, and, implicitly, that the sane are distinguishable from the insane. More recently, however, this belief has been questioned. Based in part on theoretical and anthropological considerations, but also on philosophical, legal, and therapeutic ones, the view has grown that psychological categorization of mental illness is useless at best and downright harmful, misleading, and pejorative at worst. Psychiatric diagnoses, in this view, are in the minds of the observers and are not valid summaries of characteristics displayed by the observed (3–5).

Gains can be made in deciding which of these is more nearly accurate by getting normal people (that is, people who do not have, and have never suffered, symptoms of serious psychiatric disorders) admitted to psychiatric hospitals and then determining whether they were discovered to be sane and, if so, how. If the sanity of such pseudopatients were always detected, there would be prima facie evidence that a sane individual can be distinguished from the insane context in which he is found. Normality (and presumably abnormality) is distinct enough that it can be recognized wherever it occurs, for it is carried within the person. If, on the other hand, the sanity of the pseudopatients were never discovered, serious difficulties would arise for those who support traditional modes of psychiatric diagnosis. Given that the hospital staff was not incompetent, that the pseudopatient had been behaving as sanely as he had been outside of the hospital, and that it had never been previously suggested that he belonged in a psychiatric hospital, such an unlikely outcome would support the view that psychiatric diagnosis betrays little about the patient but much about the environment in which an observer finds him.

This article describes such an experiment. Eight sane people gained secret admission to 12 different hospitals (6). Their diagnostic experiences constitute the data of the first part of this article; the remainder is devoted to a description of their experiences in psychiatric institutions. Too few psychiatrists and psychologists, even those who have worked in such hospitals, know what the experience is like. They rarely talk about it with former patients, perhaps because they distrust information coming from the previously insane. Those who have worked in psychiatric hospitals are likely to have adapted so thoroughly to the settings that they are insensitive to the impact of that experience. And while there have been occasional reports of researchers who submitted themselves to psychiatric hospitalization (7), these researchers have commonly remained in the hospitals for short periods of time, often with the knowledge of the hospital staff. It is difficult to know the extent to which they were treated like patients or like research colleagues. Nevertheless, their reports about the inside of the psychiatric hospital have been valuable. This article extends those efforts.

PSEUDOPATIENTS AND THEIR SETTINGS

The eight pseudopatients were a varied group. One was a psychology graduate student in his 20's. The remaining seven were older and "established." Among them were three psychologists, a pediatrician, a psychiatrist, a painter, and a housewife. Three pseudopatients were women, five were men. All of them employed pseudonyms, lest their alleged diagnoses embarrass them later. Those who were in mental health professions alleged another occupation in order to avoid the special attentions that might be accorded by staff, as a matter of courtesy or caution, to ailing colleagues (8). With the exception of myself (I was the first pseudopatient and my presence was known to the hospital administrator and chief psychologist and, so far as I can tell, to them alone), the presence of pseudopatients and the nature of the research program was not known to the hospital staffs (9).

The settings were similarly varied. In order to generalize the findings, admission into a variety of hospitals was sought. The 12 hospitals in the sample were located in five different states on the East and West coasts. Some were old and shabby, some were quite new. Some were research-oriented, others not. Some had good staff-patient ratios, others were quite understaffed. Only one was a strictly private hospital. All of the others were supported by state or federal funds or, in one instance, by university funds.

After calling the hospital for an appointment, the pseudopatient arrived at the admissions office complaining that he had been hearing voices. Asked what the voices said, he replied that they were often unclear, but as far as he could tell they said "empty," "hollow," and "thud." The voices were unfamiliar and were of the same sex as the pseudopatient. The choice of these symptoms was occasioned by their apparent similarity to existential symptoms. Such symptoms are alleged to arise from painful concerns about the perceived meaninglessness of one's life. It is as if the hallucinating person were saying, "My life is empty and hollow." The choice of these symptoms was also determined by the *absence* of a single report of existential psychoses in the literature.

Beyond alleging the symptoms and falsifying name, vocation, and employment, no further alterations of person, history, or circumstances were made. The significant events of the pseudopatient's life history were presented as they had actually occurred. Relationships with parents and siblings, with spouse and children, with people at work and in school, consistent with the aforementioned exceptions, were described as they were or had been. Frustrations and upsets were described along with joys and satisfactions. These facts are important to remember. If anything, they strongly biased the subsequent results in favor of detecting sanity, since none of their histories or current behaviors were seriously pathological in any way.

Immediately upon admission to the psychiatric ward, the pseudopatient ceased simulating *any* symptoms of abnormality. In some cases, there was a brief period of mild nervousness and anxiety, since none of the pseudopatients really believed that they would be admitted so easily. Indeed, their shared fear was that they would be immediately exposed as frauds and greatly embarrassed. Moreover, many of them had never visited a psychiatric ward; even those who had, nevertheless had some genuine fears about what might happen to them. Their nervousness, then, was quite appropriate to the novelty of the hospital setting, and it abated rapidly.

Apart from that short-lived nervousness, the pseudopatient behaved on the ward as he "normally" behaved. The pseudopatient spoke to patients and staff as he might ordinarily. Because there is uncommonly little to do on a psychiatric ward, he attempted to engage others in conversation. When asked by staff how he was feeling, he indicated that he was fine, that he no longer experienced symptoms. He responded to instructions from attendants, to calls for medication (which was not swallowed), and to dining-hall instructions. Beyond such activities as were available to him on the admissions ward, he spent his time writing down his observations about the ward, its patients, and the staff. Initially these notes were written "secretly," but as it soon became clear that no one much cared, they were subsequently written on standard tablets of paper in such public places as the dayroom. No secret was made of these activities.

The pseudopatient, very much as a true psychiatric patient, entered a hospital with no foreknowledge of when he would be discharged. Each was told that he would have to get out by his own devices, essentially by convincing the staff that he was sane. The psychological stresses associated with hospitalization were considerable, and all but one of the pseudopatients desired to be discharged almost immediately after being admitted. They were, therefore, motivated not only to behave sanely, but to be paragons of cooperation. That their behavior was in no way disruptive is confirmed by nursing reports, which have been obtained on most of the patients. These reports uniformly indicate that the patients were "friendly," "cooperative," and "exhibited no abnormal indications."

THE NORMAL ARE NOT DETECTABLY SANE

Despite their public "show" of sanity, the pseudopatients were never detected. Admitted, except in one case, with a diagnosis of schizophrenia (*10*), each was discharged with a diagnosis of schizophrenia "in remission." The label "in remission" should in no way be dismissed as a formality, for at no time during any hospitalization had any question been raised about any pseudopatient's simulation. Nor are there any indications in the hospital records that the pseudopatient's status was suspect. Rather, the evidence is strong that, once labeled schizophrenic, the pseudopatient was stuck with that label. If the pseudopatient was to be discharged, he must naturally be "in remission"; but he was not sane, nor, in the institution's view, had he ever been sane.

The uniform failure to recognize sanity cannot be attributed to the quality of the hospitals, for, although there were considerable variations among them, several are considered excellent. Nor can it be alleged that there was simply not enough time to observe the pseudopatients. Length of hospitalization ranged from 7 to 52 days, with an average of 19 days. The pseudopatients were not, in fact, carefully observed, but this failure clearly speaks more to traditions within psychiatric hospitals than to lack of opportunity.

Finally, it cannot be said that the failure to recognize the pseudopatients' sanity was due to the fact that they were not behaving sanely. While there was clearly some tension present in all of them, their daily visitors could detect no serious behavioral consequences — nor, indeed, could other patients. It was quite common for the patients to "detect" the pseudopatients' sanity. During the first three hospitalizations, when accurate counts were kept, 35 of a total of 118 patients on the admissions ward voiced their suspicions, some vigorously. "You're not crazy. You're a journalist, or a professor [referring to the continual note-taking]. You're checking up on the hospital." While most of the patients were reassured by the pseudopatient's insistence that he had been sick before he came in but was fine now, some continued to believe that the pseudopatient was sane throughout his hospitalization (*11*). The fact that the patients often recognized normality when staff did not raises important questions.

Failure to detect sanity during the course of hospitalization may be due to the fact that physicians operate with a strong bias toward what statisticians call the type 2 error (*5*).

This is to say that physicians are more inclined to call a healthy person sick (a false positive, type 2) than a sick person healthy (a false negative, type 1). The reasons for this are not hard to find: it is clearly more dangerous to misdiagnose illness than health. Better to err on the side of caution, to suspect illness even among the healthy.

But what holds for medicine does not hold equally well for psychiatry. Medical illnesses, while unfortunate, are not commonly pejorative. Psychiatric diagnoses, on the contrary, carry with them personal, legal, and social stigmas (*12*). It was therefore important to see whether the tendency toward diagnosing the sane insane could be reversed. The following experiment was arranged at a research and teaching hospital whose staff had heard these findings but doubted that such an error could occur in their hospital. The staff was informed that at some time during the following 3 months, one or more pseudopatients would attempt to be admitted into the psychiatric hospital. Each staff member was asked to rate each patient who presented himself at admissions or on the ward according to the likelihood that the patient was a pseudopatient. A 10-point scale was used, with a 1 and 2 reflecting high confidence that the patient was a pseudopatient.

Judgments were obtained on 193 patients who were admitted for psychiatric treatment. All staff who had had sustained contact with or primary responsibility for the patient—attendants, nurses, psychiatrists, physicians, and psychologists—were asked to make judgments. Forty-one patients were alleged, with high confidence, to be pseudopatients by at least one member of the staff. Twenty-three were considered suspect by at least one psychiatrist. Nineteen were suspected by one psychiatrist *and* one other staff member. Actually, no genuine pseudopatient (at least from my group) presented himself during this period.

The experiment is instructive. It indicates that the tendency to designate sane people as insane can be reversed when the stakes (in this case, prestige and diagnostic acumen) are high. But what can be said of the 19 people who were suspected of being "sane" by one psychiatrist and another staff member? Were these people truly "sane," or was it rather the case that in the course of avoiding the type 2 error the staff tended to make more errors of the first sort—calling the crazy "sane"? There is no way of knowing. But one thing is certain: any diagnostic process that lends itself so readily to massive errors of this sort cannot be a very reliable one.

THE STICKINESS OF PSYCHODIAGNOSTIC LABELS

Beyond the tendency to call the healthy sick—a tendency that accounts better for diagnostic behavior on admission than it does for such behavior after a lengthy period of exposure—the data speak to the massive role of labeling in psychiatric assessment. Having once been labeled schizophrenic, there is nothing the pseudopatient can do to overcome the tag. The tag profoundly colors others' perceptions of him and his behavior.

From one viewpoint, these data are hardly surprising, for it has long been known that elements are given meaning by the context in which they occur. Gestalt psychology made this point vigorously, and Asch (*13*) demonstrated that there are "central" personality traits (such as "warm" versus "cold") which are so powerful that they markedly color the meaning of other information in forming an impression of a given personality (*14*). "Insane," "schizophrenic," "manic-depressive," and "crazy" are probably among the most powerful of such central traits. Once a person is designated abnormal, all of his other behaviors and characteristics are colored by that label. Indeed, that label is so powerful that many of the pseudopatients' normal behaviors were overlooked entirely or profoundly misinterpreted. Some examples may clarify this issue.

Earlier I indicated that there were no changes in the pseudopatient's personal history and current status beyond those of name, employment, and, where necessary, vocation. Otherwise, a veridical description of personal history and circumstances was offered.

Those circumstances were not psychotic. How were they made consonant with the diagnosis of psychosis? Or were those diagnoses modified in such a way as to bring them into accord with the circumstances of the pseudopatient's life, as described by him?

As far as I can determine, diagnoses were in no way affected by the relative health of the circumstances of a pseudopatient's life. Rather, the reverse occurred: the perception of his circumstances was shaped entirely by the diagnosis. A clear example of such translation is found in the case of a pseudopatient who had had a close relationship with his mother but was rather remote from his father during his early childhood. During adolescence and beyond, however, his father became a close friend, while his relationship with his mother cooled. His present relationship with his wife was characteristically close and warm. Apart from occasional angry exchanges, friction was minimal. The children had rarely been spanked. Surely there is nothing especially pathological about such a history. Indeed, many readers may see a similar pattern in their own experiences, with no markedly deleterious consequences. Observe, however, how such a history was translated in the psychopathological context, this from the case summary prepared after the patient was discharged.

This white 39-year-old male . . . manifests a long history of considerable ambivalence in close relationships, which begins in early childhood. A warm relationship with his mother cools during his adolescence. A distant relationship to his father is described as becoming very intense. Affective stability is absent. His attempts to control emotionality with his wife and children are punctuated by angry outbursts and, in the case of the children, spankings. And while he says that he has several good friends, one senses considerable ambivalence embedded in those relationships also. . . .

The facts of the case were unintentionally distorted by the staff to achieve consistency with a popular theory of the dynamics of a schizophrenic reaction (15). Nothing of an ambivalent nature had been described in relations with parents, spouse, or friends. To the extent that ambivalence could be inferred, it was probably not greater than is found in all human relationships. It is true the pseudopatient's relationships with his parents changed over time, but in the ordinary context that would hardly be remarkable—indeed, it might very well be expected. Clearly, the meaning ascribed to his verbalizations (that is, ambivalence, affective instability) was determined by the diagnosis: schizophrenia. An entirely different meaning would have been ascribed if it were known that the man was "normal."

All pseudopatients took extensive notes publicly. Under ordinary circumstances, such behavior would have raised questions in the minds of observers, as, in fact, it did among patients. Indeed, it seemed so certain that the notes would elicit suspicion that elaborate precautions were taken to remove them from the ward each day. But the precautions proved needless. The closest any staff member came to questioning these notes occurred when one pseudopatient asked his physician what kind of medication he was receiving and began to write down the response. "You needn't write it," he was told gently. "If you have trouble remembering, just ask me again."

If no questions were asked of the pseudopatients, how was their writing interpreted? Nursing records for three patients indicate that the writing was seen as an aspect of their pathological behavior. "Patient engages in writing behavior" was the daily nursing comment on one of the pseudopatients who was never questioned about his writing. Given that the patient is in the hospital, he must be psychologically disturbed. And given that he is disturbed, continuous writing must be a behavioral manifestation of that disturbance, perhaps a subset of the compulsive behaviors that are sometimes correlated with schizophrenia.

One tacit characteristic of psychiatric diagnosis is that it locates the sources of aberration within the individual and only rarely within the complex of stimuli that surrounds him. Consequently, behaviors that are stimulated by the environment are commonly misattributed to the patient's disorder. For example, one kindly nurse found a pseudopatient pacing the long hospital corridors. "Nervous, Mr. X?" she asked. "No, bored," he said.

The notes kept by pseudopatients are full of patient behaviors that were misinterpreted by well-intentioned staff. Often enough, a patient would go "berserk" because he had, wittingly or unwittingly, been mistreated by, say, an attendant. A nurse coming upon the scene would rarely inquire even cursorily into the environmental stimuli of the patient's behavior. Rather, she assumed that his upset derived from his pathology, not from his present interactions with other staff members. Occasionally, the staff might assume that the patient's family (especially when they had recently visited) or other patients had stimulated the outburst. But never were the staff found to assume that one of themselves or the structure of the hospital had anything to do with a patient's behavior. One psychiatrist pointed to a group of patients who were sitting outside the cafeteria entrance half an hour before lunchtime. To a group of young residents he indicated that such behavior was characteristic of the oral-acquisitive nature of the syndrome. It seemed not to occur to him that there were very few things to anticipate in a psychiatric hospital besides eating.

A psychiatric label has a life and an influence of its own. Once the impression has been formed that the patient is schizophrenic, the expectation is that he will continue to be schizophrenic. When a sufficient amount of time has passed, during which the patient has done nothing bizarre, he is considered to be in remission and available for discharge. But the label endures beyond discharge, with the unconfirmed expectation that he will behave as a schizophrenic again. Such labels, conferred by mental health professionals, are as influential on the patient as they are on his relatives and friends, and it should not surprise anyone that the diagnosis acts on all of them as a self-fulfilling prophecy. Eventually, the patient himself accepts the diagnosis, with all of its surplus meanings and expectations, and behaves accordingly (5).

The inferences to be made from these matters are quite simple. Much as Zigler and Phillips have demonstrated that there is enormous overlap in the symptoms presented by patients who have been variously diagnosed (16), so there is enormous overlap in the behaviors of the sane and the insane. The sane are not "sane" all of the time. We lose our tempers "for no good reason." We are occasionally depressed or anxious, again for no good reason. And we may find it difficult to get along with one or another person—again for no reason that we can specify. Similarly, the insane are not always insane. Indeed, it was the impression of the pseudopatients while living with them that they were sane for long periods of time—that the bizarre behaviors upon which their diagnoses were allegedly predicated constituted only a small fraction of their total behavior. If it makes no sense to label ourselves permanently depressed on the basis of an occasional depression, then it takes better evidence than is presently available to label all patients insane or schizophrenic on the basis of bizarre behaviors or cognitions. It seems more useful, as Mischel (17) has pointed out, to limit our discussions to *behaviors*, the stimuli that provoke them, and their correlates.

It is not known why powerful impressions of personality traits, such as "crazy" or "insane," arise. Conceivably, when the origins of and stimuli that give rise to a behavior are remote or unknown, or when the behavior strikes us as immutable, trait labels regarding the *behaver* arise. When, on the other hand, the origins and stimuli are known and available, discourse is limited to the behavior itself. Thus, I may hallucinate because I am sleeping, or I may hallucinate because I have ingested a peculiar drug. These are termed sleep-induced hallucinations, or dreams, and drug-induced hallucinations, respectively. But when the stimuli to my hallucinations are unknown, that is called craziness, or schizophrenia—as if that inference were somehow as illuminating as the others.

THE EXPERIENCE OF PSYCHIATRIC HOSPITALIZATION

The term "mental illness" is of recent origin. It was coined by people who were humane in their inclinations and who wanted very much to raise the station of (and the public's sympathies toward) the psychologically disturbed from that of witches and "crazies" to one that was akin to the physically ill. And they were at least partially successful, for the treatment of the mentally ill *has* improved considerably over the years. But while treatment has improved, it is doubtful that people really regard the mentally ill in the same way that they view the physically ill. A broken leg is something one recovers from, but mental illness allegedly endures forever (*18*). A broken leg does not threaten the observer, but a crazy schizophrenic? There is by now a host of evidence that attitudes toward the mentally ill are characterized by fear, hostility, aloofness, suspicion, and dread (*19*). The mentally ill are society's lepers.

That such attitudes infect the general population is perhaps not surprising, only upsetting. But that they affect the professionals — attendants, nurses, physicians, psychologists, and social workers — who treat and deal with the mentally ill is more disconcerting, both because such attitudes are self-evidently pernicious and because they are unwitting. Most mental health professionals would insist that they are sympathetic toward the mentally ill, that they are neither avoidant nor hostile. But it is more likely that an exquisite ambivalence characterizes their relations with psychiatric patients, such that their avowed impulses are only part of their entire attitude. Negative attitudes are there too and can easily be detected. Such attitudes should not surprise us. They are the natural offspring of the labels patients wear and the places in which they are found.

Consider the structure of the typical psychiatric hospital. Staff and patients are strictly segregated. Staff have their own living space, including their dining facilities, bathrooms, and assembly places. The glassed quarters that contain the professional staff, which the pseudopatients came to call "the cage," sit out on every dayroom. The staff emerge primarily for caretaking purposes — to give medication, to conduct a therapy or group meeting, to instruct or reprimand a patient. Otherwise, staff keep to themselves, almost as if the disorder that afflicts their charges is somehow catching.

So much is patient-staff segregation the rule that, for four public hospitals in which an attempt was made to measure the degree to which staff and patients mingle, it was necessary to use "time out of the staff cage" as the operational measure. While it was not the case that all time spent out of the cage was spent mingling with patients (attendants, for example, would occasionally emerge to watch television in the dayroom), it was the only way in which one could gather reliable data on time for measuring.

The average amount of time spent by attendants outside of the cage was 11.3 percent (range, 3 to 52 percent). This figure does not represent only time spent mingling with patients, but also includes time spent on such chores as folding laundry, supervising patients while they shave, directing ward cleanup, and sending patients to off-ward activities. It was the relatively rare attendant who spent time talking with patients or playing games with them. It proved impossible to obtain a "percent mingling time" for nurses, since the amount of time they spent out of the cage was too brief. Rather, we counted instances of emergence from the cage. On the average, daytime nurses emerged from the cage 11.5 times per shift, including instances when they left the ward entirely (range, 4 to 39 times). Late afternoon and night nurses were even less available, emerging on the average 9.4 times per shift (range, 4 to 41 times). Data on early morning nurses, who arrived usually after midnight and departed at 8 a.m., are not available because patients were asleep during most of this period.

Physicians, especially psychiatrists, were even less available. They were rarely seen on the wards. Quite commonly, they would be seen only when they arrived and departed, with the remaining time being spent in their offices or in the cage. On the average, physicians emerged on the ward 6.7 times per day (range, 1 to 17 times). It proved difficult to make an accurate estimate in this regard, since physicians often maintained hours that allowed them to come and go at different times.

The hierarchical organization of the psychiatric hospital has been commented on before (*20*), but the latent meaning of that kind of organization is worth noting again. Those with the most power have least to do with patients, and those with the least power are most involved with them. Recall, however, that the acquisition of role-appropriate behaviors occurs mainly through the observation of others, with the most powerful having the most influence. Consequently, it is understandable that attendants not only spend more time with patients than do any other members of the staff—that is required by their station in the hierarchy—but also, insofar as they learn from their superiors' behavior, spend as little time with patients as they can. Attendants are seen mainly in the cage, which is where the models, the action, and the power are.

I turn now to a different set of studies, these dealing with staff response to patient-initiated contact. It has long been known that the amount of time a person spends with you can be an index of your significance to him. If he initiates and maintains eye contact, there is reason to believe that he is considering your requests and needs. If he pauses to chat or actually stops and talks, there is added reason to infer that he is individuating you. In four hospitals, the pseudopatient approached the staff member with a request which took the following form: "Pardon me, Mr. [or Dr. or Mrs.] X, could you tell me when I will be eligible for grounds privileges?" (or ". . . when I will be presented at the staff meeting?" or ". . . when I am likely to be discharged?"). While the content of the question varied according to the appropriateness of the target and the pseudopatient's (apparent) current needs, the form was always a courteous and relevant request for information. Care was taken never to approach a particular member of the staff more than once a day, lest the staff member become suspicious or irritated. In examining these data, remember that the behavior of the pseudopatients was neither bizarre nor disruptive. One could indeed engage in good conversation with them.

The data for these experiments are shown in Table 1, separately for physicians (column 1) and for nurses and attendants (column 2). Minor differences between these four institutions were overwhelmed by the degree to which staff avoided continuing contacts that patients had initiated. By far, their most common response consisted of either a brief response to the question, offered while they were "on the move" and with head averted, or no response at all.

The encounter frequently took the following bizarre form: (pseudopatient) "Pardon me, Dr. X. Could you tell me when I am eligible for grounds privileges?" (physician) "Good morning, Dave. How are you today?" (Moves off without waiting for a response.)

It is instructive to compare these data with data recently obtained at Stanford University. It has been alleged that large and eminent universities are characterized by faculty who are so busy that they have no time for students. For this comparison, a young lady approached individual faculty members who seemed to be walking purposefully to some meeting or teaching engagement and asked them the following six questions.

1) "Pardon me, could you direct me to Encina Hall?" (at the medical school: ". . . to the Clinical Research Center?").

2) "Do you know where Fish Annex is?" (there is no Fish Annex at Stanford).

3) "Do you teach here?"

4) "How does one apply for admission to the college?" (at the medical school: ". . . to the medical school?").

5) "Is it difficult to get in?"

6) "Is there financial aid?"

Without exception, as can be seen in Table 1 (column 3), all of the questions were answered. No matter how rushed they were, all respondents not only maintained eye contact, but stopped to talk. Indeed, many of the respondents went out of their way to direct or take the questioner to the office she was seeking, to try to locate "Fish Annex," or to discuss with her the possibilities of being admitted to the university.

Similar data, also shown in Table 1 (columns 4, 5, and 6), were obtained in the hospital. Here too, the young lady came prepared with six questions. After the first question, however, she remarked to 18 of her respondents (column 4), "I'm looking for a psychia-

TABLE 1. Self-Initiated Contact by Pseudopatients With Psychiatrists and Nurses and Attendants, Compared to Contact With Other Groups.

CONTACT	PSYCHIATRIC HOSPITALS		UNIVERSITY CAMPUS (NONMEDICAL)	UNIVERSITY MEDICAL CENTER PHYSICIANS		
	(1) Psychiatrists	(2) Nurses and Attendants	(3) Faculty	(4) "Looking for a Psychiatrist"	(5) "Looking for an internist"	(6) No additional Comment
Responses						
Moves on, head averted (%)	71	88	0	0	0	0
Makes eye contact (%)	23	10	0	11	0	0
Pauses and chats (%)	2	2	0	11	0	10
Stops and talks (%)	4	0.5	100	78	100	90
Mean number of questions answered (out of 6)	*	*	6	3.8	4.8	4.5
Respondents (No.)	13	47	14	18	15	10
Attempts (No.)	185	1283	14	18	15	10

*Not applicable.

trist," and to 15 others (column 5), "I'm looking for an internist." Ten other respondents received no inserted comment (column 6). The general degree of cooperative responses is considerably higher for these university groups than it was for pseudopatients in psychiatric hospitals. Even so, differences are apparent within the medical school setting. Once having indicated that she was looking for a psychiatrist, the degree of cooperation elicited was less than when she sought an internist.

POWERLESSNESS AND DEPERSONALIZATION

Eye contact and verbal contact reflect concern and individuation; their absence, avoidance and depersonalization. The data I have presented do not do justice to the rich daily encounters that grew up around matters of depersonalization and avoidance. I have records of patients who were beaten by staff for the sin of having initiated verbal contact. During my own experience, for example, one patient was beaten in the presence of other patients for having approached an attendant and told him, "I like you." Occasionally, punishment meted out to patients for misdemeanors seemed so excessive that it could not be justified by the most radical interpretations of psychiatric canon. Nevertheless, they appeared to go unquestioned. Tempers were often short. A patient who had not heard a call for medication would be roundly excoriated, and the morning attendants would often wake patients with, "Come on, you m-----f-----s, out of bed!"

Neither anecdotal nor "hard" data can convey the overwhelming sense of powerlessness which invades the individual as he is continually exposed to the depersonalization of the psychiatric hospital. It hardly matters *which* psychiatric hospital—the excellent public ones and the very plush private hospital were better than the rural and shabby ones in this regard, but, again, the features that psychiatric hospitals had in common overwhelmed by far their apparent differences.

Powerlessness was evident everywhere. The patient is deprived of many of his legal rights by dint of his psychiatric commitment (21). He is shorn of credibility by virtue of his psychiatric label. His freedom of movement is restricted. He cannot initiate contact with the staff, but may only respond to such overtures as they make. Personal privacy is minimal. Patient quarters and possessions can be entered and examined by any staff member, for whatever reason. His personal history and anguish is available to any staff member (often including the "grey lady" and "candy striper" volunteer) who chooses to read his folder, regardless of their therapeutic relationship to him. His personal hygiene and waste evacuation are often monitored. The water closets may have no doors.

At times, depersonalization reached such proportions that pseudopatients had the sense that they were invisible, or at least unworthy of account. Upon being admitted, I and other pseudopatients took the initial physical examinations in a semipublic room, where staff members went about their own business as if we were not there.

On the ward, attendants delivered verbal and occasionally serious physical abuse to patients in the presence of other observing patients, some of whom (the pseudopatients) were writing it all down. Abusive behavior, on the other hand, terminated quite abruptly when other staff members were known to be coming. Staff are credible witnesses. Patients are not.

A nurse unbuttoned her uniform to adjust her brassiere in the presence of an entire ward of viewing men. One did not have the sense that she was being seductive. Rather, she didn't notice us. A group of staff persons might point to a patient in the dayroom and discuss him animatedly, as if he were not there.

One illuminating instance of depersonalization and invisibility occurred with regard to medications. All told, the pseudopatients were administered nearly 2100 pills, including Elavil, Stelazine, Compazine, and Thorazine, to name but a few. (That such a variety of medications should have been administered to patients presenting identical symptoms is itself worthy of note.) Only two were swallowed. The rest were either pocketed or deposited in the toilet. The pseudopatients were not alone in this. Although I have no precise records on how many patients rejected their medications, the pseudopatients frequently found the medications of other patients in the toilet before they deposited their own. As long as they were cooperative, their behavior and the pseudopatients' own in this matter, as in other important matters, went unnoticed throughout.

Reactions to such depersonalization among pseudopatients were intense. Although they had come to the hospital as participant observers and were fully aware that they did not "belong," they nevertheless found themselves caught up in and fighting the process of depersonalization. Some examples: a graduate student in psychology asked his wife to bring his textbooks to the hospital so he could "catch up on his homework"—this despite the elaborate precautions taken to conceal his professional association. The same student, who had trained for quite some time to get into the hospital, and who had looked forward to the experience, "remembered" some drag races that he had wanted to see on the weekend and insisted that he be discharged by that time. Another pseudopatient attempted a romance with a nurse. Subsequently, he informed the staff that he was applying for admission to graduate school in psychology and was very likely to be admitted, since a graduate professor was one of his regular hospital visitors. The same person began to engage in psychotherapy with other patients—all of this as a way of becoming a person in an impersonal environment.

THE SOURCES OF DEPERSONALIZATION

What are the origins of depersonalization? I have already mentioned two. First are attitudes held by all of us toward the mentally ill—including those who treat them—attitudes characterized by fear, distrust, and horrible expectations on the one hand, and benevolent intentions on the other. Our ambivalence leads, in this instance as in others, to avoidance.

Second, and not entirely separate, the hierarchical structure of the psychiatric hospital facilitates depersonalization. Those who are at the top have least to do with patients, and their behavior inspires the rest of the staff. Average daily contact with psychiatrists, psychologists, residents, and physicians combined ranged from 3.9 to 25.1 minutes, with an overall mean of 6.8 (six pseudopatients over a total of 129 days of hospitalization). Included in this average are time spent in the admissions interview, ward meetings in the presence of a senior staff member, group and individual psychotherapy contacts, case presentation conferences, and discharge meetings. Clearly, patients do not spend much time in interpersonal contact with doctoral staff. And doctoral staff serve as models for nurses and attendants.

There are probably other sources. Psychiatric installations are presently in serious financial straits. Staff shortages are pervasive, staff time at a premium. Something has to give, and that something is patient contact. Yet, while financial stresses are realities, too much can be made of them. I have the impression that the psychological forces that result in depersonalization are much stronger than the fiscal ones and that the addition of more staff would not correspondingly improve patient care in this regard. The incidence of staff meetings and the enormous amount of record-keeping on patients, for example, have not been as substantially reduced as has patient contact. Priorities exist, even during hard times. Patient contact is not a significant priority in the traditional psychiatric hospital, and fiscal pressures do not account for this. Avoidance and depersonalization may.

Heavy reliance upon psychotropic medication tacitly contributes to depersonalization by convincing staff that treatment is indeed being conducted and that further patient contact may not be necessary. Even here, however, caution needs to be exercised in understanding the role of psychotropic drugs. If patients were powerful rather than powerless, if they were viewed as interesting individuals rather than diagnostic entities, if they were socially significant rather than social lepers, if their anguish truly and wholly compelled our sympathies and concerns, would we not *seek* contact with them, despite the availability of medications? Perhaps for the pleasure of it all?

THE CONSEQUENCES OF LABELING AND DEPERSONALIZATION

Whenever the ratio of what is known to what needs to be known approaches zero, we tend to invent "knowledge" and assume that we understand more than we actually do. We seem unable to acknowledge that we simply don't know. The needs for diagnosis and remediation of behavioral and emotional problems are enormous. But rather than acknowledge that we are just embarking on understanding, we continue to label patients "schizophrenic," "manic-depressive," and "insane," as if in those words we had captured the essence of understanding. The facts of the matter are that we have known for a long time that diagnoses are often not useful or reliable, but we have nevertheless continued to use them. We now know that we cannot distinguish insanity from sanity. It is depressing to consider how that information will be used.

Not merely depressing, but frightening. How many people, one wonders, are sane but not recognized as such in our psychiatric institutions? How many have been needlessly stripped of their privileges of citizenship, from the right to vote and drive to that of handling their own accounts? How many have feigned insanity in order to avoid the criminal consequences of their behavior, and, conversely, how many would rather stand trial than live interminably in a psychiatric hospital — but are wrongly thought to be mentally ill? How many have been stigmatized by well-intentioned, but nevertheless erroneous, diagnoses? On the last point, recall again that a "type 2 error" in psychiatric diagnosis does not have the same consequences it does in medical diagnosis. A diagnosis of cancer that has been found to be in error is cause for celebration. But psychiatric diagnoses are rarely found to be in error. The label sticks, a mark of inadequacy forever.

Finally, how many patients might be "sane" outside the psychiatric hospital but seem insane in it — not because craziness resides in them, as it were, but because they are responding to a bizarre setting, one that may be unique to institutions which harbor nether people? Goffman (4) calls the process of socialization to such institutions "mortification" — an apt metaphor that includes the processes of depersonalization that have been described here. And while it is impossible to know whether the pseudopatients' responses to these processes are characteristic of all inmates — they were, after all, not real patients — it is difficult to believe that these processes of socialization to a psychiatric hospital provide useful attitudes or habits of response for living in the "real world."

SUMMARY AND CONCLUSIONS

It is clear that we cannot distinguish the sane from the insane in psychiatric hospitals. The hospital itself imposes a special environment in which the meanings of behavior can easily be misunderstood. The consequences to patients hospitalized in such an environment—the powerlessness, depersonalization, segregation, mortification, and self-labeling—seem undoubtedly countertherapeutic.

I do not, even now, understand this problem well enough to perceive solutions. But two matters seem to have some promise. The first concerns the proliferation of community mental health facilities, of crisis intervention centers, of the human potential movement, and of behavior therapies that, for all of their own problems, tend to avoid psychiatric labels, to focus on specific problems and behaviors, and to retain the individual in a relatively nonpejorative environment. Clearly, to the extent that we refrain from sending the distressed to insane places, our impressions of them are less likely to be distorted. (The risk of distorted perceptions, it seems to me, is always present, since we are much more sensitive to an individual's behaviors and verbalizations than we are to the subtle contextual stimuli that often promote them. At issue here is a matter of magnitude. And, as I have shown, the magnitude of distortion is exceedingly high in the extreme context that is a psychiatric hospital.)

The second matter that might prove promising speaks to the need to increase the sensitivity of mental health workers and researchers to the *Catch 22* position of psychiatric patients. Simply reading materials in this area will be of help to some such workers and researchers. For others, directly experiencing the impact of psychiatric hospitalization will be of enormous use. Clearly, further research into the social psychology of such total institutions will both facilitate treatment and deepen understanding.

I and the other pseudopatients in the psychiatric setting had distinctly negative reactions. We do not pretend to describe the subjective experiences of true patients. Theirs may be different from ours, particularly with the passage of time and the necessary process of adaptation to one's environment. But we can and do speak to the relatively more objective indices of treatment within the hospital. It could be a mistake, and a very unfortunate one, to consider that what happened to us derived from malice or stupidity on the part of the staff. Quite the contrary, our overwhelming impression of them was of people who really cared, who were committed and who were uncommonly intelligent. Where they failed, as they sometimes did painfully, it would be more accurate to attribute those failures to the environment in which they, too, found themselves than to personal callousness. Their perceptions and behavior were controlled by the situation, rather than being motivated by a malicious disposition. In a more benign environment, one that was less attached to global diagnosis, their behaviors and judgments might have been more benign and effective.

REFERENCES AND NOTES

1. P. Ash, *J. Abnorm. Soc. Psychol.* **44,** 272 (1949); A. T. Beck, *Amer. J. Psychiat.* **119,** 210 (1962); A. T. Boisen, *Psychiatry* **2,** 233 (1938); N. Kreitman, *J. Ment. Sci.* **107,** 876 (1961); N. Kreitman, P. Sainsbury, J. Morrisey, J. Towers, J. Scrivener, *ibid.,* p. 887; H. O. Schmitt and C. P. Fonda, *J. Abnorm. Soc. Psychol.* **52,** 262 (1956); W. Seeman, *J. Nerv. Ment. Dis.* **118,** 541 (1953). For an analysis of these artifacts and summaries of the disputes, see J. Zubin, *Annu. Rev. Psychol.* **18,** 373 (1967); L. Phillips and J. G. Draguns, *ibid.* **22,** 447 (1971).
2. R. Benedict, *J. Gen. Psychol.* **10,** 59 (1934).
3. See in this regard H. Becker, *Outsiders: Studies in the Sociology of Deviance* (Free Press, New

York, 1963); B. M. Braginsky, D. D. Braginsky, K. Ring, *Methods of Madness: The Mental Hospital as a Last Resort* (Holt, Rinehart & Winston, New York, 1969); G. M. Crocetti and P. V. Lemkau, *Amer. Sociol. Rev.* **30,** 577 (1965); E. Goffman, *Behavior in Public Places* (Free Press, New York, 1964); R. D. Laing, *The Divided Self: A Study of Sanity and Madness* (Quadrangle, Chicago, 1960); D. L. Phillips, *Amer. Sociol. Rev.* **28,** 963 (1963); T. R. Sarbin, *Psychol. Today* **6,** 18 (1972); E. Schur, *Amer. J. Sociol.* **75,** 309 (1969); T. Szasz, *Law, Liberty and Psychiatry* (Macmillan, New York, 1963); *The Myth of Mental Illness: Foundations of a Theory of Mental Illness* (Hoeber, Harper, New York, 1963). For a critique of some of these views, see W. R. Gove, *Amer. Sociol. Rev.* **35,** 873 (1970).

4. E. Goffman, *Asylums* (Doubleday, Garden City, N.Y., 1961).

5. T. J. Scheff, *Being Mentally Ill: A Sociological Theory* (Aldine, Chicago, 1966).

6. Data from a ninth pseudopatient are not incorporated in this report because, although his sanity went undetected, he falsified aspects of his personal history, including his marital status and parental relationships. His experimental behaviors therefore were not identical to those of the other pseudopatients.

7. A. Barry, *Bellevue Is a State of Mind* (Harcourt Brace Jovanovich, New York, 1971); I. Belknap, *Human Problems of a State Mental Hospital* (McGraw-Hill, New York, 1956); W. Caudill, F. C. Redlich, H. R. Gilmore, E. B. Brody, *Amer. J. Orthopsychiat.* **22,** 314 (1952); A. R. Goldman, R. H. Bohr, T. A. Steinberg, *Prof. Psychol.* **1,** 427 (1970); unauthored, *Roche Report* **1** (No. 13), 8 (1971).

8. Beyond the personal difficulties that the pseudopatient is likely to experience in the hospital, there are legal and social ones that, combined, require considerable attention before entry. For example, once admitted to a psychiatric institution, it is difficult, if not impossible, to be discharged on short notice, state law to the contrary notwithstanding. I was not sensitive to these difficulties at the outset of the project, nor to the personal and situational emergencies that can arise, but later a writ of habeas corpus was prepared for each of the entering pseudopatients and an attorney was kept "on call" during every hospitalization. I am grateful to John Kaplan and Robert Bartels for legal advice and assistance in these matters.

9. However distasteful such concealment is, it was a necessary first step to examining these questions. Without concealment, there would have been no way to know how valid these experiences were; nor was there any way of knowing whether whatever detections occurred were a tribute to the diagnostic acumen of the staff or to the hospital's rumor network. Obviously, since my concerns are general ones that cut across individual hospitals and staffs, I have respected their anonymity and have eliminated clues that might lead to their identification.

10. Interestingly, of the 12 admissions, 11 were diagnosed as schizophrenic and one, with the identical symptomatology, as manic-depressive psychosis. This diagnosis has a more favorable prognosis, and it was given by the only private hospital in our sample. On the relations between social class and psychiatric diagnosis, see A. deB. Hollingshead and F. C. Redlich, *Social Class and Mental Illness: A Community Study* (Wiley, New York, 1958).

11. It is possible, of course, that patients have quite broad latitudes in diagnosis and therefore are inclined to call many people sane, even those whose behavior is patently aberrant. However, although we have no hard data on this matter, it was our distinct impression that this was not the case. In many instances, patients not only singled us out for attention, but came to imitate our behaviors and styles.

12. J. Cumming and E. Cumming, *Community Ment. Health* **1,** 135 (1965); A. Farina and K. Ring, *J. Abnorm. Psychol.* **70,** 47 (1965); H. E. Freeman and O. G. Simmons, *The Mental Patient Comes Home* (Wiley, New York, 1963); W. J. Johannsen, *Ment. Hygiene* **53,** 218 (1969); A. S. Linsky, *Soc. Psychiat.* **5,** 166 (1970).

13. S. E. Asch, *J. Abnorm. Soc. Psychol.* **41,** 258 (1946); *Social Psychology* (Prentice-Hall, New York, 1952).

14. See also I. N. Mensh and J. Wishner, *J. Personality* **16,** 188 (1947); J. Wishner, *Psychol. Rev.* **67,** 96 (1960); J. S. Bruner and R. Tagiuri, in *Handbook of Social Psychology*, G. Lindzey, Ed. (Addison-Wesley, Cambridge, Mass., 1954), vol. 2, pp. 634–654; J. S. Bruner, D. Shapiro, R. Tagiuri, in *Person Perception and Interpersonal Behavior*, R. Tagiuri and L. Petrullo, Eds. (Stanford Univ. Press, Stanford, Calif., 1958), pp. 277–288.

15. For an example of a similar self-fulfilling prophecy, in this instance dealing with the "central" trait of intelligence, see R. Rosenthal and L. Jacobson, *Pygmalion in the Classroom* (Holt, Rinehart & Winston, New York, 1968).

16. E. Zigler and L. Phillips, *J. Abnorm. Soc. Psychol.* **63,** 69 (1961). See also R. K. Freudenberg and J. P. Robertson, *A.M.A. Arch. Neurol. Psychiatr.* **76,** 14 (1956).

17. W. Mischel, *Personality and Assessment* (Wiley, New York, 1968).

18. The most recent and unfortunate instance of this tenet is that of Senator Thomas Eagleton.

19. T. R. Sarbin and J. C. Mancuso, *J. Clin. Consult. Psychol.* **35,** 159 (1970); T. R. Sarbin, *ibid.* **31,** 447 (1967); J. C. Nunnally, Jr., *Popular Conceptions of Mental Health* (Holt, Rinehart & Winston, New York, 1961).

20. A. H. Stanton and M. S. Schwartz, *The Mental Hospital: A Study of Institutional Participation in Psychiatric Illness and Treatment* (Basic, New York, 1954).
21. D. B. Wexler and S. E. Scoville, *Ariz. Law Rev.* **13,** 1 (1971).
22. I thank W. Mischel, E. Orne, and M. S. Rosenhan for comments on an earlier draft of this manuscript.

A large number of letters were received by the journal which published the Rosenhan article regarding what was seen as a critical attitude toward mental hospitals and the profession of psychiatry. It was pointed out that it is not unusual for a person to display extreme behavior disorders when at large in society, only to have these symptoms disappear quite quickly and completely once he has been hospitalized. Also, the fact that the person presented himself to an admitting office is an abnormal occurrence in and of itself, and the admitting psychiatrist would have been derelict had he not admitted the pseudopatient.

Rosenhan acknowledges these points, but argues that the diagnostic leap from a single symptom, hallucination, to a diagnostic categorization, schizophrenia, is the troublesome fact. Rosenhan, in his reply, makes it clear that his purpose is not to vilify psychiatry but to lead the profession to institute beneficial changes by making it more aware of the crucial issues in diagnosis and treatment that were brought out in his report.

Rosenhan's study illustrates the unique advantage of field observational techniques. There is literally no other way that the problem he was interested in could have been approached. Outside study would not have revealed the problems of diagnosing mental illness or the experience of being a psychiatric patient in the detail that was possible here with field observation. Admittedly, this study did not concern itself with some of the areas usually under examination in field observational methods. The examination of staff-patient relationships (at least as given in this report) was limited in scope, and no discussion at all is given of the patterns of relationships that exist within the patient group. A study of longer duration would undoubtedly have investigated these relationships and attempted a model of functioning which would show in more detail the patterns of patient groups, staff groups, and their relationship within the mental hospital. However, as Rosenhan points out in his commentary on the experience of being a patient, field work is not without its occupational hazards and stresses, and the objective of the study—the assessment of psychiatric diagnostic procedures—was accomplished in a very direct manner.

THE "VALIDITY" OF FIELD OBSERVATIONS

Strictly speaking, it is inappropriate to refer to the "validity" of field observations, since the validity of an individual's observations is not meaningful in the sense in which we have discussed validity in the preceding chapters. We may question the accuracy of a field worker's reports, or be startled by his interpretations, but there are no criteria for assessing validity as there are in other methods of research.

Basically the field research worker offers us his evidence and opinion and invites us to judge it. This is similar to the procedure used by an historical researcher who reads the reports and statements of others and then attempts to assess the "worth" of the evidence. The field worker attempts to assess the evidence presented both directly and indirectly to him by the group he is observing. His evaluations are undoubtedly to some extent colored with his biases and his outlook on life, no matter how he may strive to be objective. In his support, it should be emphasized that a competent field worker will make every effort to specify his biases and predispositions — to say, in effect, "I have such and such an outlook and am looking for evidence relevant to the following areas." When this is done, it is possible to better assess the material presented in its own right and also to compensate for the outlook of the field worker.

There are problems and limitations in field work that may be unrelated to the field worker's biases. The male anthropologist studying a culture in which sex roles are highly differentiated and in which sexual matters are kept highly secret cannot hope to come up with the same detailed and accurate account of women's lives that a female anthropologist studying the same culture would encounter. The female anthropologist would, of course, face the same problem in learning about events pertaining to men. Some of these problems are intrinsic to field work and, in reading accounts, they should be kept in mind. However, we should also remember that no approach other than the field method provides such a direct, in depth picture of how people in a given setting interact with others and manage their lives. Without the efforts of the field worker and his initial insights, many experimentally oriented research programs would have never had a starting point.

FOOTNOTES

[1]Marida Hollos, Community, family and cognitive development in rural Norway. Unpublished Ph.D. Dissertation, University of California, Berkeley, 1971.

[2]D. Katz, *Field studies*. In L. Festinger and D. Katz (Eds.), *Research Methods in the Behavioral Sciences*. New York: Dryden Press, 1953.

chapter seven

fundamental concepts in understanding statistical inference

Drawing by Dedini. © 1974 The New Yorker Magazine, Inc.

The article by Rhine, Hill, and Wandruff (Chapter 2) contained a considerable amount of technical shorthand, and we have already given a rather condensed explanation of this terminology. This chapter will provide the background information necessary to interpret such statements as "Girls correctly identified a mean of 5.24 good and bad pictures and the boys had a mean of 4.72, a difference producing a $t = 1.03$, $df = 48$, $p > .10$."

In order to understand such statements as the above, you must have some knowledge of the assumptions that are made when inferential statistical methods are used to reach a decision. It will also be helpful for you to master certain simple, fundamental calculations in order to understand the process of statistical inference. If you have ever had any course work in statistics, you should recognize the material presented in this chapter. If this material evokes traumas originally developed in statistics courses, we can offer at least the consolation that these are the only numerical calculations that you will be required to follow in this text. Unfortunately, there is simply no way to discuss statistical inference without considering these basic calculations.

Before presenting the steps involved in making statistical inferences, a few remarks about the outlook you should adopt may be helpful. First of all, you will have to take our word for it that numbers really behave as we say they do. Except for very simple demonstrations, you will have to take on faith our statements about what happens to sets of numbers when certain things are done, what happens to calculations when a few scores are picked at random from a larger set, and so forth. The alternative to accepting these things on faith is to undertake formal instruction in statistics.

As an opening step, you will have to review two fundamental concepts discussed earlier: *population* and *sample.* You will learn how to calculate two simple statistics—the arithmetic mean and the standard deviation—and you will become acquainted with some characteristics of these two measures.

POPULATION AND SAMPLE

The concepts of population and sample were first introduced in Chapter 2. Since these concepts are fundamental to understanding statistical inference, they will be repeated here.

A *population* is defined as all of the members of a given class or set of events. Populations can be defined in a variety of ways and can be a very small or an extremely large number of things. For example, the population of interest to us may be all the students enrolled in a given university course—a relatively small population. A larger population would be all children between the ages of 3 and 5 living within the geographical limits of the city of Stockholm, Sweden. Another population of interest could be all blue-eyed males in the United States—a large population. At the extreme, our population of interest could be all living human beings on Earth.

Only in the first two examples would it be feasible to measure some characteristic of all of the members of the population. The latter two populations are too large to make such a measurement practical.

Consequently, if we want to know something about a large population, we face the problem of never being able to make the appropriate measurements on everyone. The cost in time and money, let alone the availability of the population at a given time, clearly makes this impossible. What must be done is to select members of the population in such a way that they represent that population and will allow us to reach the most accurate conclusions possible about the characteristics of everyone in the population. Such a selection procedure is called *sampling*.

A *sample* is defined as those members of the population on whom measurements of some characteristic have actually been made. If we are to use only a few individuals to find out what we think is true of a very large number of people, then we want to be as certain as possible that the individuals we select are representative of the total population.

There are a variety of methods used to select samples. Organizations such as the Gallup Poll select their samples in such a way that they are representative of such things as political affiliation and income level. If we wanted to survey attitudes among active churchgoers we would want to make up our sample only from individuals who actually attend church services regularly.

There are many ways of obtaining a sample that is representative of a population, and we will discuss some of these in detail a bit later. At present we will discuss how to select cases for a sample by making a random selection from a population of individuals. This process is called *random sampling*.

Random Sampling

The concept of random sampling is fundamental to the process of statistical inference. A sample is considered to be random when the following two conditions are met:

1. Every individual in the population has an equal chance of being included in the sample.

2. Selecting one individual in no way affects the chances of any other individual to be included in the sample.

To illustrate, suppose you have a population of 1000 people, consisting of all the employees of a small factory. The management wishes to institute a profit-sharing plan with the employees. Under the proposed plan, employees would share in the company's profit in an amount proportionate to the number of years they have been employed. You want to interview a representative sample of these individuals to find out opinions about the new profit-sharing plan. However, in the time you have to do this, you can interview only 20 people. How can you select them?

The distribution of the number of years employed is shown in Figure 7–1. The simplest way to obtain a random sample would be to use a table of random numbers (see Table 7–3, p. 112, for an example of such a table). Figure 7–2 shows the location of a sample of 20 subjects within a population of 1000 persons selected by use of such a random number table.

On the basis of appearance, at least, the selection would seem to be reasonably representative. However, there are some other checks we can make. We want to be quite sure that our sample is representative of the *average* number of years employed. Using information from employment records, we can find the average known as the *arithmetic mean* by adding the years of employment of all the employees and dividing by 1000 (the number of employees). If we did this, we would find that the mean number of years employed is 15.5 years. When we add up the years of employment of our sample of 20 and calculate the mean, we find that the mean is equal to 14.8 years.

The fact that the population mean and the sample mean are very close is

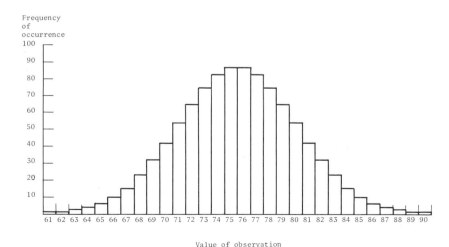

Value of observation

Figure 7–1 A distribution of number of years employed for all the employees of a small factory.

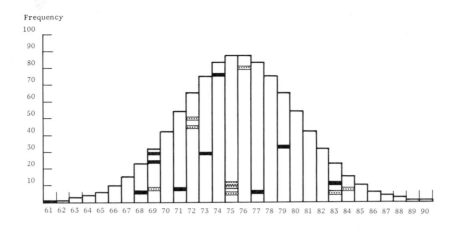

Figure 7-2   Location of 20 sample cases within a population drawn by random selection.

no accident. A sample drawn at random from a population will almost invariably provide a value reasonably close to the actual population mean. You are asked to accept this on faith, since the proof would require an excursion into calculations of the sort we wish to avoid in this book. However, to show you that this will actually happen, we have provided a way for you to demonstrate it to yourself. At the end of this chapter there is an addendum with a table of 1000 scores (a population), a random number table, and directions for their use. You can try drawing a sample from the population, calculating the mean, and seeing how close your sample mean comes to the population mean. Try it and see what happens.

Statistical inference has been defined as the process of making as wise a decision as possible on the basis of very little information. In our example, since we could not interview every employee, we took precautions to see that the people we did interview were representative of the total population. Proper selection of the sample to be studied is basic to making a valid statistical inference. If a sample is chosen in such a way that it is unrepresentative of the population, then quantities calculated from the sample (such as the arithmetic mean) will not be an accurate estimate of the population value.

Understanding the relationship of the sample to the population is one of the first steps in understanding the process of statistical inference. However, before we can proceed further with the other steps involved in making an inference, you must learn how to calculate and interpret the arithmetic mean and the standard deviation.

THE ARITHMETIC MEAN

You are already somewhat familiar with the arithmetic mean; it was defined in Chapter 2 and discussed again in our example of random sampling.

The arithmetic mean of a set of numbers is obtained by adding them all together and dividing the sum by the total number of numbers in the set. The average of the numbers 2, 3, 5, and 6 is obtained by adding them together, resulting in a sum of 16, and dividing by 4 (since there are 4 numbers), resulting in an answer of 4, which is the arithmetic mean.

Suppose that we have the numbers 2, 3, 6, and 13. When the sum of these (24) is divided by 4, the result is as follows: 24/4 = 6. Thus, the arithmetic mean of these numbers is 6.

If we have a larger set of numbers, we can expect that the mean will tell us something about the general location of most of the scores. For example, suppose that a class of 25 students was given an examination on which 20 points were possible. If we then drew a graph with the scores on the horizontal line (called the abscissa, or x axis) and the frequency with which they occurred on the vertical line (called the ordinate, or y axis), it might look like Figure 7–3.

For this example, adding all the scores together results in a sum of 350. Dividing this sum by 25 (the number of students) results in an arithmetic mean of 14. Looking at the graph, we can see that the most frequently occurring score is 14 and that the next most frequently occurring scores are 13 and 15. Our calculation in this case provides us with a good estimate of how well most people did on the exam. Suppose a second class took the same exam and had the scores shown in Figure 7–4. For this second class, adding all the scores together results in a sum of 225. Dividing this sum by 25 (the number of students in the class), we obtain a mean of 9. From these results, we immediately know that the first class did much better on the test than the second.

One of the interesting properties of the arithmetic mean is that it always reflects the exact algebraic center of the numbers on which it is calculated. To illustrate what is meant by this, take again the numbers 2, 3, 5, and 6, which had a mean of 4, and subtract the calculated mean from each of them. The fol-

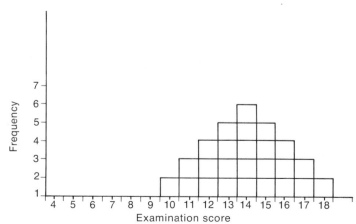

Figure 7–3 A frequency distribution of examination scores for a class of 25 students.

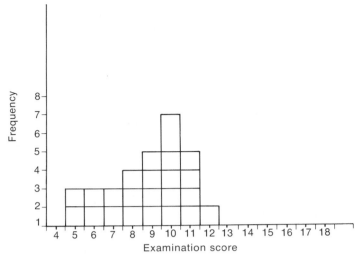

Figure 7–4 A frequency distribution of examination scores for another class of 25 students.

lowing difference scores will be obtained:

$$2 - 4 = -2$$

$$3 - 4 = -1$$

$$5 - 4 = +1$$

$$6 - 4 = +2$$

If we now add up the difference scores (-2, -1, $+1$, $+2$), we find that their sum is zero. This will always happen with a set of numbers on which a mean is calculated; if it does not, then the mean has not been calculated correctly. Try this with any set of numbers and demonstrate the point for yourself.

Central Tendency

The purpose of calculating the difference scores and demonstrating that they sum to zero is to illustrate that the arithmetic mean is a measure of the *central tendency* of the scores. In the previous example of two classes taking the same examination, we know from looking at the means for the two groups of students that the first group, with a mean of 14, did better than the second group, which had a mean of 9. An individual student, even if he is a member of the group which has the low mean, may have a very high score on the examination. Yet, if we are interested in characterizing the performance of one group relative to another, the mean is one of the best indices to use.

There are situations in which the mean is inappropriate as a measure of central tendency. The mean of the numbers 2, 2, 2, 2, 3, 3, 4, 4, 4, 672 is 69.8 and, obviously, does not reflect the central tendency of the distribution of scores well at all; it is a gross overestimate of the value of the majority of scores. Although there are other kinds of averages suitable for such problems (such as the median and the mode), we are not including discussions of them here, since we do not need them to follow the line of reasoning used in making statistical inferences.

THE STANDARD DEVIATION

We have now presented some basic information regarding the most commonly used measure of central tendency in statistics—the arithmetic mean—and have given a brief account of some of its properties. The calculation of another important statistic must now be presented. This statistic is the *standard deviation.*

Dispersion. The standard deviation is a measure of how much scores disperse or spread around a mean. The mean, while informative about the general level of a set of scores, provides no information about how much *variation* exists. For example, the distributions of scores shown in Figure 7–5 all

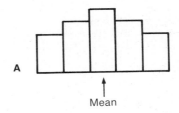

A

Mean

Figure 7–5 Representation of three sets of scores with the same mean and different standard deviations.

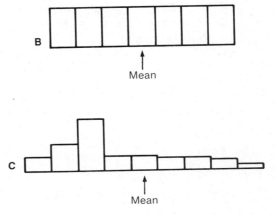

B

Mean

C

Mean

have the same arithmetic mean. However, an examination of the distributions indicates that there is a large difference in how much these scores disperse around their arithmetic means. Set A has no scores very far above or below the arithmetic mean; the dispersion is very slight. Set B has many more scores at extreme positions above and below the mean than does set A, and set C has many more scores at one extreme of the distribution than at the other. Clearly, some way to express these differences would be useful. To use a different sort of illustration, it is not enough to know that a river you wish to wade across has a mean depth of 3 feet. The depth of the river could actually vary from less than an inch to over 50 feet—a matter of some concern if you do not know how to swim.

Ideally, a measure of dispersion should provide a reasonable index of all the dispersion. It should not give greater importance to some scores in relation to others. Also, it should have a discernible relationship to the arithmetic mean and be understandable in relation to it. Finally, it should be as general a measure as possible—that is, it should be useful in making inferences about a population from a sample. The measure best fulfilling these criteria is the standard deviation. The standard deviation is a number which becomes larger as the spread of scores around the mean becomes greater. It is related to the arithmetic mean and is calculated using the mean as a reference point.

To illustrate this relationship, we will use the earlier demonstration of differences around the mean. We pointed out that if you calculate the mean for a set of scores and then subtract the mean from each score, keeping track of signs, the sum of these differences is zero. As in our earlier example where the mean is 4:

$$2 - 4 = -2$$
$$3 - 4 = -1$$
$$5 - 4 = +1$$
$$6 - 4 = \underline{+2}$$
$$0$$

As an average index of dispersion, this is clearly not very satisfactory, since its value is zero. However, we can overcome this problem by squaring each of the differences. This will give us all positive numbers. (A negative number, when multiplied by another negative number, becomes positive.) For the above example:

$$-2 \times -2 = +4$$
$$-1 \times -1 = +1$$
$$+1 \times +1 = +1$$
$$+2 \times +2 = \underline{+4}$$
$$\overline{+10}$$

This new value (+10) is known as the *sum of squares*.

Variance.   If we now divide the sum of the squares by the number of scores, we have a mean of the squared differences: $10/4 = 2.50$. This mean, or average, of the squared difference is known as the *variance*. This value will increase as the dispersion of scores around the mean increases. The larger the variance, the greater the dispersion of scores around the mean. The variance is a very useful quantity in statistical calculations and will be discussed in more detail in later chapters. However, it is not a completely satisfactory measure of the dispersion of a set of scores. Ideally, some unit of measurement should be found that would allow us both to indicate dispersion and to tell how far scores range from the mean in some unit that makes sense no matter how many scores we have.

Calculation of the Standard Deviation.   Exactly such a unit can be obtained by one more simple calculation. We take the variance and calculate its square root: $2.50 = 1.58$. This is the standard deviation.

The preceding example shows you how the standard deviation is calculated.[1] To illustrate how it is used, we will consider yet another example.

TABLE 7–1   Calculation of the Standard Deviation

SCORE	DIFFERENCE (score minus arithmetic mean)	DIFFERENCE SQUARED*
10	−4	16
11	−3	9
11	−3	9
12	−2	4
12	−2	4
12	−2	4
13	−1	1
13	−1	1
13	−1	1
13	−1	1
14	0	0
14	0	0
14	0	0
14	0	0
14	0	0
15	+1	1
15	+1	1
15	+1	1
15	+1	1
16	+2	4
16	+2	4
16	+2	4
17	+3	9
17	+3	9
18	+4	16
Sum = 350	Sum = 0	Sum = 100

$$\text{Mean} = \frac{350}{25} = 14.0 \qquad \text{Variance} = \frac{100}{25} = 4.0$$

$$\text{Standard Deviation} = \sqrt{4.0} = 2.0$$

*Remember that two negative numbers multiplied together will yield a positive number ($-4 \times -4 = +16$) while a positive number multiplied by a negative number will yield a negative value ($-4 \times 4 = -16$).

The calculations of the mean and standard deviation for a set of scores are given in Table 7–1 so that you can follow the process in detail if you wish. The procedure is exactly the same as shown in the earlier example. Once the mean is calculated, it is subtracted from every score, keeping track of signs. These differences are then squared and added, and the process continues as before. We take the mean of these squared differences (4.0) and then the square root of that mean (2.0). This is the standard deviation for the set of scores.

What does this number mean and how is it used? At this point, some technical definition is unavoidable — in statistics, a standard deviation is known as *a measure of the dispersion of scores around the arithmetic mean in the original score units.* For an illustration of what this actually means, see Figure 7–6.

Figure 7–6 is a graph of the scores on which the standard deviation was calculated. The mean of 14.0 is marked on the illustration to show where it falls in the distribution of the scores.

Take the value for the standard deviation that we obtained in the earlier calculation and add it to the mean (14.0 + 2.0 = 16.0). This sum equals the value of the score that is one standard deviation above the mean, and it is this value that is indicated in Figure 7–7. Now take the value of the standard deviation and *subtract* it from the mean (14.0 − 2.0 = 12.0). This value is one standard deviation below the mean, and it is also indicated in Figure 7–7. If we were to take twice the value of the standard deviation and add it to the mean (14.0 + 4.0 = 18.0) and then subtract twice the value of the standard deviation (14.0 − 4.0 = 10.0), we would have the values indicated in Figure 7–8. Note that more and more of the scores are included as we move additional standard deviation units from the mean. In fact, all of the scores in this distribution occur between plus and minus 2 standard deviations from the mean. You should also note that you can find the value of any score if you know the value of the standard deviation, since the standard deviation is expressed in original score units. For this example, if you know that the mean is 14.0 and the standard deviation is 2.0, you can determine the value of any score. If you are told that the highest score is two standard deviations above the mean, you

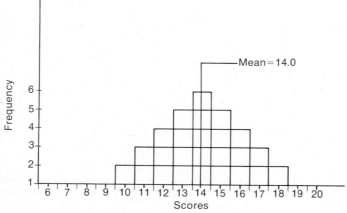

Figure 7–6 Location of the arithmetic mean in a distribution of scores.

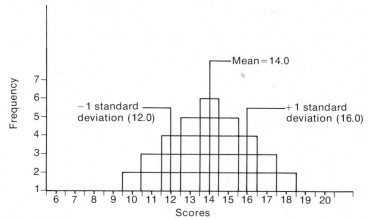

Figure 7–7 Locations of one standard deviation above the mean and one standard deviation below the mean.

have only to perform the addition $14.0 + 2.0 + 2.0 = 18.0$ to determine that the highest score is 18.

The percentage of scores that lie between plus and minus 1, 2, and 3 standard deviations is fairly constant for large numbers of scores that are grouped in the manner shown so far. As an illustration of this, look at the graph of a new set of scores in which the dispersion around the mean is much greater than for the previous example (see Figure 7–9).

As can be seen from inspection of Figure 7–9, the range of scores around the mean is much greater, and, as a result, the size of the standard deviation is also larger. You will also note that the number of cases occurring between plus and minus 1 standard deviation from the mean is about the same, and that all of the scores again occur between plus and minus 2 standard deviations.

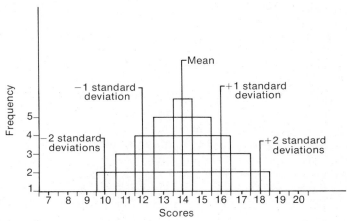

Figure 7–8 Location of two standard deviations above and below the mean.

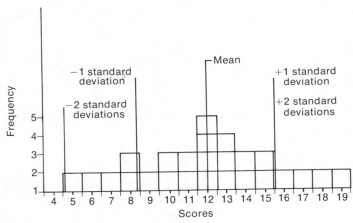

Figure 7–9 Location of the mean and plus and minus 2 standard deviations for a set of scores with greater dispersion around the mean.

For symmetrically distributed sets of scores, the percentages of cases occurring between the mean and different standard deviation distances from the mean remain relatively constant. There are exceptions, of course, but we will not be concerned with these in our present discussion. We are emphasizing the point that a relatively constant percentage of cases are found between fixed standard deviations from the mean because the fixed nature of these relationships plays an important part in statistical inference.

By now, you may have concluded that this chapter is all quite technical and that if the rest of the book is like this, your chances of getting through it and remembering anything useful are extremely remote. However, these preliminaries are essential if you are to be able to follow the logic that will be developed in the next sections of this chapter. For example, although driving a car may be fun, the practice of eye, hand, and foot coordination necessary to learn to drive is scarcely exhilarating. However, such detailed practice is absolutely necessary. Much the same problem is present here. The logic and procedures of statistical inference can be an interesting challenge and even enjoyable, but some basic background is a prerequisite to understanding what is being talked about. Our detailed discussion of some of the properties of the mean and standard deviation is the fundamental background required to understand the discussion that will follow. If you do not have a thorough grasp of the material presented to this point, we suggest that you reread it and review it until you are reasonably comfortable with it. Otherwise much of what will be presented in the remainder of this book will make little sense.

We are now ready to begin our discussion of the material that is central to the logic of statistical inference. Three topics will be covered and their relationship to one another will be discussed. In order of presentation, these topics are the *normal curve, probability,* and *random sampling distributions.* The relationship of this material to the arithmetic mean and standard deviation will be developed as we proceed and should be clear by the end of the chapter.

THE NORMAL CURVE

If you have ever had any course work in statistics or in tests and measurement, you have probably encountered the theoretical mathematical concept known as the *normal curve*. It is also referred to as the *bell-shaped curve* and the *normal probability curve*. Its properties are central to so much of statistical inference that it is frequently difficult to remember that the normal curve is just a mathematical equation that is used as a model of reality. The fact that it is useful in making decisions about events in the real world is simply a fortunate coincidence — one of those rare cases when a theoretical mathematical concept can be used to predict and to help us understand events in the real world.

A graph of the normal curve is shown in Figure 7–10.

The usefulness of the normal curve lies in the fact that we can use some of the relationships established in it to make inferences about events in the real world. To illustrate this point, consider how some of the statistics you have learned about can be interpreted in relation to the normal curve. For example, if we know the arithmetic mean and the size of the standard deviation for a normal curve, we can determine just what percentage of scores would fall between the mean and one standard deviation above the mean. Similar determinations can be made for one standard deviation below the mean, for two standard deviations, three standard deviations, and so forth. The percentage of cases to be found for each of these relationships is shown in Figure 7–11.

As can be seen in Figure 7–11, 34.13% of the cases are found between the mean and plus 1 standard deviation. Between plus and minus 1 standard deviation, 68.26% of the cases are found; between plus and minus 2 standard deviations, 95.45%; and between plus and minus three standard deviations, 99.73%. These percentages will be the same for any normal curve.

You may be puzzled at this point as to why we are emphasizing these relationships and why we are interested in determining the percentage of cases to

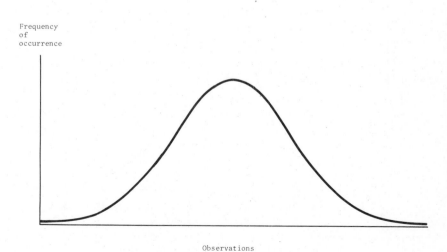

Frequency
of
occurrence

Observations

Figure 7–10 Theoretical normal curve.

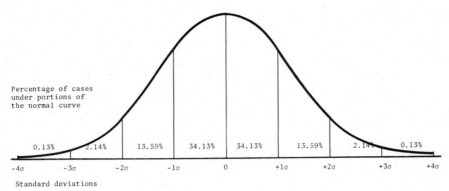

Percentage of cases
under portions of
the normal curve

| 0.13% | 2.14% | 13.59% | 34.13% | 34.13% | 13.59% | 2.14% | 0.13% |

| -4σ | -3σ | -2σ | -1σ | 0 | +1σ | +2σ | +3σ | +4σ |

Standard deviations

Figure 7–11   Percentages of cases under portions of the normal curve. (From Bernstein, Allen L. *A handbook of statistics solutions for the behavioral sciences.* Copyright © 1964 by Holt, Rinehart & Winston, Inc., and reprinted with their permission.)

be found between given standard deviations. The reason is actually quite simple: The normal curve can be used to help us make intelligent estimates about events in the real world because many events in the real world, if represented by a graph, would distribute in a shape so close to the normal curve, that we can use the properties of the curve to help us make judgments. As examples, look at Figures 7–12 and 7–13. Figure 7–12 represents the distribution of intelligence test (IQ) scores of children tested with the Stanford-Binet intelligence test. Figure 7–13 is on quite a different level — it depicts the weight gain of 100 pigs over a given period of time. Both of these sets of scores are actually close enough in shape to the normal curve to allow us to use some

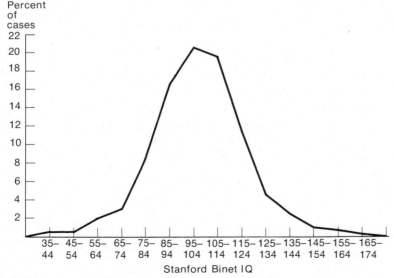

Percent
of
cases

Stanford Binet IQ

Figure 7–12   Stanford-Binet IQ's of 2904 unselected children between the ages of 2 and 18. (From Terman, Lewis M., and Merrill, Maud, A. *Measuring intelligence.* Copyright © 1937 by Houghton Mifflin Company, and reprinted with their permission.)

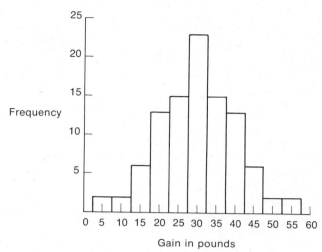

Figure 7–13 Graphical representation of array of 100 normally distributed gains in weight in pigs. (From Snedecor, G. *Statistical methods.* Copyright © 1956 by Iowa State University Press, and reprinted with their permission.)

of the properties of the normal curve to infer things. For example, if we want to know what percentage of pigs would be expected to gain more than a certain number of pounds, we can calculate the mean and standard deviation and find out how many pigs are above a given poundage in relation to the standard deviation. Then, reference to the normal curve will give us an immediate es-

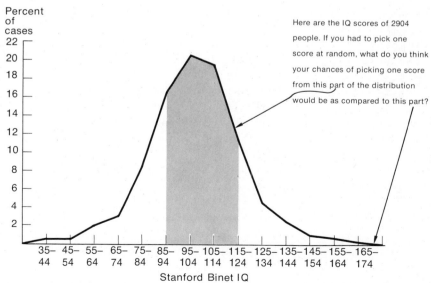

Here are the IQ scores of 2904 people. If you had to pick one score at random, what do you think your chances of picking one score from this part of the distribution would be as compared to this part?

Figure 7–14 Stanford-Binet IQ's of 2904 unselected children between the ages of 2 and 18. (From Terman, Lewis, M., and Merrill, Maud, A. *Measuring intelligence.* Copyright © 1937 by Houghton Mifflin Company, and reprinted with their permission.)

timate of what percentage of cases would be expected above a given standard deviation. Similarly, if we wanted to know how often an IQ score of a given magnitude would be expected to occur, we can calculate the mean and standard deviation for the IQ scores and again refer to the normal curve. For example, in the distribution of intelligence test scores shown in Figure 7–12, an IQ score of 165 or greater is more than 3 standard deviations above the mean. Reference to the normal curve shows us that only 0.13% of the scores are above 3 standard deviations. Clearly we would not expect scores this large to occur very frequently. By contrast, we *would* expect scores in the IQ range of 85 to 124 to occur frequently, since these values lie within one standard deviation above and below the mean, and 68% of the cases are to be found in this range of the normal distribution.

Another example: If we wished to know the chance of obtaining a score of a given magnitude, we could easily determine it by finding what percentage of the scores in the distribution would be expected to occur beyond the limits of the score in question. For example, in the distribution of intelligence test scores shown in Figure 7–12, an IQ of 165 or greater occurs less than 1% of the time. Clearly our chances of picking such a score out of the entire set of 2904 scores just by chance is not very great. By contrast, our chances of picking a score in the IQ range of 85 to 124 would be much better, simply because so many children achieve scores between 85 and 124. In the next section we will see how the normal curve is used to determine how often something occurs by chance—i.e., its probability.

PROBABILITY

We have already encountered the concept of probability in the earlier discussion of the article by Rhine et al. Probability is defined as the ratio of the number of ways an event can happen to the total number of ways it can and *cannot* happen. Numerically, probability can range from .000 (the event never happens) to 1.000 (the event always happens). If an event can happen in 5 ways and not happen in 10, the probability of the event happening is 5/(5 + 10) = 5/15 = .333.

An example may help to illustrate. If you wanted to know the probability of obtaining tails when a coin is tossed 3 times in a row, you would first determine the number of ways it could and could not happen. What are the possible outcomes? If we write them out, we have the following:

TTT
HTH
HHT
THH
THT
TTH
HTT
HHH

These are all of the outcomes possible when a coin is tossed 3 times. Applying the probability formula above, we have 1 way that the event can happen and 7 ways that it cannot. Consequently, we have $1/(1 + 7) = 1/8 = .125$. There is only 1 way to get 3 tails: TTT. Let us take a closer look at the ways in which you *cannot* get 3 tails. There is only 1 way to get 3 heads, (HHH), but there are 3 ways to get 2 heads and a tail (HHT):

> HTH
> HHT
> THH

There are also 3 ways to get 2 tails and a head:

> THT
> TTH
> HTT

Thus, some events have a higher probability of occurrence than others. If we wanted to know the probability of getting 2 tails and a head in any order in 3 coin tosses, the probability would $3/8$ or $.375$.

Suppose you wanted to know the probability of tossing a coin 10 times and having it come up tails every time. Since it would take several pages to list all the possible outcomes as we did for 3 coins, perhaps you would be willing to take our word for it that there is a total of 1024 possible outcomes and that they are distributed as follows:

> 1 way to get 10 heads and 0 tails
> 10 ways to get 9 heads and 1 tail
> 45 ways to get 8 heads and 2 tails
> 120 ways to get 7 heads and 3 tails
> 210 ways to get 6 heads and 4 tails
> 252 ways to get 5 heads and 5 tails
> 210 ways to get 4 heads and 6 tails
> 120 ways to get 3 heads and 7 tails
> 45 ways to get 2 heads and 8 tails
> 10 ways to get 1 head and 9 tails
> 1 way to get 0 heads and 10 tails
> _____
> 1024 possible outcomes

The total number of ways the event can and cannot happen is 1024, and the probability of tossing tails 10 times in a row is equal to $1/1024$, or $.00098$.

Now look at some other aspects of the ways in which the events can happen. Note that the occurrences are regular and symmetrical. There are exactly as many ways to get 7 heads and 3 tails as there are to get 3 heads and 7 tails. In fact, if we were to plot the number of ways things can happen as though they were a set of scores, it would look like Figure 7–15A for the example of 3 coins, and like Figure 7–15B for the example of 10 coins.

If you continued to plot these examples for larger and larger sequences of coin tosses, as your number of events gets larger and larger, you would end up with a frequency distribution exactly like that shown in Figure 7–16.

If you refer back to page 89, you will see that Figure 7–10 (the normal curve) is identical to the one just shown. The fact that the frequencies with which *chance* events occur distribute themselves in exactly the same form as

Frequency

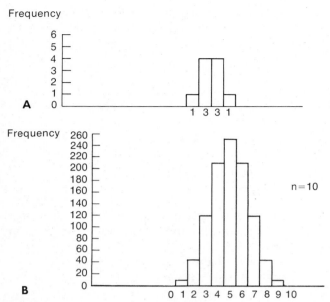

Figure 7–15 *A*, Graphical representation of the number of tails expected when 3 coins are tossed. *B*, Graph of the number of tails expected when 10 coins are tossed.

the mathematical concept known as the normal curve is a remarkable and useful coincidence between the real world and a mathematical equation.

How does this similarity between the normal curve and the frequency with which events occur help us to determine the expected probability of events occurring or not occurring?

Remember that earlier we emphasized the percentage of cases to be found between given standard deviation distances from the means. For the normal curve, 68.3% of the cases are between plus and minus 1 standard deviation; 95.4% between plus and minus 2 standard deviations, and 99.7% between plus and minus 3 standard deviations. Now, if you will refer back to the discussion of IQ scores on page 91, you will see that an IQ of 165 or greater occurs less than 1% of the time and that the chances of picking an individual

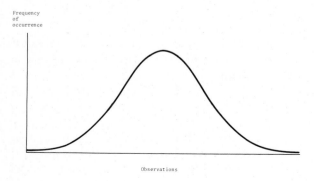

Figure 7–16 Graphical representation of an infinite number of coin tosses.

with that high an IQ at random from a population of 2904 persons are not very good. On the other hand, the chances of picking 1 person out of 2904 with an IQ between 95 and 104 are quite high because IQ values within that range occur quite frequently. The IQ values of 95 and 104 are within the range of plus and minus 1 standard deviation, which is where 68.3% of the cases are to be found. Clearly, our chances of picking one person with a given IQ score at random from 2904 people are much higher if we are picking from the range in which 68.3% occur than if we pick from a range in which less than .01% occur. As a probability, we can compare it to the chances of tossing 5 heads and 5 tails when tossing 10 coins as compared to the chances of tossing 10 heads and no tails.

Since so many different kinds of measurements and observations in the real world do distribute themselves in a normal fashion (or close enough to it), we can take advantage of this to estimate the probability of obtaining given values. To use the IQ example again, if we know that the IQ scores of the 2904 children are normally distributed and if we know the mean and the standard deviation, we can estimate the number of children having any given IQ score. Thus, we can establish the probability of finding an individual with an IQ of, say, 165—a very unlikely occurrence in a normally distributed population, such as one in which the mean IQ is 100 and the standard deviation is 15.

At this point in the text, you have encountered one basic type of statistical inference: using information gained from a sample to estimate the probability of occurrence in the population at large. The next step will be to see how inferences are made in experiments; in short, how someone who studies two groups of individuals treated differently in some way comes to the conclusion that the differences between the two groups are greater than can be expected by chance alone. To understand this you will have to understand the concepts of a *random sampling distribution.*

RANDOM SAMPLING DISTRIBUTION

We have already discussed population and sample at the beginning of this chapter, and an account of the process of *random sampling* was also presented. If you have forgotten these concepts, we suggest that you review them before proceeding with this section, since many of the same procedures are used here as were discussed in that part of the chapter.

You are already familiar with the fact that you take a sample from a population in order to know something about the population. Usually, your knowledge of the population is limited to what you know about the sample. To illustrate the ways in which random sampling distributions work and the manner in which they are developed, we will use something with which you are already familiar. Let us use the distribution from page 000 of the number of years 1000 people working in a small factory have been employed. This is a population within the limits of the definitions given earlier. The years employed distribute as shown in Figure 7–17.

For this population, we know the mean (15.5), the standard deviation (4.5), and we know that 68.3% of the people are between plus and minus 1 standard deviation; 95.4% are between plus and minus 2 standard deviations,

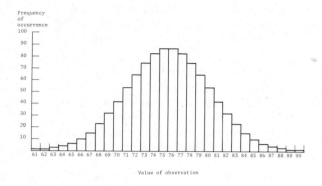

Figure 7-17 A distribution of number of years employed for all the employees of a small factory.

and 99.7% are between plus and minus 3 standard deviations. These are the same percentages that are between the standard deviation points in the normal curve. A real population might not correspond this perfectly to the ideal, but for many situations, the correspondence would be extremely close. We use an idealized example because it simplifies the process of understanding.

To understand how random sampling distributions are developed, it is necessary to introduce the idea of *random sampling with replacement.* The conditions are exactly the same as were discussed on pages 78 to 80, with the difference that once a case or score has been selected, it is then replaced in the population from which it is drawn. This means that a given score could be selected randomly 2 or more times in a row. In fact, in drawing a random sample of 30 scores with replacement, it would be possible to draw the identical score 30 times in a row! The chances of this happening are remote, but the point is that the conditions for random sampling are such that each and every score has an equal chance of being selected each time a score is selected from the population. To illustrate how this works and how it is used in statistical inference, we will use the population shown in Figure 7–17 to construct a random sampling distribution of arithmetic means.

To do this, we first decide what our sample size should be. For this example, let us use samples of size 30. We then select a score (in this case the "score" represents the number of years employed) by means of a random number table, note the score, select the next one, note it, and so forth, until we have 30 scores selected from the population of 1000. If we select the same person twice or more in drawing our sample, he or she is included as many times as selected under the rules of replacement.

The next step is to calculate the arithmetic mean for these 30 numbers and note it. When this is done we go through the same process of selecting another 30 scores, calculating the mean, and noting it. We repeat this procedure 1000 times, at the end of which we have 1000 arithmetic means calculated on samples of size 30.[2]

Before continuing with the process, there is one additional point to make. Since we replace each score after selecting it, our population of 1000 can, for all practical purposes, be considered infinitely large, since it does not diminish in size as we select samples from it. In selecting 1000 samples of 30 each, it is obvious that every score appears much more than once. However, we could go ahead and draw several hundred thousand samples of size 30, if we

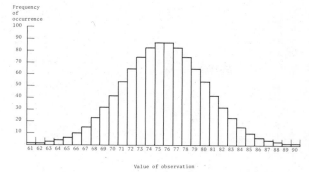

Figure 7–18 Normal distribution of means.

wished, without affecting the population, as long as we follow the rule of re-placement.

Now let us continue with the development of a random sampling dis-tribution of means. If we take the 1000 arithmetic means and plot them as scores just as we did for the original scores, we will have a distribution that looks like that shown in Figure 7–18.

The following would be true of this distribution:

1. Its arithmetic mean would be the same as the mean of the original pop-ulation of 1000 scores. (You may boggle at the idea of calculating an arithmetic mean on a set of means, but there is nothing wrong with thinking of a calculated statistic, such as a mean, as a score in another context.)

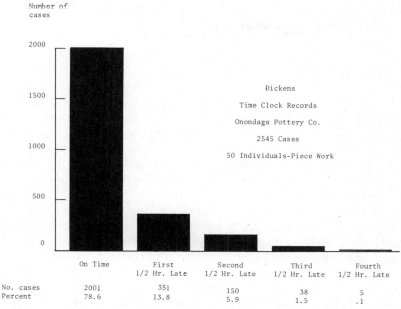

Figure 7–19 A distribution of the times people arrive for work in a factory. (From Allport, F. H. *The J-curve hypothesis of conforming behavior.* In E. E. Maccoby (Ed.), *Readings in social psychology.* Copyright © 1947 by Henry Holt Co., and reprinted with their permission.)

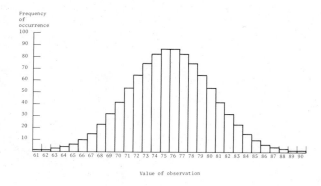

Figure 7–20 Distribution of arithmetic means.

2. Exactly 68.3% of the scores would be found between +1 and −1 standard deviations; 95.4% of the scores between +2 and −2 standard deviations; and 99.7% between +3 and −3 standard deviations. What we have done is to create by this process a random sampling distribution identical to the theoretical normal curve. Again, we see the remarkable coincidence between events in the real world and theoretical concepts essential to statistical inference.

You may well wonder whether this procedure works so marvelously when the sampling is done from some population that is not a perfect match to the normal curve. If we were to draw samples from a population such as that shown in Figure 7–19, and were to go through exactly the same sampling procedure with replacement, as described earlier on the 1000 random samples of size 30, the graph of the 1000 arithmetic means would be as shown in Figure 7–20. Thus statistics (such as means) calculated on non-normal curve populations still distribute as the normal curve. It is this fact that makes normal curve methods so useful.

Accuracy of Estimates

How do we use this random sampling distribution of means to make a statistical inference? You have already seen how population values are inferred from a sample, and perhaps you have wondered how a researcher who does not know the value of the population mean can be so sure that he is estimating the population mean correctly. Let us now examine how random sampling distributions enable us to evaluate the accuracy of our estimates based on sample values.

Basically, we accomplish this by taking advantage of the fact that the random sampling distribution of a statistic, such as a mean, distributes normally, and therefore has exactly the same expected percentage of cases between given standard deviations as is found in the normal curve.

The logical process is as follows: Any mean that we calculate on a sample can be seen as a single randomly selected mean from a hypothetical population of thousands of arithmetic means. In other words, we can act as if we had drawn thousands of samples and calculated means on each of them, and can consider the one mean we have obtained as being one of those thousands of means. In effect, we can proceed as though we had constructed a random sampling distribution of means, as was done earlier. Since we can be confident that a random sampling distribution of means will have a distribution identical to the normal curve, we can proceed as though we had actually constructed a random sampling distribution.

You may feel at this point as though you have entered a cloud-cuckooland where everyone goes around behaving as if certain things were true when there is no evidence whatever that they are. However, if you review the sequence, you should come to the conclusion that this procedure does make some logical and conceptual sense. This logical schema is based on the premise that we can calculate one mean based on a sample of subjects and view it as one of thousands of means that can be calculated on samples randomly drawn from the population. Having obtained that one mean, we can use its characteristics to infer something about the distribution of a large number of means drawn from the population. This is one of the fundamental premises of statistical inference.

Now we must deal with the actual process. Remember that our present purpose is to make a wise judgment about the population mean on the basis of one obtained sample. You will have to take on faith the idea that the arithmetic mean of a population can be estimated with a high degree of accuracy from a sample that is a relatively small percentage of the population. What is necessary is some way to determine the accuracy of your estimated mean value. After all, in a random sample, every score has an equal chance of being chosen, and it is quite possible that all of the scores we selected randomly came from that part of the population that is 2 standard deviations above the mean. If this is the case, then the mean calculated on those scores would also be at least 2 standard deviations above the real population mean. What we need is some way to estimate the probability that our estimate is reasonably accurate. There is such a way, but to explain it we have to introduce another simple calculation and to explain its relationship to the concepts developed at this point.

STANDARD ERROR OF THE MEAN

This calculation is known as the *standard error of the mean*, and it is obtained by dividing the standard deviation of the scores by the square root of the sample size. For a sample of 30 scores with a mean of 15 and a standard deviation of 5, the calculation would be as follows:

$$\text{Standard error of the mean} = \frac{\text{standard deviation}}{\sqrt{\text{sample size}}}$$

$$\frac{5}{\sqrt{30}} = .91$$

The standard error of the mean is the statistic we use to tell us something about how accurately we can estimate the population mean from a sample mean. To begin with, think of the standard error as a specialized kind of standard deviation. Exactly the same use is made of the standard error as we make of the standard deviation—to tell us about the dispersion of scores around the mean. However, for the standard error, the dispersion measured is that of sample means around the population mean.

If we now take a single sample of size 30 and calculate the mean, the standard deviation, and the standard error of the mean, we may proceed as follows. Suppose the mean is 15 and the standard deviation is 5. The standard error is then 5/ $\sqrt{30}$, or .91. We assume that our sample of 30 cases is a random sample from the population. Now, we want to make some estimate of how accurate we might be if we used the sample mean of 15 as an estimate of the population mean. To do this we take the mean of 15 and add the value of one standard error to it (15 + .91 = 15.91). We then take the mean and subtract the value of one standard error from it (15 − .91 = 14.09). We now have the values 15.91 and 14.09. We now repeat the process with two standard errors (15 + .91 + .91) added and two subtracted (15 − .91 − .91), yielding 16.82 and 13.18, respectively. If we do it for +3 and −3 standard errors, we get the values of 17.73 and 12.27. Just as we know that 99.7% of all the scores lie between +3 and −3 standard deviations in a normal distribution, we can now say that the probability is less than .001 that the actual value of the population mean is either smaller than 12.27 or larger than 17.73.

Perhaps a comment about the sequence in which you should think about these things would be of help. Remember that a random sampling distribution of means will take the shape of the normal curve, and the percentages of cases between plus and minus 1, 2, and 3 standard deviations are the same as in the normal curve. In other words, over 99% of all the means in the random sampling distribution will be between +3 and −3 standard deviations in the random sampling distribution. *The standard error is the statistic we use to make the best estimate possible of the numerical values of the standard deviation of the random sampling distribution of means.* Since we know that 99% of all the means are between +3 and −3 standard deviations, and since our one mean is one of the thousands of random samples possible, setting the limits of +3 and −3 standard errors allows us to be 99% sure that the actual value of the population will be somewhere between 12.27 and 17.73.

Let us review the process briefly. Suppose that we have one sample of 30 scores. Our population may be 300 or 30,000 or three million or even larger. We would like to know the arithmetic mean of this population of scores, but can only obtain a random sample of 30 scores. We know that, even in small samples, estimates of the mean of a population will be fairly accurate if the sample is drawn randomly. However, we would like to be able to put some limits on our estimate and say that the probability is .95 that the population mean is between two values. What we have to work with is one arithmetic mean, one standard deviation, and one standard error—all calculated on a sample of 30 scores. How are we able to make statements about an entire population from this tiny amount of information?

We can assume that our sample mean is one of a set of thousands that could be calculated. The distribution of these thousands of means will have a shape identical to the normal curve. The mean of this distribution of sample means will be identical to that of the underlying population of scores and the

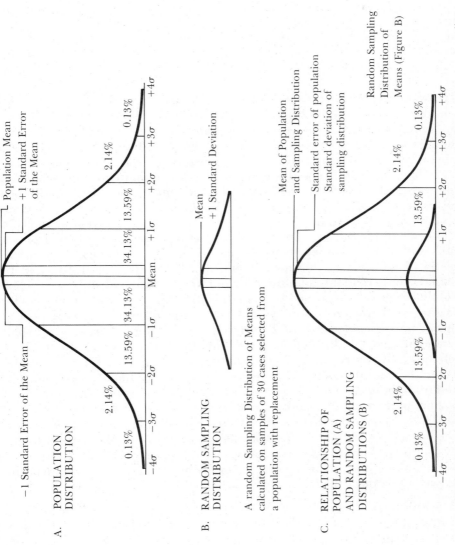

Figure 7-21 Graphic representation of the relationship between a population distribution and a random sampling distribution of means calculated on samples drawn from that population.

standard deviation of this distribution is the standard error of the distribution of the population mean. This relationship is shown graphically in Figure 7–21.

From this one sample, we wish to make as informed a judgment as possible about the value of the arithmetic mean for an entire population. It is not possible to test everyone, so a sample is taken from which we wish to estimate how everyone else *not* tested would do. If we had unlimited time and money, we could test everyone and find out what the true average for the population would be. Since this is impossible in most cases, we must use statistical theory to make the best judgment we can about the entire population. To do this we assume that the mean of the sample we take is just one of an infinite number of means that could be calculated on samples taken from our population.

How does this information allow us to make probability statements? Remember that some values occur with much greater frequency than others. In the symmetrical types of distributions that we have been talking about, the arithmetic mean is located at the center of the distribution. To use the example of coin tossing again, if 10 coins are tossed, the combination of 5 heads and 5 tails is the one that occurs most frequently. Similarly, frequencies of 6 heads and 4 tails or 6 tails and 4 heads also occur much more frequently than 10 heads or 10 tails. The point here is that in picking one toss of 10 coins out of a population of a thousand tosses of 10 coins each, you are much more likely to pick one of 5 heads and 5 tails or 6 heads and 4 tails, than you are to pick one of 10 tails and 0 heads, simply because the others occur so much more often. Since 95.4% of the expected mean values fall between +2 and −2 standard deviations of the random sampling distribution of means and since we can estimate this standard deviation by calculating the standard error of the mean for our sample, all we have to do to make an estimate with a 95% chance of including the actual population value is to take our sample mean and add to it the standard error multiplied by 2.00. This gives us an upper limit above which only 2.5% of the means in the random sampling distribution would be expected to be located. The same standard error multiplied by 2.00 and subtracted from the mean will give us the lower limit below which only 2.5% of the means in the random sampling distribution of means would be expected to lie. Thus, we can say that the probability that the actual population value will be outside these limits is less than .05. Another way to think about this is to say that if we were to draw 100 samples of 30 scores each, only 5 times out of 100 would we have an arithmetic mean that was larger or smaller than the limits we set by our calculations.

You will be relieved to know that we have now covered the basic logic involved in the process of statistical inference. If you have been able to follow the process to this point, you now have a grasp of the most important concepts involved in making statistical inferences. There are other aspects to consider, of course, but these largely represent variations on the material covered so far. As an illustration of the variations that play an important part in types of statistical inference, let us consider some other types of random sampling distributions.

DIFFERENCE DISTRIBUTIONS

Suppose we were to draw a random sample of 30 scores, calculate the mean, then draw another random sample of 30 scores, calculate that mean, and then subtract the mean of the second sample from the mean of the first. If we did this we would have what is known as a difference score based on means. If we were to repeat this process several thousand times, we could develop a random sampling distribution of difference scores. Such a distribution would display the characteristics of the normal curve, and we would thus know the percentage of scores expected to occur between plus and minus 1, 2, and 3 standard deviations. However, the mean of this distribution is zero. Why is this? Remember that the accuracy of estimating the population mean from random samples is quite good. It follows, therefore, that any two random samples should both be quite good estimates of the population mean, and that if we subtract the mean of one sample from another the most likely result would be a difference close to or equal to zero. For example, if we were to actually draw 1000 samples of 30 persons each from a defined population, test them on something, and take the average for each sample of 30, then subtract the mean of sample 2 from that of sample 1, the mean of sample 4 from that of sample 3, and so forth, we would have 50 difference scores. The mean of these pairs of differences would be very close to zero, and approximately 68% of the difference scores would be between plus and minus 1 standard deviation. Only 1% of these differences would be so large as to fall outside the points marking plus and minus 3 standard deviations. Such a distribution could be used to assess the meaningfulness of differences between groups in an experiment.

Now let us consider a somewhat fanciful example. Suppose you were to draw, as before, a random sample of 30 scores, calculate the mean, draw a second sample of 30 scores, calculate its mean, subtract the mean of the second sample from the first, then add your current age to the difference score you now have, and divide that result by your weight on your 16th birthday. If you were to do this several thousand times, you would again have a random sampling distribution identical in shape to the normal curve. The mean of this distribution would be equal to your current age divided by your weight on your 16th birthday. Remember that normally the mean of a set of difference scores is zero, and that you are adding to zero your current age divided by your weight on your 16th birthday.

Clearly such a distribution would not be of much use in statistical inference. However, it does illustrate that random sampling distributions can be constructed under a variety of conditions and will always assume the shape of a normal curve.

For example, suppose we draw, as before, a random sample of 30 scores, which we call sample A. We calculate the mean and the variance of sample A (see page 000 for a description of the calculation of the variance). We then draw a second sample of 30 scores, which we call sample B, and calculate its mean and variance. Next we subtract the mean of sample B from the mean of sample A to obtain a *difference score of means*. We now carry out another calculation, as follows:

$$\sqrt{\frac{\text{Variance of sample A}}{\text{Sample size (30)}} + \frac{\text{Variance of sample B}}{\text{Sample size (30)}}} = \frac{\text{Standard error of}}{\text{the mean difference}}$$

We take the variance of sample A and divide it by the number of scores in the sample (30); divide the variance of sample B by the number of scores in the sample (again 30); add these two calculations together; and take the square root. This gives a new quantity which statisticians call the standard error of the difference since it is an estimate of the standard deviation of a distribution of difference scores based on means. We have one final step remaining: to divide our mean difference score by the standard error of the difference:

$$\frac{\text{Difference score of means}}{\text{Standard error of the mean difference}}$$

THE *t* STATISTIC

Just in case you are wondering whether this is another fanciful exercise involving inserting your age and weight into calculations, let us assure you that it is not. You have just gone through the process of calculating a well-known statistic for determining whether in fact two independent samples are really significantly different from each other statistically. This statistic is known as *t*, and you encountered it in the Rhine et al. article and at the beginning of this chapter.

At this point let us re-examine the statement from Rhine et al. that was quoted in the opening paragraph of this chapter. Since the nature of an experimental procedure determines what type of statistical calculations will be made, perhaps we should also give some account of the assumptions a research worker is making when he evaluates the statistical significance of a mean difference between two groups. Look at the original Rhine et al. statement summarizing one of their findings: "Girls correctly identified a mean of 5.24 good and bad pictures and the boys had a mean of 4.72, a difference producing a $t = 1.03$, $df = 48$, $p > .10$."

First of all, what is the experimenter doing when he examines a difference such as the one between boys and girls just noted? In examining such a difference he asks a question as to whether or not the difference between the average scores of boys and girls is large enough to conclude that there may be a real difference between boys and girls on this measure. In other words, is it possible that the ability of girls of the age studied to correctly identify actions usually labeled "good" and "bad" is different from that of boys of the same age? Or is this difference between the average scores no more than might occur by sheer chance? What is needed here is a way to estimate the probability with which this difference occurs by chance.

The *t* statistic is one method we can use to estimate this probability. This statistic is the ratio of the difference between two arithmetic means to the expected dispersion around those means. The concept of dispersion was presented in our discussion of the standard deviation, but a review of this material in relation to a specific problem may be helpful.

Suppose we were to take the scores on picture identification obtained by Rhine et al. and plot them on a graph, with order of magnitude on the horizontal axis and the frequency with which they occur on the vertical axis. In other words, we construct a frequency distribution. Plotted separately for boys and girls, the distributions might look like this:

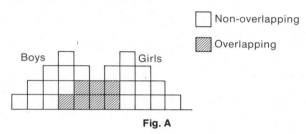

Fig. A

Obviously there is a good deal of overlap in that there are several boys and girls who have identical scores. Does this mean that there are no sex differences on this measure? What if the distributions looked like the following?

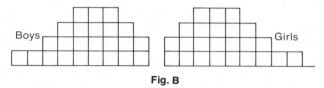

Fig. B

If the distributions had looked like this, it would be pretty safe to conclude that boys and girls differ, since there is no overlap of scores—the lowest score by a girl is higher than the highest score made by a boy, indicating that girls clearly do better on this measure. However, suppose the distributions had looked like this:

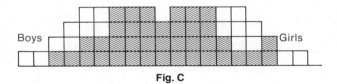

Fig. C

We would probably conclude that there is no difference between boys and girls on identifying concepts of good and bad.

As we mentioned earlier, the t statistic is a measure of the difference between means relative to the dispersion around these means, and it can be used to find out how often a given difference would occur by chance. Some rather complex mathematics were necessary to develop the t statistic. However, these need not concern us, as it is not necessary to know the mathematics in order to interpret the meaning of the statistic.

An experimenter uses the statistical formula which you saw on page 104.

to calculate a numerical value for t. That formula is represented as follows:

$$t = \frac{\text{Difference between two means}}{\sqrt{\dfrac{\text{Variance of sample A}}{\text{Size of sample A}} + \dfrac{\text{Variance of sample B}}{\text{Size of sample B}}}}$$

$$= \frac{\text{Difference between two means}}{\text{Standard error of the difference}}$$

In the example from Rhine et al., this difference would be calculated by subtracting the average score for boys from the average score for girls (mean for boys = 4.72; for girls = 5.24):

$$
\begin{array}{r}
5.24 \\
-\,4.72 \\
\hline
0.52
\end{array}
$$

Thus, the difference between the two means is equal to .52. This difference is then divided by the appropriate measure of dispersion (the standard error of the difference) to calculate the statistic. Remember that the standard error of the difference is an estimate of the variability of a distribution of mean differences, assuming that the pairs of means on which it is based are drawn from the same population. When we make this assumption we are assuming that the two means are from the same population—i.e., that there is no difference between them. We do this because we know that if this assumption is true, the mean difference is zero, and any result other than zero is the result of chance sampling differences. To test this assumption, we then use the t statistic, which takes into account both the size of the mean difference and the amount of variability of the distribution of differences.

When t has been calculated, the experimenter then consults a book of statistical tables,[3] specifically, a table entitled "t distribution." The statistical table of the t distribution is simply a list of values indicating how often the value of t would be expected to reach a given size by chance alone. An agreed upon convention by statisticians is to accept as a real difference those values of the t statistic which would be expected to occur 5% or less of the time by chance alone. An alternate, more stringent choice is to accept those values expected to occur 1% or less of the time by chance.

The experimenter enters the section of the table appropriate for his sample size. The Rhine et al. example was based on 50 subjects—25 in each group. The value in the appropriate section of the table which would be expected to occur 5% of the time by chance alone is 2.00, and the value that would be expected to occur 10% of the time by chance alone is 1.29. Since the calculated value, the t found by Rhine et al., is only 1.03, the conclusion is that there is no real difference between boys and girls on this measure. This conclusion is expressed in the statement: "Girls correctly identified a mean of 5.24 good and bad pictures and the boys had a mean of 4.72, a difference producing a $t = 1.03$, $df = 48$, $p > .10$." In other words, the value that Rhine et al. obtained by calculation is one that would be expected to occur more than 10% of the time by chance alone.

What determines the choice of the .05 and .01 levels to indicate a real difference? Obviously, there is no single point at which a difference is suddenly more meaningful or "significant." The choice of the .05 and .01 levels is simply an agreed upon convention by statisticians. There are times where it may be appropriate to select a less extreme level than .05 and other times when it may be decided that a proof of difference requires a value that would be expected to occur only .001 of the time by chance alone. These decisions are made in reference to what is being studied and with consideration to the cost of making a mistaken inference; they are not statistical problems per se.

Just in case the relationship is not entirely clear between the calculations carried out by Rhine et al. and the process of inference, let us look at it from a slightly different point of view. What does the value of the t statistic calculated by Rhine et al. indicate in relation to the material presented so far? How do we relate it to random sampling distributions and how do we make judgments of statistical significance (or lack of it)?

In the discussion of random sampling distributions, it was emphasized that you could construct practically any kind of random sampling distribution (including one for age divided by your weight on your 16th birthday). For the Rhine et al. example, let us assume that we could draw samples of 25 children from a huge population of boys and girls, ages 2 to 6, and test them with the picture identification task used by Rhine et al. Remember that we are randomly sampling from a population of boys and girls and that any given randomly drawn sample is likely to have fairly equal numbers of each sex. Our procedure would be to draw a sample of 25 children, test them, and calculate the mean and variance; draw a second sample of 25, test them, calculate the mean and variance; find the difference between the mean of the first sample and the mean of the second sample; and do the calculations necessary to arrive at the t statistic. If we were to do this several thousand times, what would we have? By now you already know the answer—we would have a random sampling distribution of the t statistic for differences between two independent groups based on samples of 25 subjects. The mean of this distribution would be zero. (If this puzzles you, go back and read the section on difference distributions, beginning on page 103.)

Said another way, we have constructed a distribution of a statistic in which there are no differences between the groups other than what may be expected by chance alone. Suppose girls actually are better than boys at identifying concepts of good and bad. We are sampling randomly from a population of equal numbers of boys and girls so that any given sample of 25 will have approximately equal numbers of boys and girls. Consequently, any large mean differences could occur only by chance. For such a difference to occur, one sample would have to be drawn just from that section of the population in which those boys and girls who have scores predominantly above the population mean are located. The other sample would have to be drawn from that section of the population in which the children have scores that are predominantly lower than those of the first samples. Two such samples would have a large mean difference, and if the variability within each of the two samples was relatively small, the value of the t statistic would be quite large. (Remember that the t statistic is a number that increases in magnitude as the size of the mean difference increases and the variability—which is divided into the mean difference—decreases.) How often does such a difference occur in drawing random samples? For now let us just say, not very often.

At this point, we should introduce a topic which you may encounter in discussions of research—the *null hypothesis*. We have, without going into detail, discussed how to test for differences between groups. However, when you test to see whether there are specific differences between groups, it implies the idea that there is some specific value that you are testing against. This is the *null hypothesis*—the idea that there is *no* difference between the groups being studied.

The null hypothesis, as is true of many other notions in statistical hypothesis testing, is somewhat confusing upon first examination. Usually, if you have carried out an experiment in which you have randomly selected an experimental and control group, you are actively interested in any differences that may appear. Why, then, the idea of the null hypothesis—the idea that there is no difference between the groups being studied?

The advantage of the null hypothesis is that it provides an exact and concrete value—zero—to work with. It is difficult to specify that one group does better than another in terms of some measured attribute, unless some standard can be found that would make such differences meaningful. The null hypothesis provides just such a standard. A person testing the null hypothesis is saying that there is zero difference between his experimental and control groups in statistical terms, no matter what the absolute value of the measured attribute. Of course, although he states the hypothesis that there is no difference, he might hope that the groups really do differ. In the Rhine et al. study, the experimenters were undoubtedly hopeful that the study would show differences between the groups, but their tests were done using the null hypothesis—that is, on the premise that there was zero difference between the groups.

Having reviewed this, let us go back to the specific statistic calculated by Rhine et al. They wished to determine whether or not there was a specific difference between boys and girls on their particular measure. To determine this, they calculated the t statistic. One of their assumptions should be made quite clear. They assumed, for the purposes of making the statistical test, that there was zero difference between the boys and girls. This may seem confusing at first, but the reason is one of specifying the difference exactly, and the logic is as follows. In a random sampling distribution with samples of 25 children and an equal number of boys and girls in each sample, we know how often large differences occur by chance simply because of the percentage of cases bounded by plus and minus 1, 2, and 3 standard deviations in the normal curve. This is the distribution that we would get if there were no real differences. We have separated our subjects into boys and girls and calculated a t statistic. If the value of our t statistic is one that would occur by chance only 5% of the time or less, then we can be rather confident that there is a real difference between boys and girls, since under conditions in which no difference exists, t statistic values this large occur only 5 times out of 100 or less. Put another way, if we drew random samples with equal numbers of boys and girls, we would get a value as large as the one obtained only 5 times out of 100.

Since Rhine et al. obtained a *t* equal to 1.03, the question now arises: how often does a difference this large occur by chance? Table 7–2 shows a segment of the standard table of the distribution of the *t* statistic, as it is found in most statistics texts.

The table is read as follows: The column at the far left, labeled "Degrees of Freedom" refers to the total number of subjects in the sample. For technical statistical reasons, the value used in this calculation is 2 less than the actual number of subjects. (You will recall that although Rhine et al. had 50 subjects, their statement refers to "*df* = 48.") The reason for using *df* rather than the actual number of subjects will not be discussed here, since it is not fundamental to your understanding of the process of inference.

The percentages represent probability levels. Another way to think of probability is in terms of percentages of occurrence under conditions of no difference. Thus, for 48 *df* in the column at the far left and in the column headed 5%, we find the value 2.010. What this means is that for this number of

TABLE 7–2 Values of *t* at the 5% and 1% Levels of Significance*

DEGREES OF FREEDOM	5%	1%	DEGREES OF FREEDOM	5%	1%
1	12.706	63.657	32	2.037	2.739
2	4.303	9.925	34	2.032	2.728
3	3.182	5.841	36	2.027	2.718
4	2.776	4.604	38	2.025	2.711
5	2.571	4.032	40	2.021	2.704
6	2.447	3.707	42	2.017	2.696
7	2.365	3.499	44	2.015	2.691
8	2.306	3.355	46	2.012	2.685
9	2.262	3.250	48	2.010	2.681
10	2.228	3.169	50	2.008	2.678
11	2.201	3.106	55	2.005	2.668
12	2.179	3.055	60	2.000	2.660
13	2.160	3.012	65	1.998	2.653
14	2.145	2.977	70	1.994	2.648
15	2.131	2.947	80	1.990	2.638
16	2.120	2.921	90	1.987	2.632
17	2.110	2.898	100	1.984	2.626
18	2.101	2.878	125	1.979	2.616
19	2.093	2.861	150	1.976	2.609
20	2.086	2.845	200	1.972	2.601
21	2.080	2.831	300	1.968	2.592
22	2.074	2.819	400	1.966	2.588
23	2.069	2.807	500	1.965	2.586
24	2.064	2.797	1000	1.962	2.581
25	2.060	2.787	∞	1.960	2.576
26	2.056	2.779			
27	2.052	2.771			
28	2.048	2.763			
29	2.045	2.756			
30	2.042	2.750			

*From Fisher, R. A. *Statistical Methods for Research Workers*, 14th ed. (Copyright © 1972 by Hafner Press.)

subjects under conditions of random sampling from the same population (in other words, when there is no difference between groups) a calculated t statistic (the number arrived at by the calculations on page 106) as large or larger than the value 2.010 occurs only 5% of the time by chance alone. In other words, if we drew 1000 pairs of samples from the same population and calculated the t statistic, only 50 times would we expect to get a difference this large on the basis of chance alone.

Moving over to the next column (headed 1%), we find the value of 2.681. The process is the same. In the 1000 pairs of samples mentioned above, we would expect to find a value as large as 2.681 only 10 times by chance alone. As we mentioned earlier, there are agreed upon conventions for deciding when a difference is so large that it will be decided that it is not a chance difference—the normal convention is to accept the value of 5%. In other words, once a t statistic is as large as the value found in the 5% column, we can feel fairly comfortable in concluding that there is a real difference between the groups. If an even more stringent level is demanded, the value of 1% is used.

Since the Rhine et al. t statistic has a smaller value than that found in the 5% column, the conclusion is that the difference between boys and girls is not statistically significant, since the difference they found would be expected to occur more than 10% of the time as a result of chance sampling error.

You may wonder why different values of the t statistic occur for different numbers of subjects. This is a topic of considerable complexity, and a complete treatment of it would lead us into a more conventional course on statistics. For our purposes, it is simplest to think of the values in the table as representing different random sampling distributions of t for different numbers of subjects. The values we see in the tables are the parts of these distributions that are of use to us in doing experiments—the values that would be expected to occur with the specified probability by chance alone when no real difference exists.

One more aspect of the t statistic remains to be covered. To illustrate it, we will use another quote from the statistical statements made by Rhine et al.:

> A two-factor analysis [of variance] was performed with 6 month age intervals as one factor and good or bad pictures as the second. . . . The criterion measure was the number of correct responses to the pictures. The difference between age levels is significant (F = 5.33, df = 7.42, p < .001).

Thus far our discussion of random sampling distributions has been almost exclusively concerned with the t distribution. The statistic F, mentioned in the above quote, has another kind of random sampling distribution; we will have more to say about it in a later chapter. It is mentioned here primarily to illustrate the overall similarity of the process of inference when using random sampling distributions. For our present purposes, let us simply say that the random sampling distribution of F is used in much the same way as t, and the pattern of interpretation is similar. Those values which occur 5% or less of the time by chance are tabled, and the calculated F statistic is examined with reference to these tables to see if the value obtained is equal to or greater than the tabled value of F. For Rhine et al., the calculated value of F is equal to 5.33, which for the number of subjects and conditions involved would be expected to occur less than one-tenth of one percent of the time by chance alone. Clearly, Rhine and coworkers are justified in concluding that the scores associated with the age differences they found did not occur by chance alone and that there is a real difference between the age groups.

We have now presented all the basic steps involved in making a statistical inference. Essentially, we estimate the probability of obtaining mean differences of a given size, taking into account the variability of the distributions of scores. We have a theoretical model, the normal distribution, which applies to the distribution of statistics and which provides a powerful analytic tool with which to estimate the probability of obtaining differences of various magnitudes. The ability to apply this model to samples allows us to make generalizations regarding underlying realities far more rationally and confidently than we could by relying on intuition alone.

In the next chapter we will discuss a wide variety of common statistics in terms of their operating characteristics, their uses, and their limitations. The basic logic underlying all of these inferential statistics has been developed here, and what follows merely represents applications of the basic logic presented in this chapter.

FOOTNOTES

[1]The nature of the calculation may strike you as being tedious. There are easier ways to calculate the standard deviation, but this book is not meant to teach methods of calculation. In the few calculations remaining, we will use calculation methods which clarify the nature of the basic statistic rather than using formulas that are simpler to calculate but are intuitively more difficult to understand.

[2]You might conclude from this that we really enjoy incredibly dull and repetitive tasks. Fortunately, computers have no sense of boredom and can do a task such as this in about one third of a minute. The mathematical statisticians who first developed random sampling distributions did it mathematically and not by the procedure we are describing. However, the end result is the same, whether done mathematically or by random selection procedures. Since the repeating procedure is much easier to follow than calculus, we have chosen this way to illustrate the process.

[3]Sets of such tables can be found in C. Hardyck and L. Petrinovich, *Introduction to statistics for the behavioral sciences*. Philadelphia: W. B. Saunders Company, 1970.

ADDENDUM: RANDOM SAMPLING

On page 80 of this chapter, we claimed that a sample selected randomly would always provide a reasonably good estimate of the population mean. As a way of demonstrating this, we have provided the following exercise.

On pages 112 and 113 you will find two tables. Table 7–3 is a table of random numbers. Table 7–4 is a table of 1000 scores, arranged to form a normal distribution with a mean of 75.5 and a standard deviation of 4.55. The subjects in Table 7–4 are numbered from subject number 000 to subject number 999. To try your hand at drawing a random sample, go through the following procedure: Pick some point of entry in Table 7–3. (With a table of random numbers it does not matter where you start or what direction you choose to read in.) Read a sequence of 3 digits and write them down, read another 3

TABLE 7–3   Random Numbers*

10097	32533	76520	13586	34673	54876	80959	09117	39292	74945
37542	04805	64894	74296	24805	24037	20636	10402	00822	91665
08422	68953	19645	09303	23209	02560	15953	34764	35080	33606
99019	02529	09376	70715	38311	31165	88676	74397	04436	27659
12807	99970	80157	36147	64032	36653	98951	16877	12171	76833
66065	74717	34072	76850	36697	36170	65813	39885	11199	29170
31060	10805	45571	82406	35303	42614	86799	07439	23403	09732
85269	77602	02051	65692	68665	74818	73053	85247	18623	88579
63573	32135	05325	47048	90553	57548	28468	28709	83491	25624
73796	45753	03529	64778	35808	34282	60935	20344	35273	88435
98520	17767	14905	68607	22109	40558	60970	93433	50500	73998
11805	05431	39808	27732	50725	68248	29405	24201	52775	67851
83452	99634	06288	98083	13746	70078	18475	40610	68711	77817
88685	40200	86507	54801	36766	67951	90364	76493	29609	11062
99594	67348	87517	64969	91826	08928	93785	61368	23478	34113
65481	17674	17468	50950	58047	76974	73039	57186	40218	16544
80124	35635	17727	08015	45318	22374	21115	78253	14385	53763
74350	99817	77402	77214	43236	00210	45521	64237	96286	02655
69916	26803	66252	29148	36936	87203	76621	13990	94400	56418
09893	20505	14225	68514	46427	56788	96297	78822	54382	14598
91499	14523	68479	27686	46162	83554	94750	89923	37089	20048
80336	94598	26940	36858	70297	34135	53140	33340	42050	82341
44104	81949	85157	47954	32979	26575	57600	40881	22222	06413
12550	73742	11100	02040	12860	74697	96644	89439	28707	25815
63606	49329	16505	34484	40219	52563	43651	77082	07207	31790
61196	90446	26457	47774	51924	33729	65394	59593	42582	60527
15474	45266	95270	79953	59367	83848	82396	10118	33211	59466
94557	28573	67897	54387	54622	44431	91190	42592	92927	45973
42481	16213	97344	08721	16868	48767	03071	12059	25701	46670
23523	78317	73208	89837	68935	91416	26252	29663	05522	82562
04493	52494	75246	33824	45862	51025	61962	79335	65337	12472
00549	97654	64051	88159	96119	63896	54692	82391	23287	29529
35963	15307	26898	09354	33351	35462	77974	50024	90103	39333
59808	08391	45427	26842	83609	49700	13021	24892	78565	20106
46058	85236	01390	92286	77281	44077	93910	83647	70617	42941
32179	00597	87379	25241	05567	07007	86743	17157	85394	11838
69234	61406	20117	45204	15956	60000	18743	92423	97118	96338
19565	41430	01758	75379	40419	21585	66674	36806	84962	85207
45155	14938	19476	07246	43667	94543	59047	90033	20826	69541
94864	31994	36168	10851	34888	81553	01540	35456	05014	51176
98086	24826	45240	28404	44999	08896	39094	73407	35441	31880
33185	16232	41941	50949	89435	48581	88695	41994	37548	73043
80951	00406	96382	70774	20151	23387	25016	25298	94624	61171
79752	49140	71961	28296	69861	02591	74852	20539	00387	59579
18633	32537	98145	06571	31010	24674	05455	61427	77938	91936
74029	43902	77557	32270	97790	17119	52527	58021	80814	51748
54178	45611	80993	37143	05335	12969	56127	19255	36040	90324
11664	49883	52079	84827	59381	71539	09973	33440	88461	23356
48324	77928	31249	64710	02295	36870	32307	57546	15020	09994
69074	94138	87637	91976	35584	04401	10518	21615	01848	76938

*This table is reproduced with permission from the RAND Corporation: *A Million Random Digits*, 1955.

TABLE 7–4   Identification Numbers and Test Scores for 1000 Students

000	61	255 ↓ 329	73	938 ↓ 960	83		
001	62						
002	63	330 ↓ 412	74	961 ↓ 975	84		
003	63						
004* ↓ 007	64	413 ↓ 499	75	976 ↓ 985	85		
008 ↓ 013	65	500 ↓ 586	76	986 ↓ 991	86		
014 ↓ 023	66	587 ↓ 669	77	992 ↓ 995	87		
024 ↓ 038	67	670 ↓ 744	78	996	88		
				997	88		
039 ↓ 061	68	745 ↓ 809	79	998	89		
				999	90		
062 ↓ 093	69	810 ↓ 863	80				
094 ↓ 135	70	864 ↓ 905	81				
136 ↓ 189	71	906 ↓ 937	82				
190 ↓ 254	72						

*Subjects 004 through 007 all have scores of 64. The same convention applies to all ↓ groupings.

digits, write them down, and so forth, until you have twenty 3-digit numbers. If you had begun in the upper left hand corner of the table, and read the first row, you would have a sequence such as 100, 973, 253, 376, 520, 135, etc. Note that there is one restriction—you cannot skip about in the table and pick single digits. To do so would destroy the element of randomness.

Now turn to Table 7–4. Let your first random 3-digit number stand for that person in Table 7–4. Look up his score and write it beside his subject number. Using the sequence we gave above, the score for individual #100 is 70, for individual #973, 84, and so forth. Continue this process until you have 20 scores. Add them together and calculate the arithmetic mean. The value you obtain should be between the values of 78.13 and 72.87, 99 times out of 100 based on normal curve expectations. If you follow the rules as given above and you actually obtain a value outside those we have specified for a sample of 20 cases, send your calculations to the publisher* and he will refund the price of your book!

Earlier we commented that statistical inference was often the process of making wise decisions on the basis of little information. Hopefully, this demonstration has provided you with some believable evidence about the power of random sampling techniques to accurately assess the parameters of a population.

*If you do obtain such a value, send your calculations to the Psychology Editor, W. B. Saunders Co., West Washington Square, Philadelphia, Pennsylvania 19105. Give your sequence of random numbers and indicate the page, column, and row where you started your random sequence. If your solution is the first received by the publisher, he will refund the current retail price of the book.

chapter eight

testing for the significance of differences between groups

"Seventy-three percent are in favor of one through five, forty-one percent find six unfair, thirteen percent are opposed to seven, sixty-two percent applauded eight, thirty-seven percent . . ."

In this chapter we will discuss the statistical methods most frequently used in contemporary social science to evaluate the significance of group differences. Our goal is to provide you with information on the use of each kind of statistic and enough knowledge to enable you to understand it within the perspective of the material covered in Chapter 7.

Since we presented the basic logic of statistical methods in terms of random sampling distributions, we will, whenever helpful, provide you with some information on the sampling distribution of the statistic as well. Since there are limitations on the ways in which certain types of statistical methods can be used, we will point out such restrictions when they occur. Finally, we will indicate some common types of misuse of each statistic which you might encounter in the research literature.

t STATISTIC FOR REPEATED MEASURES

In Chapter 7 we developed the logic of statistical methods using the statistic known as *t* applied to testing the significance of a mean difference between two independent groups. This statistic is probably the most common one used to test for the significance of a difference between two groups. In view of the detail presented in Chapter 7, it scarcely seems necessary to elaborate further on ways to test differences between two independent groups. The only caution we should emphasize is that the two independent groups must be comparable in terms of the trait to be measured at the outset of the experiment. If they are not, it is impossible to tell if the difference appearing at the end of the experiment is due to the experimental treatment or if it is a function of biased subject selection.

There is another type of research design in which the *t* statistic is frequently used. Sometimes only one group of subjects is used in an experiment. The procedure in such cases is to measure the subjects before the experiment, carry out some experimental procedure, and then measure the subjects again to see if there has been a change in the variable being measured.

Still another design involves matching the subjects in two independent groups on a related variable. If we are interested in evaluating the efficiency of two different methods of teaching reading to first grade children, it might be advantageous to match pairs of individuals in each of the groups in terms of intelligence. This matching would reduce the amount of variability present, assuming that intelligence is related to ability to read—a likely assumption.

The random sampling distribution of the statistic used to test for such changes would be a population of difference scores. The logic of this procedure is identical to that discussed earlier when the distributions of random sampling differences were discussed (Chapter 7, p. 103). Two samples drawn at random from the same population should be equally good estimates of the mean. In Chapter 7 we said that the process of drawing random sample A from a population, calculating its mean, drawing sample B from the same population, calculating its mean, and then subtracting the mean of sample B from the mean of sample A would most often produce a value of zero. This process, repeated thousands of times, would produce a normal distribution of differences with the mean equal to zero. Exactly the same result occurs if sample A consists of 20 randomly drawn scores and sample B of 20 randomly drawn scores; then we subtract the first score in sample B from the first score in sample A, and continue until we have 20 difference scores. If we add these difference scores and find the mean, we are likely to get a value of zero, just as we did when subtracting the mean of sample B from the mean of sample A.

If we repeated this process thousands of times, we would have a normal distribution of difference scores identical to the one discussed in Chapter 7, page 103. In practice, what the research worker does is to find the mean of the scores for his subjects and the standard error of the mean (Chapter 7, p. 99) and then to carry out the following calculation.

$$t = \frac{\text{mean of difference scores}}{\text{standard error of the mean difference}}$$

The resulting value of the *t* statistic can be evaluated in exactly the same way as the *t* for independent groups: it is compared with the values listed in a table of the *t* statistic. If the calculated value exceeds the value in the table, at one of the accepted significance levels, the researcher can conclude that a real change has occurred in his subjects from the first measurement to the second.

The *t* statistic is considered by statisticians to be exceptionally "robust." This means that there are relatively few types of distributions of scores under which this statistic would result in misleading probability estimates. In other words, if you conclude on the basis of the *t* statistic that there is a statistically meaningful difference between two groups, you will seldom be wrong.

As we continue our discussion of types of measurements, we will frequently encounter statistics for which the data must have certain characteristics if the statistic calculated is to be meaningful. Some statistics are meaningless if calculated using too few subjects; others require that the distribution of the data have a particular form and so on. The t statistic is remarkable in that it can be used with relatively little concern for the characteristics of the data.

One- and Two-Tailed Tests

In the Rhine, Hill and Wandruff article reprinted in Chapter 2, mention is made of a two-tailed sign test. (The sign test is discussed on p. 143.) The distinction between one- and two-tailed tests occurs in behavioral sciences research literature with moderate frequency, and is quite a simple one. With the two-tailed sign test, when an investigator reports that a difference is significant at the 5% level, he is making no judgment about the direction of the mean difference. The 5% column in the table of values of t (Chapter 7, p. 109) is interpreted as being the sum of the 2.5% at the extreme upper end of the distribution and the 2.5% at the extreme lower end of the distribution. In other words, the research worker makes no prediction as to which of his groups, A or B, will have the higher (or lower) mean.

By contrast, in a one-tailed test, the research worker does make a prediction regarding the direction of the difference. He states, before carrying out the calculations, that group A (or group B) will have the higher mean. By predicting the direction of the difference, he need obtain only half as large a value of t to claim significance at the 5% level of significance. For example, a t statistic of at least 2.080 is necessary to claim significance at the 5% level for 21 degrees of freedom. If a one-tailed test is done, the value of t at the same level need be no larger than 1.040 for 21 degrees of freedom.

One-tailed tests are a controversial matter in the social sciences, and statisticians are generally opposed to using them. For an investigator to predict the direction of a difference in a research study implies that he has an extremely well-developed theory capable of making rather specific predictions—a situation which does not occur very often in the social sciences. Studies where one-tailed tests are reported should be examined rather carefully to see if such a prediction is really warranted by the conditions of the study.

ANALYSIS OF VARIANCE

The analysis of variance is probably used more than any other statistical technique in contemporary social science research. If you wish to read journals publishing experimental research articles, you will probably encounter more varieties of analysis of variance techniques than you will any other method. This statistic allows one to plan experiments of great intricacy and to examine possibilities that could not be studied by any other method. It is a statistic of considerable complexity on which entire volumes have been written. In this presentation, we will necessarily be limited to a discussion of the basic logic underlying analysis of variance and of the most common uses of the method.

The concept of variance was introduced rather briefly in Chapter 7, when the process of calculating the standard deviation was illustrated. As you (hopefully) remember from one of the first examples, once the mean is calculated, the next step is to subtract it from all the scores. In the first example in Chapter 7, where the mean is 4:

$$2 - 4 = -2$$
$$3 - 4 = -1$$
$$3 - 4 = +1$$
$$6 - 4 = +2$$

The sum of the difference $= 0$

The next step is to square each difference:
$$-2 \times -2 = +4$$
$$-1 \times -1 = +1$$
$$+1 \times +1 = +1$$
$$+2 \times +2 = +4$$

The sum of the squares $= +10$

We next take the sum of these squared differences and find the mean:

$$10/4 = 2.50$$

This quantity (2.50) is known as the *variance*. You can see even from this brief example that the greater the dispersion of scores around the mean, the larger the variance will be.

Sampling Distribution of Variances. We can construct a random sampling distribution of the F statistic (the final step in the computation of the analysis of variance) by drawing a random sample from a population, calculating its mean and variance, and then drawing another random sample and calculating its mean and variance.

The next step is to take the two variances and divide one by the other. If we were to do this the thousands of times necessary to construct a sampling distribution, we would have a distribution that looks rather different from anything we have seen so far. This sampling distribution of the ratio of two variances is shown in Figure 8–1.

The mean of this distribution is 1.00, and the values distribute positively from a minimum value of zero. If the shape of this sampling distribution puzzles you, remember that there is no such thing as a negative variance. The variation of a set of scores around a mean may be zero—you may have a situation where all the scores are exactly the same—but you cannot have less than no variation.

Why is the mean 1.00? Review the process you go through to obtain this sampling distribution. You draw a random sample, calculate the mean, and then calculate the variance of the scores around that mean. You do the same thing for a second sample. Just as two means are estimates of the population mean, the two variances are estimates of the population variance. Most of the time we would expect the two variances to be quite similar to each other, just as we expect the two means to be quite similar. The result of dividing two almost identical quantities by one another is 1.00, and this is the value of the mean of this sampling distribution.

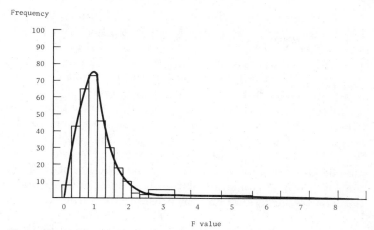

Figure 8–1 Comparison of theoretical F distribution (smooth line) for 9 and 98 degrees of freedom with the distribution (bar graph) of 1000 F ratios for 9 and 98 degrees of freedom.

A large value in this distribution of variances would be obtained if the first sample drawn happened to contain scores which came from the extremes of the population, resulting in a large variance, and the second sample happened to contain scores all drawn from one restricted section of the population, resulting in a very small variance. If the variance of the first sample is divided by the variance of the second sample, the resulting value will be considerably larger than 1.00. It is also the case that such values occur with steadily decreasing frequency as they become larger and larger.

A Sample Experiment Using Analysis of Variance

We mentioned at the beginning of this section that the analysis of variance is a complex technique. For you to understand how it is used in experiments, it will be necessary to lead you through a simple example, as if you were doing an experiment and using the analysis of variance to evaluate your results.

To begin, the experimenter selects a sample of 30 subjects from a population suitable for his purposes. These subjects are randomly assigned to one of three groups. Since the assignment of a person to a given group is completely by chance, it is quite safe to assume that the three groups do not differ on the variable he wishes to study. Let us suppose that the experimenter is interested in whether people will improve more in a physical skill, such as throwing a ball at a target, if they are paid on the basis of how much their performance improves.

The experimental procedure consists of two minutes' practice throwing a ball at a target followed by throwing of the ball at the target 20 times, with the number of hits within a certain area of the target being counted. The three groups are defined as follows: *Group A* is the control group, which receives no pay for doing this. Group B goes through the identical procedure but is paid 25 cents for each hit during the testing period. Group C also goes through the procedure, but is paid 50 cents for each hit.

If payment to the subjects makes no difference in how accurate they are at their task, there should be no difference in the mean number of hits scored by groups A, B, and C. In other words, their average scores should not be different from what we would expect if we had all three groups go through the same procedure without payment. Table 8–1 shows the calculation of the mean and variance for each of the three groups.

What can the experimenter conclude by looking at Table 8–1? The first thing to note is that Group A has the lowest mean number of hits, Group B does better than Group A, and Group C does best of all at hitting the target. From this information the experimenter is safe in concluding that paying the subjects does seem to result in some improvement at the tasks. However, this type of simple inspection of the data does not tell him whether these differences are large enough to represent a real difference or if they are merely the result of chance variations. Perhaps if he had had all three groups go through the procedure without payment, he would still have obtained mean differences as large as these.

Keep in mind that what is being done here is basically the same as finding out whether the means of two groups are really different. The analysis of variance is a way to assess the meaningfulness of *differences between means when more than two groups are involved.* The arrangement of the arithmetic is somewhat different, but the purpose and the logic are the same.

To see what is meant by "arrangement of the arithmetic," look at Table 8–2.

Table 8–2 contains the same 30 scores that are present in Table 8–1. However, here we have combined them and calculated the mean and variance for all 30 subjects as one group. Now, see how these results compare with the results of the calculations in Table 8–1.

The mean for all 30 subjects is close in value to the mean for Group B, which is midway between the means of Groups A and C. However, when the sums of the squared difference scores for Groups A, B, and C are added together (4.00 + 6.00 + 18.00 = 28.00) the total is smaller than the sum we ob-

TABLE 8–1   Scores Indicating the Number of Times a Target Is Hit Accurately

	GROUP A			GROUP B			GROUP C	
Score	Score minus mean	Score minus mean squared	Score	Score minus mean	Score minus mean squared	Score	Score minus mean	Score minus mean squared
3	−1	1	5	−1	1	9	−2	4
3	−1	1	5	−1	1	10	−1	1
4	0	0	5	−1	1	10	−1	1
4	0	0	6	0	0	10	−1	1
4	0	0	6	0	0	11	0	0
4	0	0	6	0	0	11	0	0
4	0	0	6	0	0	11	0	0
4	0	0	7	+1	1	12	+1	1
5	+1	1	7	+1	1	12	+1	1
5	+1	1	7	+1	1	14	+3	9
Sums 40	0	4	Sums 60	0	6	Sums 110	0	18

Mean = 4.00 Variance = 0.40 Mean = 6.00 Variance = 0.60 Mean = 11.00 Variance = 1.80

TABLE 8–2   Scores Indicating the Number of Times a Target is Hit Accurately: Groups A, B, and C Combined

Score	Score minus mean	Score minus mean squared
3	−4	16
3	−4	16
4	−3	9
4	−3	9
4	−3	9
4	−3	9
4	−3	9
4	−3	9
5	−2	4
5	−2	4
5	−2	4
5	−2	4
5	−2	4
6	−1	1
6	−1	1
6	−1	1
6	−1	1
7	0	0
7	0	0
7	0	0
9	+2	4
10	+3	9
10	+3	9
10	+3	9
11	+4	16
11	+4	16
11	+4	16
12	+5	25
12	+5	25
14	+7	49
Sum 210	0	Sum of squared 288 differences
Mean = 7.00		Variance = 9.60

tain for all 30 scores treated as one group (288.00). How can this happen when exactly the same scores entered into both sets of calculations?

Understanding why this difference occurs is the key to understanding what happens in an analysis of variance. This basic idea is that the variation present in a set of scores can be broken into two parts, and these parts can be compared with each other in the same way as when we take the variances of two samples drawn randomly and divide one by the other.

We have already discussed one of these sources of variation—the variation of a set of scores around their mean. We have three illustrations of this in the sums of the squared differences for Groups A, B, and C. (We will continue to work with these sums, to keep our explanation as simple as possible.) These sums are 4.00 for Group A, 6.00 for Group B, and 18.00 for Group C, the total for all three groups being 28.00.

The new source of variation is obtained by adding all the groups together and calculating one mean for all 30 subjects. This variation can be found by going through the following steps:

1. Take the mean of Group A and subtract it from the mean calculated on

all 30 subjects (hereafter called the *total mean*):

Group A	Total Mean	Group A Mean	Difference	Squared Difference
	7.00	4.00	3.00	9.00

2. Multiply the squared difference by the number of subjects in Group A:

$$10 \times 9.00 = 90.00$$

3. Repeat these steps for Groups B and C, as shown below:

Group	Total Mean	Group Mean	Difference	Squared Difference
B	7.00	6.00	1.00	$1.00 \times 10 = 10.00$
C	7.00	11.00	4.00	$16.00 \times 10 = 160.00$

When the three numbers obtained by these processes are added up, the total is 260.00 ($90.00 + 10.00 + 160.00 = 260.00$). When this new total is added to the sums of the squared differences for Groups A, B, and C (28.00), our total is 288—exactly the same as the sum of the squared differences found when we treated all 30 subjects as one group (Table 8-2).

Thus, the variation present in the 30 scores has been broken into two parts. The first part is the variation present in Groups A, B, and C. It is just that—the variation of the scores in Group A around the mean of Group A plus the variation of the scores in Group B around the mean of Group B plus the variation of the scores in Group C around the mean of Group C. The sum of the variations for these three groups is called the *within groups sum of squares*.

The other source of variation is the one we obtained when we subtracted the mean of Group A from the *total mean*, squared the difference, and multiplied it by the number of subjects in Group A. Repeating this process for Groups B and C, and then adding the figures obtained for all three groups, we get what is known as the *between groups sum of squares*. The ratio of the two sums of squares, divided by the appropriate number of degrees of freedom (the *within groups variance* and the *between groups variance*) is used to determine whether or not the differences between the group means are greater than would be expected by chance.

A mean value of each sum of squares is calculated by dividing it by the appropriate degrees of freedom. The ratio of these two mean values, or *mean squares*, as they are called, is then used to determine whether or not the differences between the group means are greater than would be expected by chance.

How does this work? Keep in mind that the *between groups variance* and the *within groups variance* are supposed to be estimates of the same thing—the variation present in a set of scores. The variation *within* groups is the variation we expect to find in a set of scores because of individual differences. In the target accuracy experiment, for example, we would expect some people to be a little better at the task than others; however, we would *not* expect one group to do better than another if all groups received the same treatment. If all three groups were run on the experiment, with no group being paid, we would expect that the means of Groups A, B, and C would differ only very slightly, if at all. Under these circumstances, if we subtracted the mean of Group A from the total mean, that of Group B from the total mean, and so forth, we would expect to end up with a rather small sum. If people actually do better on this task when paid, however, then the mean differences should be quite large. The larger the differences between the means of the groups are, the larger the sum of squared differences for the between groups variance will be. In other words, if the variation *between* groups is not much greater than the variation *within* groups, clearly the groups are not very different from one another,.

Analysis of Variance Table.   There are a few more steps remaining in the calculation of the final statistic (F), and these can be illustrated by what is called an *analysis of variance table*. If the experiment on target accuracy that we have been using as an example were one that you were reading in a journal, the results might be expressed in an analysis of variance table such as the following:

Source of Variance	Sum of Squares	df	Mean Square	F	p
between groups	260.00	2	130.00	126.21	.01
within groups	28.00	27	1.03		
Total	288.00	29			

The first quantities under the heading "Sum of Squares" are already familiar to you. The "between groups" sum is that obtained by subtracting the means of the groups from the total mean, squaring the differences, and multiplying by the number of subjects. The "within groups" sum is obtained by methods you became familiar with in Chapter 7: Calculate the mean for Group A, subtract it from each score in Group A, square the differences, and sum them. Repeat this process for Groups B and C. (If you are at all puzzled about where these quantities come from, review pages 120–122 before proceeding.)

You have also run across the notation "*df*" before and been told that it stands for *degrees of freedom*. We will not delve into the meaning of the concept of degrees of freedom here, since it is not essential for our purposes. In the analysis of variance, the average, or mean, variance is calculated by dividing each sum of squares by the appropriate *df*. For the between groups sum of squares, the *df* is equal to the number of groups minus 1. Since we have three groups, the *df* is equal to 2. For the within groups sum of squares, the *df* is equal to the number of subjects minus the number of groups. Since we have 30 subjects and three groups, the *df* is equal to 27.

When the sums of squares are divided by the degrees of freedom, the results are as shown in the column headed "Mean Square."

One final step remains: The between groups mean square is divided by the within groups mean square to produce the statistic known as F. The last column in the table indicates the probability that the obtained value of F would occur by chance alone.

You can see that, although the arrangement of the arithmetic is quite a bit more complicated, this process is not very different from the process of calculating a t statistic for determining whether or not two groups are significantly different.

The F statistic is interpreted in much the same way as the t statistic. Once the value of F has been calculated, the experimenter consults published tables of the F statistic to see whether his value is equal to or greater than those values of F that occur 5% or 1% of the time by chance for conditions of three groups and 30 subjects. If his value is equal to or larger than the tabled value, he will conclude that there is a real difference between his groups. In the study we have presented, a value of F equal to 5.45 would be expected to occur by chance only 1 out of 100 times. Consequently, the experimenter would conclude that paying subjects *does* have a significant effect on the improvement of accuracy and that, within the limits studied, increasing the amount of pay results in still more improvement in accuracy.

This, then, is the basic logic underlying analysis of variance. The essential concept is that the variation of the scores around the total mean can be separated into components, and these components can be identified and then compared. In the example just given, we separated the *total* variation into the variation existing *within* each sample and that existing *between* samples. If our experimental treatment had had no effect, the variation existing between the three groups would have been equal or nearly equal to that existing within the groups.

As mentioned earlier, one of the major advantages of the analysis of variance technique is that comparisons are possible with it that could not be done with any other statistic. For example, suppose we were interested in sex differences in education and wished to find out whether particular teaching methods were more effective with girls than with boys. We have three methods we wish to compare and will use the analysis of variance method. Our experiment may be set up in the following manner.

	Teaching Method A	Teaching Method B	Teaching Method C	
Boys	$n = 10$ $\bar{X} = 46.4$	$n = 10$ $\bar{X} = 30.2$	$n = 10$ $\bar{X} = 17.8$	$\bar{X}$ Boys $= 31.5$
Girls	$n = 10$ $\bar{X} = 36.8$	$n = 10$ $\bar{X} = 37.8$	$n = 10$ $\bar{X} = 21.4$	$\bar{X}$ Girls $= 32.0$
	$\bar{X} = 41.6$ Method A	$\bar{X} = 34.0$ Method B	$\bar{X} = 19.6$ Method C	

$n =$ the number of subjects in each condition.

$\bar{X} =$ the mean of the scores. The value of 46.4 is the mean for boys taught by Method A, and 36.8 is the mean for girls taught by Method A. The value of 41.6 is the mean for Method A over both boys and girls. The values of 31.5 and 32.0 at the far right are the means for boys over all methods and for girls over all methods. The symbol $\bar{X}$ is a generally accepted statistical symbol for the mean.

At the end of the period during which we use the different methods, we give a common examination to all the students and separate the scores as shown above. Using analysis of variance, we can make three kinds of comparisons. We can look at the main conditions first. For example, do boys and girls differ regardless of the type of teaching method used? The other main question would be: is one type of teaching method better than the others, regardless of the sex of the student? Finally, we come to the question that can only be answered by the analysis of variance method: Is there a particular method that is more effective with one sex than with the other? For example, do girls do better under Method B than under Method A? This is called an *interaction*, and it is the power to test for such interactions that makes analysis of variance such a useful statistical tool.

The summary of the analysis of variance might be reported in the following manner:

Source of Variation	Sum of squares	df	Mean Square	F	p
Sex	4.2	1	4.2	.35	NS
Teaching Methods	4994.1	2	2497.0	209.8	.01
Interaction	810.2	2	405.1	34.0	.01
Variation within groups	643.2	54	11.9		
Total	6451.7	59			

The calculations are quite similar to those in the first example. The sums of squares are divided by their respective degrees of freedom to obtain the mean squares. The F statistics are calculated by dividing the mean square for each of the sources of variation by the mean square for variation within groups, as follows:

$$4.2/11.9 = \quad .35$$
$$2497.0/11.9 = 209.8$$
$$405.1/11.9 = \quad 34.0$$

In each of these calculations, two sources of variation are being compared. The variation within groups is the variation we expect when there are no differences.

In the first comparison—that of differences between boys and girls—we find that the difference between the means of boys and girls is less than the variation within the groups and conclude that there are no differences attributable to sex. The letters "NS" in the column headed "p" (probability) stand for "not significant," indicating that there is no meaningful difference.

The next comparison—teaching methods—is a different story. The value of the F statistic that occurs 1% of the time for this type of comparison is 5.04. Since we have an F of 209.8, this difference is highly significant.

If we look at the means for the different teaching methods we see that the highest scores are obtained by the group taught by Method A and the next best by that taught by Method B, while the group taught by Method C clearly did less well. On the basis of this finding, we would conclude that Method A seems superior to the other methods of instruction, regardless of the sex of the student.

However, there is also a significant interaction between sex and type of teaching method. The value of the F statistic that occurs 1% of the time by chance for this comparison is the same as that found for the teaching methods comparison—5.04. The value found for the interaction is 405.1—clearly a highly significant value.

A significant interaction here means that there is a relationship between a particular teaching method and the sex of the students. One way to interpret such a finding is to prepare a graph on which the mean values for boys and girls for each teaching method are plotted and connecting lines are drawn. This has been done in Figure 8–2. At the bottom of the graph, the letters A, B, and C refer to the three teaching methods. Along the side of the graph are the

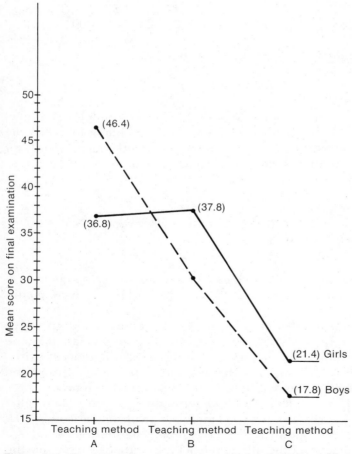

Figure 8–2 The interaction of sex and teaching method. Numbers in parentheses are the means for boys and girls for each of the teaching methods.

mean values of each of the cells. The mean value for boys taught by Method A is 46.4, and that value is plotted above the letter A at the point where the value of 46.4 would lie. The mean values for B and C are plotted in the same fashion and a line is drawn connecting the three points. The same procedure is repeated for the means of the girls.

By examining Figure 8–2, we can easily see the reason for finding a significant interaction. The mean values of boys and girls change position between Methods A and B, indicating that boys do better when taught by Method A and girls do better when taught by Method B.

What conclusion should be drawn by the research worker on the basis of these results? Should he conclude that girls should be taught by a different method from boys? On the basis of these data, he would not be justified in suggesting this, since the girls taught by Method B do not really do much better than those taught by Method A. The significance of the interaction is primarily due to the fact that *boys* do somewhat better when taught by Method A.

Perhaps the most important thing to remember about this example is the interaction. This combination of two separate variables could not have been found by other statistical designs. The ability to evaluate interactions is the primary reason for the frequency with which analysis of variance designs are used.

One additional illustration will be provided. Suppose we wanted to elaborate on the study just done to investigate the effectiveness of different teaching materials as well. Such a study would be arranged as follows:

	Teaching Method 1		Teaching Method 2		Teaching Method 3	
	Teaching Material A	Teaching Material B	Teaching Material A	Teaching Material B	Teaching Material A	Teaching Material B
Boys	N = 10	N = 10	N = 10	N = 10	N = 10	N = 10
Girls	N = 10	N = 10	N = 10	N = 10	N = 10	N = 10

Our procedure is much the same as with the first example, since we give a common exam to all students at the end of the study and arrange the scores in the manner shown above.

We have three main questions that can be asked: Are there differences among teaching methods, regardless of sex and type of teaching material? Are there differences in ease of learning the two materials, regardless of sex and type of teaching method? Are there differences between the sexes, regardless of teaching methods and materials?

With this design, additional testing of interactions is possible. For example, we can ask if there are particular combinations of teaching methods and materials that seem to be particuarly effective. We can even ask if there is a particular combination of teaching method and teaching materials that is more effective with one sex or the other.

The results of such an experiment would be reported in the following manner:

Source of Variation
Material (A)
Method (B)
Sex (C)
A × B Interaction
A × C Interaction
B × C Interaction
A × B × C Interaction
Within Groups Variation
Total

The degree of complexity of design possible with analysis of variance is quite high. It is perfectly possible to design experiments involving four or five conditions. However, trying to understand the meaning of a significant four- or five-way interaction is a task of considerable difficulty for the experimenter as well as for the person reading the published results.

You can expect some difficulty in trying to understand the results of some of the more complicated analysis of variance models; knowledgeable experimenters as well as beginners have difficulty in untangling some of the results in complex designs. The only general advice we can offer is to keep the main conditions in mind and to see whether the interactions make sense conceptually.

ANALYSIS OF COVARIANCE

Occasionally found in the research literature is a technique known as the *analysis of covariance*. Covariance is a rather specialized technique that is quite useful for solving certain types of problems. Suppose an experiment is planned using three groups of subjects. The subjects are to be tested at the beginning of the experiment and again at the end. When we finish collecting the test scores, we find that one group has such high scores at the beginning of testing that it is evident it is not really comparable to the other two groups. This creates a problem, since our statistical methods require us to assume that prior to the experiment these were three samples from the same population. Given these initial differences, it appears that we cannot test for changes at the end. However, the analysis of covariance allows us to adjust the scores of the groups in such a way that we can estimate very precisely what the scores at the end *would* have been if the three groups had been comparable to begin with. The results of covariance analysis are F statistics and are interpreted in exactly the same way.

MULTIPLE COMPARISONS

A new type of analysis known as multiple comparisons has begun to appear in the research literature in recent years. Its purpose is to further identify differences among groups once an analysis of variance has been performed.

For example, suppose an experiment is run involving five groups of subjects and the experimenter, finding a statistically significant value of the F statistic, concludes that there is an overall significant difference between the groups. He would also like to know just where the differences occur. Is Group 1 significantly different from Group 2? Are Groups 2 and 3 significantly different from one another? Is Group 1 significantly different from Groups 2 and 3? Multiple comparison methods are designed to answer questions of this type. There are several varieties of multiple comparison methods, and mathematical statisticians are in sharp disagreement about the worth of some of them. The methods you will encounter most frequently are usually identified by the name of the statistician who developed them. They are given below in alphabetical order.

Duncan   Dunnett   Newman-Keuls   Scheffé   Tukey

In addition, the t test is sometimes used for multiple comparisons of the groups taken two at a time.

Without going into great detail, here is our evaluation of multiple comparison techniques. Recent research indicates that some of these techniques can be seriously misleading and can lead to wrong conclusions. For example, if the t test is used to make multiple comparisons, there is a very good chance that the experimenter will conclude that two groups are significantly different when in fact they are not. Much the same statement can be made about the Duncan test and, to a lesser extent, the Newman-Keuls method. By contrast, the Scheffé and Tukey methods seem to be free of this problem. What this means in practice is that interpretations of data which utilize t tests to do multiple comparisons (keep in mind that the t test is an excellent and very powerful statistical technique; it is simply not appropriate for this particular use) or which use the Duncan technique have to be regarded rather suspiciously, since the chances of the experimenter drawing an incorrect conclusion are rather high. To a lesser extent, this is true of the Newman-Keuls method as well. However, if it is concluded that there is a significant difference between groups based on the use of the Scheffé or Tukey methods, we can have a high degree of confidence in the conclusions.

We have not mentioned the Dunnett technique until now because it is more specialized in nature. It is a statistic for comparing several groups with a single group. In other words, in pairs of comparisons, several groups are, in turn, compared with one other group. Usually a control group is compared against several experimental groups. The statistic is quite trustworthy, and there is little danger of drawing false conclusions from it.

CAUTIONS AND LIMITATIONS OF THE ANALYSIS OF VARIANCE TECHNIQUE

In general, our remarks about the "robustness" of the t test are directly applicable to the analysis of variance technique (the t test is actually a specialized form of analysis of variance). Very few assumptions need be made about the distribution of the scores, and the power of the method to detect differences has already been discussed. As in most statistics, the larger the sample size, the more reliable the conclusions. However, the analysis of variance can be used with small samples with no great loss of power to detect differences.

Other Considerations. Until now, we have been concerned with explaining the logic of hypothesis testing and clarifying what is meant by statistical significance. Before continuing, it would be wise to emphasize that these are simply conventions which statisticians accept and that there is nothing sacred about them. For example, suppose that a *t* test is performed and the value falls just short of the tabled value indicating significance at the 5% level. Is it sensible to conclude that there is no difference between the groups? The answer is, of course, no, since it is evident that the groups *do* differ somewhat. The agreed upon significance levels serve a useful function as guidelines for evaluating results, but they are not absolute. In the last analysis, a statistical technique is used to discover and evaluate findings—not to interpret them or to pass judgment on their meaningfulness. Real significance, as opposed to statistical significance, is a judgment that can only be made by the researcher and the people who read the results of his work.

As an exercise in understanding analysis of variance designs, you are asked to read the article reprinted below. In reading it, you should not only note the nature of the results and how they were obtained but you should also try to estimate how many separate experiments would be required if this study were done by comparing independent groups two at a time. Remember that analysis of variance designs allow comparisons that cannot be made as efficiently by any other method. Such factors as interactions between variables are not detectable by other techniques.

Retardation, School Strata, and Learning Proficiency*†

WILLIAM D. ROHWER, JR., Ph.D., AND STEVE LYNCH, University of California, Berkeley

ABSTRACT

The study compares paired-associate learning efficiency in institutionalized retardates and in a variety of samples of children. The total sample of 432 was comprised of 48 Ss drawn from each of nine populations: retarded adults,

*This work was supported, in part, by a contract with the U. S. Office of Education (OE6-10-273) through Project Literacy. The report was prepared at the Institute of Human Learning which is supported by grants from the National Science Foundation and the National Institutes of Health.

†An expanded version of this paper was presented at the annual meeting of the American Association of Mental Deficiency, Denver, Colorado, 1967.

This article originally appeared in the *American Journal of Mental Deficiency*, Vol. 73, No. 1, July, 1968, and is reprinted with permission.

and upper- and lower-strata kindergarten, first-, third-, and sixth-grade children. The learning task was administered to all Ss under one of four experimental conditions. Learning efficiency was lower in the retardate sample than in any other, including both an equal-MA group and a lower-MA group. The pattern of differences produced by experimental conditions, however, was consistent across all samples.

As measured by performance on tests of intelligence or of school achievement, the proportion of retarded children (IQ range 50 to 70) among low-strata populations is larger than that among high-strata populations (Burt, 1961). One question regarding these findings is whether or not scores on such tests reflect underlying learning proficiency as accurately for the former as is the case for the latter. If not, then intelligence tests cannot be relied upon as singularly sufficient devices for the intellectual classification of children. The diagnostic problem is that of distinguishing among retarded children those persons who have learned relatively little during a given number of years because they are true slow learners from those who have learned equally little because of a corresponding deficiency in their opportunity to learn. One potential solution to the problem is the use of learning tasks as diagnostic instruments in conjunction with standardized tests of intelligence. But before this solution can be recommended, it is necessary to show that groups of retardates suspected to be adequate learners perform better on such learning tasks than groups of retardates thought to be inherently slow learners, when the two are equated for mental age (MA).

This stipulation raises a second issue for which the present study has relevance, namely, that of the psychological nature of retardation in cases for which neither specific gene defects nor specific organic defects can be identified as determinants (such cases are hereafter referred to as retardates). If Zigler (1967) is correct, groups of normal learners and of retardates, equated for MA should not perform differently on learning tasks when care is taken to equate for motivational factors. As advanced by Zigler (1967) this assertion is based on the assumption that retardates and normals, equated for level of cognitive development, as is roughly the case in equal-MA comparisons, are characterized by the same kinds of cognitive functioning. In contrast, the position taken here is that equal-MA comparisons should not yield equal levels of performance by retardates and normals on cognitive tasks, in particular, learning tasks since one of the defining characteristics of such retardation is low learning efficiency.

Evidence already available is consistent with such a position. Jensen (1966) found that normal school children performed at a higher level than institutionalized retardates (characterized by no known organic defect) on both a serial and on a PA learning task. It must admitted that in terms of Zigler's analysis this study confounds the variables of intelligence and institutionalization thereby rendering the conclusion indefinite. Another study (Rapier, in press), however, does not have this limitation. A comparison is made of serial and PA learning efficiency as between high- and low-strata children (that is, children drawn from public schools serving low- and high-SES residential areas) where both samples were retarded and non-institutionalized. The low-strata group performed significantly better than the high-strata group on both learning tasks, indicating that equal MAs do not imply equality of learning proficiency. Furthermore, the low-strata retarded group learned as efficiently as equal-CA groups of normal, low- and high-strata children. The design of the present study permits another examination of this issue incorporating the possibility of comparisons among samples of institutionalized retardates, low-strata children, and high-strata children. Our prediction was that both the low- and the high-strata children would learn more efficiently than the retardates.

The experiment was also designed to assess the assertion that similar kinds of cognitive structures are operative for Ss across the three samples. Using a set of pictorial PA materials, Rohwer, Lynch, Levin, and Suzuki (in press) found that random samples of high- and low-strata elementary school children (grades 1, 3, and 6) not only performed at the same level but responded similarly to various experimental conditions under which the task was presented. That is to say, a Depiction factor (Still vs. Action pictures of each pair) and a Verbalization factor (names of the two objects in each pair vs. phrases containing the names vs. sentences containing those names) were associated with the same kinds of performance differences in both samples. In all cases, action pictures and sentence descriptions produced more efficient learning than any of the other conditions. From these results it may be inferred that the same kinds of cognitive structures are available to low- and high-strata children within the age range sampled, if it is granted that response to the experimental conditions represents a valid index of some corresponding cognitive structures. On this assumption, the present experiment examines this same issue for younger children and for institutionalized retardates as well. We expected that all three samples, retardates, low-strata, and high-strata children, would be consistent in their response to the experimental conditions.

> *In the opening section of their report, Rohwer and Lynch review previous research on the topic of retardation and learning and outline differing theoretical points of view.*

METHOD

Subjects. The total sample of 432 was comprised of 48 Ss drawn from each of nine different populations: kindergarten (K), first, third, and sixth grades in schools serving middle-class residential areas; grades K, 1, 3, and 6 in schools serving lower-class residential areas; and, retarded adults, having no known organic defects, in a public institution for the mentally retarded. Within each sample, equal numbers of Ss were assigned randomly to the four experimental conditions. Chronological age information for each of the samples is presented in Table 1. Information as to mental age is available on three of the samples: lower-strata K, upper-strata grade 3, and retarded adults. This information was obtained from the files of the respective institutions in the latter two cases: upper-strata third graders had been administered the Kuhlmann-Anderson; mentally retarded adults had been administered the Binet. For the purposes of the present study the Binet was administered to the sample of low-strata K children. The mean MA of the retarded adults and the upper-strata third-graders was equivalent ($\overline{MA}$ = 9.66 and 9.61, respectively) whereas that of the lower-strata K group was considerably below this ($\overline{MA}$ = 4.70). Thus, both an equal-MA comparison and an unequal MA comparison favoring the retarded adults could be made in terms of performance on the PA task.

> *Note that all necessary data to establish the mental age levels of the groups tested is provided, and the means by which mental age was measured is specified.*

TABLE 1. Mean Chronological Age of the Samples as a Function of Population Membership

STRATA	K	1	3	6	RETARDATES
High	5.32	6.60	8.57	11.60	25.56
Low	5.31	6.93	8.97	12.06	

Materials and design. All Ss were asked to learn the same list of 24 PAs. Each pair consisted of two familiar objects previously recorded on black-and-white movie film. Two such films were used; in one, each pair of objects had been filmed while engaged in a short action episode (e.g., a sequence showing a DOG walking to a GATE and closing it); in the other film the two objects in each pair were stationary when filmed. Thus, the first experimental factor was Depiction (Action vs. Still).

The films were constructed in accord with the requirements of a pairing-test method of presentation such that the block of 24 sequences bearing the images of the paired objects (pairing trials) were followed by 24 sequences bearing only one object from each of the pairs (test trial). The test trial materials were identical for both conditions of Depiction. Materials for two pairing and two test trials were used and on no one of the four trials was the order of presentation of the items the same as that of any other trial.

The second experimental factor, Verbalization, consisted of two levels: Names vs. Sentences. In the former, as each PA was presented during the pairing trials, E uttered aloud the names of the two objects in view (e.g., FORK-CAKE, TOWEL-PLATE, CAT-LOG), whereas, in the latter, he uttered a sentence containing those two names (The FORK cuts the CAKE, The TOWEL wipes the PLATE, The CAT jumps the LOG).[3] In sum, the design was a 9 × 2 × 2 factorial with independent groups in which the principal factors were Groups, Depiction, and Verbalization.

Procedure. The task was administered individually to each S. The instructions described the pairing-test procedure and encouraged Ss to attend to each of the pairs as it was shown and to the E's accompanying utterance during the pairing trials. It was explained that the test trials would consist of the successive presentation of one of the objects from each pair and that the Ss task was to recall and utter the name of the missing object. Examples were given orally to illustrate the procedure.

The films were presented on a beaded screen by means of a 16 mm. movie projector; accordingly the testing room was dimly illuminated. During the pairing trials, E read the appropriate verbalization as each PA appeared on the screen and during the test trials he read the name of the exposed object from each pair as it appeared on the screen. The S's task was to utter the name of the missing object from each pair immediately after E named the visible object. On both pairing and test trials, the exposure interval was 4-secs, the interitem interval was 1-sec and the intertrial interval was 4-secs. For all Ss the task was terminated after two complete trials.

All procedures and specific test materials are described in sufficient detail to provide the reader with an understanding of the procedure.

RESULTS AND DISCUSSION

Learning was measured in terms of the numbers of correct responses made on the two test trials. These scores were subjected to analysis of variance of the type suggested by Winer (1962) which permits the inclusion of a group extraneous to a balanced design in the overall analysis. In the present case, that group is, of course, the institutionalized retardates. The principal sources of variance assessed were: Populations (retardates vs. all other groups); Grades (K vs. 1 vs. 3 vs. 6); Strata (lower vs. higher); Depiction (Still vs. Action); and, Verbalization (Names vs. Sentences). A summary of the analysis of variance is presented in Table 2.

[3]A complete list of the noun pairs and the sentences may be obtained from the first author upon request.

A discussion of factorial designs was given on pages 34–35. The design used in this study is of the following form:

| | | NAMES | | SENTENCES | |
		Still	Action	Still	Action
G R O U P S	**High Strata** Kindergarten				
	First Grade				
	Second Grade				
	Sixth Grade				
	Low Strata Kindergarten				
	First Grade				
	Second Grade				
	Sixth Grade				
	Retardates				

The results pertinent to an appraisal of the relationship between learning proficiency and subject classification variables are presented in Table 3. The main effect of Populations (P) indicated that the retarded group performed less well than all other groups combined.

> *In reading the interpretation of the data, you may wonder how the authors can come to the conclusions they do about the results from the data of Table 2. To understand such a conclusion as "The main effect of Populations (P) indicated that the retarded group performed less well than all other groups combined," examine the mean values given in Table 4. The means for the retardates are lower than for any other group.*

Similarly, the main effect of Grades (G) was significant, and an application of the Scheffe method for multiple contrasts revealed that the performance of the sixth- and third-grade samples did not differ significantly but that both were superior to the first-grade group, which, in turn was superior to the kindergarten sample.[4] Neither the main effect of Strata (S), nor the interaction S × G was significant. Comparisons of the performance of the retarded group with each of the other samples were made by means of Dun-

_____

[4]This and all other comparisons made by means of either the Scheffé or the Dunnett method were computed for $p = .05$.

TABLE 2.   Summary of Analysis of Variance on Mean Numbers
of Correct Responses Per Trial

SOURCE	df	MEAN SQUARES	F
Populations (P)	1	2499.28	103.22**
Grades (G)	3	776.62	32.07**
Strata (S)	1	13.02	. . . .
G x S	3	49.49	2.04
Verbalization (V)	1	547.85	22.63**
Depiction (D)	1	1166.68	48.18**
V x D	1	444.91	18.37**
P x V	1	12.33	. . . .
P x D	1	2.84	. . . .
P x V x D	1	20.31	. . . .
G x V	3	18.65	. . . .
G x D	3	15.15	. . . .
G x V x D	3	20.31	. . . .
S x V	1	46.02	1.90
S x D	1	22.69	. . . .
S x V x D	1	126.75	5.24*
G x S x V	3	7.74	. . . .
G x S x D	3	21.01	. . . .
G x S x V x D	3	2.31	. . . .
Subjects w/groups	396	24.21	. . . .

*$p < .05$.
**$p < .01$.

nett's method for comparing an extraneous group with those in an associated balanced design. Learning was more efficient in every one of the samples of children than in the sample of institutionalized retardates. Note that this result holds for the lower-strata kindergarten comparison, a sample in which the mean MA was much lower than that of the retardates, as well as for the equal-MA comparison with the upper-strata third-grade sample.

For a brief description of the reliability of the Scheffe and Dunnett methods, review pp. 128–129.

In view of the latter results, the assertion that normals and retardates of the same MA do not differ in level of intellectual performance seems clearly invalid. It might be argued

TABLE 3.   Mean Numbers of Correct Responses Per Trial as a
Function of Population Membership

STRATA	K	1	3	6	TOTAL	RETARDATES
			GRADE			
High	13.54	15.06	16.62	16.77	15.50	9.96
Low	11.82	14.88	17.14	17.12	15.24	

MSE (396) = 24.21.

TABLE 4. Mean Numbers of Correct Responses Per Trial as a Function of Populations, Verbalization and Depiction

| | CONDITIONS | | | |
| | NAMES | | SENTENCE | |
POPULATIONS	Still	Action	Still	Action
High Strata	13.10	15.73	15.88	17.29
Low Strata	12.18	17.12	15.59	16.07
All Children	12.64	16.42	15.73	16.68
Retardates	7.71	11.29	10.21	10.62
Totals	12.09	15.85	15.12	16.01

MSE(396) = 24.21

that the inferiority of the retarded group vis-a-vis the upper-strata third-grade sample can be accounted for in terms of differences in motivational and emotional factors rather than in intellective factors. Close examination, however, indicates that this argument does not hold for the observed inferiority of the retardates to the lower-strata samples. In advancing the case for the attribution of performance differences to motivational factors, Zigler (1967) relies mainly on the notions of social deprivation and failure expectancy, both of which are higher in retarded than in upper-strata samples. But both a history of social deprivation and of failure, especially on cognitive tasks, are characteristics of lower-strata children as well as of retardates. Accordingly, an explanation of the inferior performance of the retardates on the present PA tasks in terms of motivational factors is not compelling. In contrast, the results are consistent with the assumption that retardates are inherently slow learners. If so, this characteristic rate of learning would be expected to appear in their performance on learning tasks as was clearly the case in the present experiment.

Another implication of these results is that a learning task such as that used in the present study is of potential utility in distinguishing cultural retardates from true slow learners among those who score in the retarded range of tests of intelligence. Obviously, the present results are not sufficient to warrant an immediate recommendation in this regard for all of the tasks of test construction and evaluation remain to be done. Nevertheless, the results suggest that such an effort has considerable promise.

It still remains to examine the results relevant to the issue whether normals and retardates are characterized by the same types of cognitive structures. For this purpose the appropriate tests are those involving the main effects and the interaction of the experimental conditions within each of the subject populations of the variables sampled. The effects of the experimental conditions themselves were substantial. As Table 2 reveals, the main effects of Verbalization (V) and of Depiction (D), as well as the interaction, V × D, were significant. The relevant means for these and related effects are presented in Table 4.

These main effects and the interaction hold for the retarded sample as well as for the samples of school children, that is, no one of the three interactions between experimental and subject variables was significant. This is to say that the pattern of facilitation produced by sentences and action pictures was similar for both institutionalized retardates and normal school children. The result is entirely consistent with the notion that the *kinds* of cognitive structures involved in the two samples are very similar, despite the fact that the two populations differ in level of performance.

Interactions between factors can sometimes be more easily understood if represented pictorially. The graph shown in Figure 8–3 was made from the data of Table 4 to illustrate the interaction between the factors of Verbalization and Depiction. The graph contains the

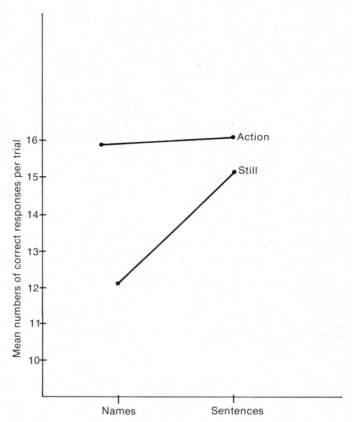

Figure 8–3 Graphic representation of the interaction between verbalization and depiction. (Data from Rohwer and Lynch.)

means for the Still and Action conditions, and the points are connected by lines. When they are plotted in this manner, we can see that the rate of improvement for the Still condition is much greater under the sentence condition. All groups do much better with Still Depictions if verbalizations are done in sentence form. By contrast, for the Action Depiction, the names vs. sentences verbalization seems to make little difference.

Among the remaining tests in the analysis of variance, only one, namely, S × V × D, was significant. An inspection of the means involved in this effect as presented in Table 4 and an application of Scheffé's method reveals that the interaction holds only in the lower-strata samples. We have no explanation for this outcome and one should probably not be attempted until the effect is replicated.

Reflection about the results of the present experiment suggests the following interpretation. Among the retardates, even optimal conditions of learning, as represented by the PA task used here, are not sufficient to improve performance to the level of that observed in equal-, or lower-MA normals. In contrast, under these same conditions, the performance of lower-strata children, inaccurately classified as slow learners on the basis of standardized test performance, belies the assumption that they cannot be proficient learners. Finally, within the age and intelligence ranges sampled, all three populations appear to share similar kinds of cognitive structures, and, thus, all benefit from the same facilitative conditions of learning.

> *On page 126 we discussed the problems encountered in interpreting complex interactions. In this article, the authors evidently feel that the interaction between Verbalization and Depiction which existed only for the lower strata is unusual enough to require replication before being accepted as a meaningful research finding. Such a situation is not unusual. A research worker may come to the conclusion that one of his findings is peculiar enough to be doubtful, and he may want to see it occur again in another study before accepting it as fact.*

REFERENCES

Burt, C. *The backward child.* London: University of London Press, 1961.

Jensen, A. R. Rote learning in retarded adults and normal children. *Amer. J. Ment. Defic.,* 1966, **69**, 828–834.

Rapier, J. L. The learning abilities of normal and retarded children as a function of social class. *J. educ. Psychol.,* in press.

Rohwer, W. D., Jr., Lynch, S., Levin, J., & Suzuki, N. Grade level, school strata and learning efficiency. *J. educ. Psychol.,* in press.

Winer, B. J. *Statistical principles in experimental design.* New York: McGraw-Hill, 1962.

Zigler, E. Familial mental retardation: A continuing dilemma. *Science,* 1967, **155**, 292–298.

Some aspects of the Rohwer and Lynch article may strike you as difficult to follow, particularly the problem of keeping track of the interrelationships among variables. Actually, the study is quite clearly presented. The tracing out of analysis of variance designs is a more time-consuming process than understanding single-variable studies, yet the amount that can be learned from research studies carried out in this manner is much greater.

COMPARISONS OF FREQUENCIES

The statistics which we have discussed to this point have all dealt with data that are in the form of measurements along some continuous scale. Quite often data are not in this form but are organized in categories. For example, we might have merely an expression of "agree" or "disagree" in response to a question, with no attempt made to ascertain the relative intensity of the agreement or disagreement. What we obtain in such research is a tallying of frequencies. We have, then, a set of responses from a sample of individuals, and these responses are categorized according to how many are in one category as compared to another.

Let us consider a concrete example. Suppose we were interested in whether or not standards of morality in the United States were different as a function of amount of education. To find out, we might ask a set of questions on moral issues to a sample of people. We could categorize these people into separate groups on the basis of their education, e.g., completed grade school; completed high school; completed college; have a higher degree. We could ask questions such as "Do you believe it is important for people to have pre-marital sexual relationships in order to attain a satisfactory sexual adjustment in marriage?" The responses could be grouped by education, and we might obtain a distribution of scores similar to the following:

	Yes	No	Total
Grade School	5	15	20
High School	14	16	30
College	16	10	26
Higher Degree	7	3	10
Totals	42	44	86

These data appear to show that the more education the subjects had, the more they tended to agree with the question. However, we are now faced with the problem of deciding whether or not the different frequencies represent a statistically significant trend; that is, can the pattern of results be taken as expressing a meaningful tendency rather than being a chance difference?

Chi Square

The most commonly used statistic with data that are in the form of frequencies is called chi square (symbolized χ^2). To illustrate its use, look at a segment of the above table. Of the 26 people who had completed college, 16 responded "yes" to our question and 10 responded "no." Is the 16 to 10 division we obtained different enough from a 13 to 13 (chance) division to conclude that there is a meaningful tendency for college-educated people to say "yes" more often than "no" to this question, or could the difference be the result of a sampling fluctuation? Since we know what to expect on the basis of chance (13 "yes" and 13 "no"), we can compare our obtained result (16 "yes" and 10 "no") to this expected distribution. We do this by computing the χ^2 statistic, which takes into account the magnitude of the differences from chance expectancy for each cell of the table. ("Cell" refers to the intersect of a particular row and column in the body of a table.)

We evaluate the χ^2 statistic in much the same manner as the statistics discussed earlier. Published tables of χ^2 distributions give the values of χ^2 that occurs 5% of the time or less by chance. If a calculated value of χ^2 exceeds the tabled value, we can conclude that our difference is significant.

Sampling Distribution of χ^2. The distribution of the values of χ^2 depends on the number of categories being examined. If responses are classified into two categories, we have two deviations possible from chance: the deviation for "yes" and the deviation for "no." We know that we can expect some variability from pure chance expectancy. The sampling distribution of χ^2 is just such a distribution. If we were to sample randomly from a population in which "Yes" and "No" answers were present in equal numbers, and we drew a sample of 30 items at a time, most often we would be quite close to 15 "yes" and 15 "no" answers. However, it is also possible to draw a sample of 2 "yes" and 28 "no" answers. The χ^2 statistic is developed from such sampling distributions and is used to determine how often a set of frequencies will have a certain ratio of "yes" answers to "no" answers under chance conditions.

The ratio of "yes" to "no" answers will also be determined by the number of categories. In the example on page 139, there are four groupings of "yes"-"no" responses, categorized on the basis of education. If education made no difference in the way persons answered the question asked, we would expect a division of answers close to 50% "yes" and 50% "no." We wish to determine the extent to which these answers differ from what would be expected by chance. Since the number of possible deviations will influence the size of χ^2 the tables are organized in such a way as to take this into account. Hence, the χ^2 table will have different distributions depending on the number of categories.

Let us now present the data we developed on page 139 in the manner in which you might encounter them in a research publication:

A χ^2 analysis was performed on the distribution of responses to the question. The χ^2 was 8.12, which is significant beyond the .05 level of significance. It appears, then, that there is a tendency to accept fewer absolute moral restrictions as education level increases.

Let us review the steps necessary to reach this conclusion. First of all, it was necessary to determine the chance distribution of the responses of the 86 people. Since the number of individuals within the different educational categories varied, this was not a simple matter of spreading the cases evenly through the table, but required some calculations. Next, the size of the differences of the obtained values from the expected values were determined. These values were substituted into the χ^2 formula, and a χ^2 value of 8.12 was obtained. Since the χ^2 value was larger than the value of 7.82 listed in the table for the .05 level of significance, a deviation of this magnitude from the expected frequencies would occur fewer than 5 times in 100 by chance alone. Therefore we can conclude that there was a tendency for the distribution of responses to differ systematically as a function of educational level. For an illustration of the use of χ^2 in research, see the article by Marascuilo and Penfield in Chapter 5.

Cautions and Limitations. The chi square is a simple statistic to calculate and can be used in a large variety of situations. However, there are several cautions which you should remember, since χ^2 tends to be misused quite often.

In order to use χ^2, the data must be in the form of frequency counts. You *cannot* use χ^2 if your data are in the form of measured magnitudes, such as test scores. Measured magnitudes should be analyzed using a statistic such as t or F.

You have to determine on some *a priori* basis the theoretical expected frequencies. In the example used here, we assumed a random chance distribution and tested our obtained frequencies against this theoretical distribution. We could, if the nature of the problem made it sensible to do so, have assumed any expected distribution we wished. For example, if there were some reason to expect it, we could have assumed that twice as many college graduates would have said "yes" than "no," and that the others would show a chance distribution. The choice of the theoretical model is dictated by logical and scientific considerations, not by statistical ones. The statistical considerations begin only after the theoretical model has been chosen on some rational grounds.

The most important consideration (and one which is often violated) is that all of the events in the table should be *independent*. This means that no two frequencies can be based on the same individual. Often investigators will have frequencies of responses from one individual or will have a situation in which any one individual might contribute more than one response. In this case you *cannot* use χ^2, since its random sampling distribution has been calculated assuming completely independent events. Again, let us emphasize that this is one of the most common misuses of χ^2 to be found in the literature, and you should be alert for it. One simple guideline is to see whether the frequencies in the χ^2 test categories are equal to the sample size. If the χ^2 frequencies add up to more than the number of subjects, χ^2 is being used incorrectly.

Fisher Exact Test

One other test is being used more and more often with frequency data. That test, the Fisher Exact Probability Test, can be used when the number of expected cell frequencies is too small to permit the use of the χ^2 statistic. Otherwise, the restrictions on its use are the same as those for χ^2. The Fisher Exact Test requires no assumptions about the theoretical distribution of the statistic other than that of random probability. The probability is not estimated as in the χ^2 statistic, but is calculated directly. Because of the immense effort involved in calculating it, the statistic has not been used very widely. However, recently it has been programmed for high speed computers, which makes its use much more feasible, and you are likely to be encountering it more often in the research literature.

You will note that the Fisher Exact Test was used in the Rhine et al. study in Chapter 2. Rhine and coworkers constructed fourfold tables with "chosen" and "not chosen" as columns and "asking for good" and "asking for bad" as rows, and calculated Fisher's Exact Test on each of the tables. Of the 40 tests made, only 2 reached the .05 level of confidence — exactly what would be expected on the basis of chance alone. Therefore, the researchers concluded that there was no significant effect present.

COMPARISON OF PERCENTAGES AND PROPORTIONS

Another form in which data are often reported is in terms of the percentage of people exhibiting and not exhibiting certain characteristics, or the proportion of people agreeing or disagreeing with certain items on an attitude scale. It would be possible in some situations to convert these percentages to frequencies and to use either χ^2 or the Fisher Exact Test. Sometimes, however, we are interested in the percentages themselves and would like to make our inferences in terms of the distribution of percentages. It is customary to transform percentages into proportions in this case. This is done by simply moving the decimal point two places to the left, letting 1.00 stand for the totality instead of expressing the data to the base 100 as with percentages.

Test for Proportions

The statistic used to make inferences regarding the distribution of proportions is the z test for proportions. This statistic can be used to test for any theoretical proportional split. We could assume that the proportion in one direction is essentially the same as the proportion in the other direction. That is, that the split is .5 to .5. Or we could, on the basis of the claims of someone else, or based on theoretical reasons, assume some other proportional split, such as .7 to .3. Once we have chosen the theoretical model we wish to test, we can determine the distribution of proportions based on samples of the size we have. We can estimate the standard error of that distribution and then proceed as we would with a t statistic by dividing the difference between our obtained proportion and the theoretical proportion by the standard error of the proportion. The values of this statistic distribute normally, so we can refer to a table of the normal curve and determine the probability of obtaining a difference as large as the one we have on the basis of chance alone.

Assume that it is claimed that 70% of the students at a given college believe that a socialistic form of government would be superior to any other. We could evaluate the likelihood of this being a true statement by taking a representative sample of 100 students at that college and asking them to agree or disagree with the statement. Assume that 55% agreed with the statement. We will then assume that the observed proportion, .55, is a random chance deviation from the true population value of .70. When we calculate the z for proportions, we obtain a value of 2.5. From reference to the table of the normal curve we find that a z deviation from the population mean as large as 2.5 would be expected to occur by chance fewer than 2 times out of 100. Hence we will conclude that the claim made is *not* true, since a difference as large as the one we obtained would occur too infrequently by chance alone.

NON-PARAMETRIC (DISTRIBUTION-FREE) TESTS

In all of our discussion of statistics so far, we have dealt exclusively with what are called "normal curve" statistical methods. They are classified as such because their properties are derived from some of the properties of the normal curve and they required that the user assume that his measurements come from a population with a normal distribution, or at the very least, that statistics calculated from that population will distribute normally. In some situations, however, assumption of a normal distribution clearly is not warranted, and specialized statistical methods, known as "non-parametric" or "distribution-free" methods, have been developed to deal with these cases. Such methods are also used when the data are expressed in terms of ranks, making it impossible to calculate the value of the mean.

The topic of non-parametric statistics is an extensive and complex one. Understanding of the logic involved requires much more knowledge of statistics than is assumed for the readers of this book. However, reference to non-parametric measures occurs frequently in the social sciences literature (see Marascuilo and Penfield, Chapter 5, p. 000), and some information regarding the specific uses of the various techniques will be useful. Consequently, we are including a brief section on some of these statistical tests, providing enough description to permit anyone encountering this terminology to at least have some frame of reference against which to evaluate it.

Tests of the Significance of Differences Between Two Groups

1. The Sign Test. The sign test takes its name from the fact that only the plus or minus sign around some reference point enters into the calculations. The sign test is evaluated by counting the number of plus or minus signs and referring to a table of probability values which specify chance levels of occurrence for the frequency of signs. It is not a powerful test and is usually used only where the data are unsuitable for other types of tests.

2. Mann-Whitney U Test. This is one of the most commonly used non-parametric methods for determining the signficance of a difference between two groups. The statistic "U" is interpreted through tables of the statistic, much as is done with the t statistic.

3. Median Test. This is another test to determine whether two groups differ significantly in terms of the value of their medians.

4. Kolmogorov-Smirnov Two-Sample Test. Another test of whether two samples have actually been drawn from the same population.

There are two tests for situations in which two groups are related, as in the case of matched pairs. These are the *McNemar test* for the significance of changes and the *Wilcoxon matched-pairs signed ranks test*. These tests are used to detect the possible statistical significance of differences between two groups.

Tests for More Than Two Groups

Two more non-parametric methods should be mentioned here. The *Friedman two-way analysis of variance* uses a statistic called χ_r^2, which is evaluated by means of a table of χ^2 to determine whether the groups differ significantly. The *Kruskal-Wallis one-way analysis of variance* uses a statistic called H, which is evaluated for significance in special tables, as with the F statistic.

The non-parametric tests just discussed are all reasonably efficient tests. In statistical terms, this means that the tests give answers very close to what the normal curve statistics would provide if their use could have been justified. There are a variety of other methods available, but many of them are sadly inefficient. If a non-parametric measure has a .45 efficiency when compared to the t statistic, this means that you have the efficiency equal to calculating the t statistic with only 45 people when the study is actually based on a sample of 100 subjects. In other words, using the non-parametric measure is equal to throwing away 55 subjects from your sample.

chapter nine

measures of how things are associated

In our discussions of research techniques and statistical methods, we have tended to focus on ways in which we determine *differences* between groups, between survey questions, and between experimental treatments. In this chapter, we will examine the ways we can find out how things change in *association* with one another, in other words, how things change *together*.

A HYPOTHETICAL EXAMPLE OF ASSOCIATION

Suppose that you had the opportunity to interview several families as part of a survey. For the purposes of the survey, households consisting of married couples between 60 and 70 years of age have been selected. As part of the survey, you ask them about their children and, as is not unusual when interviewing couples of this age, you are shown pictures of grown children. After looking at about your fifteenth family picture, you note that in the majority of the pictures, siblings of the same sex are almost all of the same height, even though the parents may be quite different in height. After a few more interviews, you are convinced that this is a definite trend, and as an additional question (after you finish doing your survey interview) you ask those parents who have two female children about the heights of the children. You note this down and do the same for the next group of families you interview. A few weeks later, you have the numbers given in Table 9–1, listing the height in centimeters of 13 pairs of sisters.

As you look over the pattern of measurements, your earlier impression of a relationship seems to be confirmed: the height of the first-born female seems to be related to the height of the second-born female. To obtain a clearer idea

145

TABLE 9-1   Heights in Centimeters of Thirteen Adult
Females (X) and Their Sisters (Y)

OLDER SISTER	YOUNGER SISTER
X	Y
187	187
167	170
180	177
177	180
176	175
160	167
180	177
167	157
167	162
162	167
162	162
162	163
165	164
N = 13	13
MEAN = 170.153	169.846
S.D. = 8.744	8.716

of how the two sets of measurements change together, you could construct a grid on which both sets of scores could be plotted. Such a grid could be drawn with the height of the first-born listed on the vertical scale and the height of the second-born on the horizontal scale. The pairs of measurements could then be plotted on the grid, placing a mark at each point where each pair of scores intersect. When completed, such a grid (in statistics, called a *scatter plot*) allows you to examine the patterns of change of the two sets of measurements in relation to each other. If the 14 pairs of measurements listed earlier were plotted in this fashion, the result would be as shown in Figure 9-1.

In Figure 9-1, we can see that the change is systematic, and that the pairs of measurements form a reasonably straight line as the heights are plotted from the shortest pair of siblings to the tallest. It is also evident that the pattern of change is fairly evenly distributed from the lowest value to the highest. Given these conditions—that the change is *linear* and *evenly distributed*—we can use the statistic known as the *Pearson product-moment correlation coefficient* to determine how closely the two sets of measurements are related.

THE PEARSON CORRELATION COEFFICIENT (PEARSON *r*)

The Pearson correlation coefficient is the principal statistic used to determine whether change in one set of measurements is associated with change in another. For the sets of measurements on siblings, the Pearson *r* (the usual symbol for this statistic) is +.87.

The calculation method for the Pearson *r* can be found in almost any introductory statistics text, and there is no need here for a detailed analysis of the calculation methods. However, several factors enter into the interpretation of

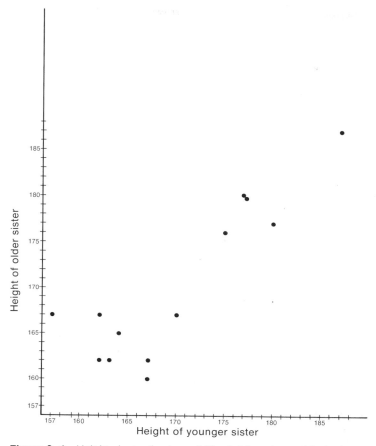

Figure 9–1   Heights in centimeters of 13 adult females and their sisters.

this coefficient, and in order to properly evaluate research using correlational methods, these should be reviewed.

The Pearson r can vary in magnitude from +1.00 to −1.00. A Pearson r of +1.00 means that changes in one set of measurements are *exactly* proportional to changes in the other set. If the example of the height relationship of siblings were perfect, each pair of sisters would have exactly the same relationship to each other in height over the entire range of height measured, without a single deviation from a perfect relationship. Such a perfect relationship, as plotted on a grid, is shown in Figure 9–2A.

The exact reverse of such a relationship is shown in Figure 9–2B. In this plot, the Pearson r is −1.00, indicating that as one measurement increases in numerical value, the other decreases by an exactly proportionate amount over the entire range.

The circumstance of no relationship at all—i.e., change in one variable is completely unrelated to change in the other variable—is shown in Figure 9–2C. As you can see, the pattern of the plots forms an almost perfect circle. In this condition, the value of r will be 0.00.

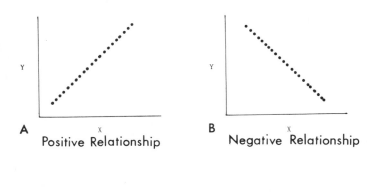

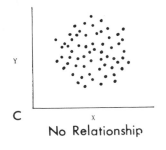

Figure 9-2   See text for explanation.

To return to the example of the correlation between heights of sisters, we can now ask how the obtained value of +.87 should be interpreted. Clearly it indicates a close relationship. A perfect relationship with no variation in the relation of one set of scores to the other would be +1.00, and our obtained r of .84 is fairly close to this value. If we compare this to another set of data, one which gives us the correlation between the heights of husbands and wives, we might find that here the Pearson r is equal to +.45. Can we conclude that the relationship between the heights of siblings is twice as high as that between husbands and wives? The answer is a straightforward "no," since the value of the correlation coefficient is *not* a value that can be interpreted linearly—an r of .60 does not indicate twice as strong a relationship as an r of .30.

One very useful way to think about the meaning of an obtained r is to look at its square. If we found the value of the square for the r between siblings, we would have a value of .75 (.87 × .87 = .75) and for the r between parents (.45 × .45 = .20) we would have the value of .20. This can be interpreted as the *percentage of association* between the two variables. For the r of .87 between siblings, we have 75% of the variation in the height of one sibling associated with the height of the other. For the r of the parents, we have 20% of the variation in the height of one parent associated with the height of the other parent. Note that in both examples, respectively 25% and 80% of the variation is not accounted for; this is variation that is due to other factors.

It should now be easy for you to see that a correlation of .30 is only one quarter as high as a correlation of .60, since the former accounts for only 9% of the variation while the latter accounts for 36% of it. With this in mind, try evaluating the size of several r's to see just how much of the variation they account for and how much they leave unexplained.

There is one other aspect of correlation that should be mentioned. One of the more important considerations in the example we chose is that there is no reason at all to assume causation on the basis of the correlation. To claim that the height of the first-born causes the height of the second-born would be absurd. Yet the most common error made in correlational research is to attribute causation on the basis of a correlational relationship. One research study in the area of criminology assumed a causal relationship for a correlation found between the occurrence of rainy weather and the frequency of house burglaries. In terms of ascribing causality, assuming that rain causes burglary is about as sensible as suggesting that a region suffering from a severe drought should import burglars.

LIMITATIONS OF CORRELATION

In our earlier discussions on such topics as the analysis of variance, we were quite casual about the nature of the assumptions to be made about the data, saying in effect that there were very few considerations that were of any concern at all. This is not true for measures of association. If the data do not meet certain specified characteristics, most coefficients are at best inappropriate, and at worst may give an incorrect notion of the degree of association.

To see some of the problems encountered with the Pearson r, look at Figure 9–3, which contains sets of plots of scores, called scatter plots. Of these, only A meets the requirements essential for computing the Pearson r and thus only in A is the calculation meaningful. It is inappropriate to calculate r on set B, because the data do not distribute themselves along a straight line. There is obviously a high degree of relationship between the two variables, but the

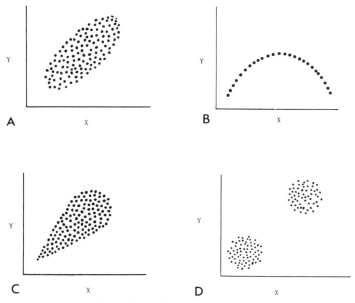

Figure 9–3 See text for explanation.

Pearson r requires that the change be *linear*, that is, that the degree of change be constant over the entire range of scores. An r calculated on B would result in a numerically low coefficient, giving a drastic underestimate of the degree of relationship. It is also inappropriate to calculate r on set C, because the scores here are not distributed evenly throughout their range. In plot D, the situation is somewhat more complicated. The data for plot D indicate that there is clearly no relationship at all—that there are two separate sets of scores which have been combined arbitrarily. However, an r calculated on these data would indicate a very high degree of relationship and would give a completely misleading picture of the pattern of association present, since the presumed relationship is merely the result of combining two sets of data which have different mean values.

At least one conclusion is obvious: measures that are correlated without determination of their scatter plots are suspect, since they invariably lead us to misleading conclusions about the level of association. With computers available, it is tempting for researchers to simply obtain all possible correlations between variables and to discuss only those that are significant—a practice that is all too common. Another tendency is to present *all* the correlations but emphasize only those that are significant, without considering how many would be significant by pure chance. One volume on creativity was examined by a well-known statistician with this problem in mind, and he found that the published correlations exactly reproduced a normal curve with its mean at 0.00. The implications of this are obvious: the authors of the book based their conclusions on chance rather than on meaningful relationships.

PREDICTION

Up to now we have discussed the correlation coefficient only as a measure of association. However, there is another very practical use for the Pearson r: it can be used to predict the value of one set of measurements from the values of another.

In the example of the correlation between heights of siblings, we initially noted that there seemed to be a strong relationship between the heights, and we confirmed this suspicion by means of the Pearson r. Knowing the value of this correlation, we can now make some predictions.

For example, suppose we have the heights of four adult women and would like to know the heights of their older sisters. The data gathered for the correlation obtained earlier can be used to develop such a prediction equation. The calculations needed are basically those for determining the equation for a straight line. The methods of calculation will not be shown here since they can be found in almost any introductory statistics text. For the data of our example, the equation is of the form $Y' = bX + a$, where the letters in the equation stand for the following quantities:

Y' = the score we would like to predict; the variable whose measurements are not known (in this example, the height of the older sister).

b = the value that indicates the rate of change of one variable in relation to another.

X = the value of the measurement we know (the height of the younger sister).

a = a constant to adjust the two regression lines to the same point (in this case, to pass the two lines through the mean of X and the mean of Y).

The heights of the four younger women are respectively 165, 180, 176, and 165 centimeters. The values for the prediction equation are:

$$Y' = .87 X + 21.8$$

(These values are based on the preceding calculation of the Pearson r.) To predict the height of the sister of the first person out of the four, we substitute her height into the equation in place of X:

$$Y' = .87 (167) + 21.8 = 167.09$$

The value of 167.09 is the predicted height of the sister. To find the predicted heights for the other three scores, the same process is repeated: For the second person the equation is $Y' = .87 (180) + 21.8$, and the result is 178.4.

How accurate are these predictions? The higher the value of the Pearson r, the more accurate the prediction, and the lower the value of r, the less accurate the prediction. If the r were +1.00 or −1.00, the prediction would be perfect. There are methods for determining the limits of the predicted value. For example, in the prediction of the sisters' heights, the results if presented in a research report would have reported the predicted height as plus or minus 4.35 centimeters, to indicate that the true value would lie between those limits. As the value of r decreases, the limits within which the prediction must be made become larger and larger.

Prediction equations are used in a variety of circumstances. For example, suppose a test exists which is quite good at selecting promising applicants for certain kinds of employment, but is expensive and time-consuming. Another measure exists which can be given very quickly and has a correlation of .85 with the first test. With this degree of association between the two tests, an applicant could be given the short test, and a prediction could be made based on his score on that test as to what his score on the longer test would have been if he had taken it. While there is some loss in accuracy, the correlation is high enough so that the loss in accuracy is not too great. There are a variety of such uses for prediction equations, and in the following discussion of other measures of association, we will note whether these measures can also be used for prediction purposes.

OTHER MEASURES OF ASSOCIATION

A variety of different methods exist to measure association. Almost without exception, they are subject to limitations of interpretation in the same way as the Pearson r is. Perhaps the simplest way to regard these other methods is as approximations to the Pearson r. These measures offer a reasonable estimate of what a Pearson r would be if the data were such that we could justify its calculation. Since these specialized measures are not often found in the literature, our description of them will be relatively brief and will focus on their interpretation.

Correlation Ratio (Eta, η)

When the data do not show a linear (straight line) pattern of change, the correlation ratio (usually symbolized by the Greek letter eta, η) is the appropriate statistic. For example, if we were to examine the relationship between strength of hand-grip and age, we would find that strength of grip first increases as age increases and then begins to decrease as old age is approached. The distribution is shown in Figure 9–4.

For such data the only appropriate measure of association is the correlation ratio, since it will indicate the maximum degree of association present between the two measures. Special methods exist for using eta to predict from one measure to another.

Biserial and Point-Biserial Correlation Coefficients

If we faced a situation where we had one variable that was continuous (such as scores on a test) and another variable that was expressed in only two categories (such as answering a question "yes" or "no"), and we wanted to know the degree of association between the two, the statistic that would most probably be used is the point-biserial r. (Biserial r, the other statistic mentioned in the heading, has numerous disadvantages and is seldom used now. It is mentioned here primarily for the sake of completeness.) The point-biserial r is equivalent to a Pearson r—in fact, if we had a set of data with one measure as scores and another measure expressed as either 1 or 0 (numerically equivalent to "yes" or "no") and we carried out the calculations for the Pearson r, we would get exactly the same value as when carrying out the

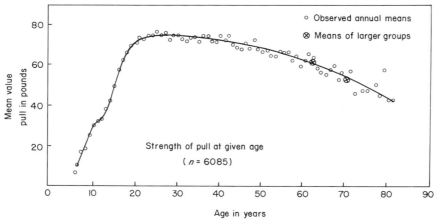

Figure 9–4 Illustration of a markedly curvilinear relationship. (From Ruger, H. A., and Stoessiger, B. On the growth curves of certain character in man (males). *Annals of Eugenics*, April, 1927, 11, 76–110.)

calculations for the point-biserial r. The point-biserial, however, cannot be used for prediction.

Tetrachoric Correlation Coefficient

The tetrachoric coefficient is a rather specialized statistic. It was designed to estimate the degree of association in cases where the things measured are basically continuous, but where only categorized "yes-no" information is present. For example, suppose we wanted to know the correlation between income and education, but the only information we had on a particular group of subjects was data such as "college educated" vs. "not college educated," and for income, such information as "income above $10,000 per year" vs. "income less than $10,000 a year." When faced with such limited data on which to calculate a measure of association, the tetrachoric coefficient is the only choice. It does not have very much power to detect association between two measures and would only be used when the limitations of the data prohibit the use of any other measure. The labor involved in calculating the tetrachoric coefficient is so tedious that it is almost always done on a digital computer.

The Contingency Coefficient

The contingency coefficient, C, is a measure of association for problems with multiple categories. For example, take the demonstration problem that was used in our discussion of the χ^2 statistic on page 139. If we wanted to know the degree of association between the answers and the education categories, the contingency coefficient would be the most appropriate statistic.

The Phi Coefficient

The phi coefficient is used to determine the degree of association between two sets of "yes-no" information. If we were interested in the correlation between two items on a test that are both answered "true" or "false," we would use the phi coefficient. The phi has the same power to detect association as the Pearson r—in fact, if a Pearson r is calculated on two measures with scores of 1 or 0, the result is identical to the phi calculation.

Rank Difference Correlation Coefficient (Rho)

Occasionally a situation arises where measurements are in the form of rank order information only. To calculate the rank difference correlation, the measurements are ranked with the highest score in each measure having the rank of I. When two such sets of ranks are obtained, the rank difference coefficient can be used to determine the degree of association between the two sets of ranks. As a measure of association, the rank difference coefficient is quite good, producing about the same coefficient as the Pearson r on the same data.

RELIABILITY AND VALIDITY

In reading published research reports, particularly those that involve tests of some kind, you will frequently come across references to the concepts of reliability and validity. There is an extensive literature on these topics, but discussion of it requires considerable background in statistics and measurement. However, some basic understanding of what is meant by reliability and validity is important in evaluating much of the work that is published in the social sciences. Since correlation methods are usually used in determining the reliability and validity of a measure, our discussion is included here in the presentation of measures of association.

In fact, one of the most important uses of measures of association is to determine the reliability and the validity of measurements. When we speak of *reliability,* we mean the likelihood of obtaining the same answer when we measure the same thing twice. If we had a perfectly reliable ruler and measured the length of the same surface over and over, we would obtain the same measurement every time. However, if the ruler were made of rubber and had to be stretched to span the surface, the measurements would differ from one reading to the next, since on one occasion we might stretch the ruler a bit further than on another. The rubber ruler, then, would be an unreliable measuring instrument since we would get different answers on different occasions. Obviously, if a test is to be of any use it must be reliable; we must get the same answer when we measure the same thing twice.

However, a test can be reliable and still not be of any use if it lacks validity. Validity means that a measuring instrument measures what it is supposed to measure. If we had a ruler that was perfectly reliable but whose units were incorrectly marked off, we would get the same answer on successive occasions, but our measurements would not be valid indicators of the length of the surface, because of the inaccuracy of the units. You can see, then, that a test can be reliable but not valid. On the other hand, a test *must* be reliable if it is to be valid.

Measures of Reliability

Equivalent Forms Method. One of the ways to establish the reliability of a test is to construct two equivalent forms of the test, administer the two forms to the same individuals, and correlate the score obtained on one form with that obtained on the other. If the test were completely reliable, the correlation between the two testings would be +1.00. This ideal, however, is never attained in practice, since many factors enter into the picture which lower the reliability estimate of even the best test. Some of these are factors affecting the individual that vary from day to day—such things as variations in motivation level from one test session to the next, variations in health and amount of sleep, and other psychological and physiological changes. In addition, chance factors can enter in as a result of misreading a question, or marking an answer in the wrong place.

Variations in the environment will also lower a test's reliability. On one testing it might be quiet and thereby conducive to concentrating on the test, while on another occasion there might be a good deal of noise and confusion, and the individual's performance would suffer as a result.

Reliability can be lowered by errors made in scoring the test or in recording the score. Also, the first testing might influence the results of the second testing, especially if items on the two tests involved a problem that an individual might be able to think through between the two testings, or if there are timed performances of the same type on each testing.

Another disadvantage of the equivalent forms method is the huge effort involved in making two complete tests to measure the same thing. It is necessary to develop a huge pool of items of comparable difficulty and content and to balance the two tests so that they are comparable.

Test-Retest Method. If the nature of the research permits, it is possible to use the same test twice. This is called the test-retest method. This method has most of the limitations of the equivalent forms method except for the fact that it does not entail as much work for the investigator. Its major disadvantage is that if there are any cumulative effects of one testing on the next, it is virtually useless as a method of establishing reliability.

Split-Half Method. The split-half method is the most common way of estimating the reliability of a test. It involves splitting the test into two halves—e.g., odd vs. even items, or first half vs. second half—and calculating the correlation coefficient between the two halves. This eliminates problems due to varying environmental and individual factors, but has one inherent limitation. The limitation is that we are interested in estimating the reliability of the *complete* test, but are obtaining only the correlation of two half-tests. Since the correlation of two half-tests will be systematically lower than the correlation of two whole tests, we must correct for this factor. To do this, the obtained correlation coefficient (which is called a reliability coefficient when used to estimate reliability) is corrected by applying a particular correction formula, the *Spearman-Brown Prophecy* formula. This formula increases the estimated correlation by an amount appropriate to correct for the bias involved when using two half-tests.

How large should reliability coefficients be in order to make a test a usable one? This depends entirely on the manner in which the test is to be used. If we are going to use the test to make predictions of individual behavior, reliability coefficients are commonly required to be in the high .90's. If the test is to be used to characterize the performance of groups of individuals, it may be acceptable to have reliabilities in the high .80's or low .90's and still have a useful measuring instrument.

Measures of Validity

Once we have established the reliability of a measuring instrument, the question of the validity of the test arises. To determine whether or not a test measures what it is supposed to measure, we must have some independent measurement of the trait or skill in question. This independent measurement is called a *criterion measure*. For example, if we wished to construct a test which would predict success in college, an appropriate criterion measure to see if the test were valid would be grades later achieved in college. We could then correlate the score on our test with the grades obtained. Such a correlation would be called a *validity coefficient.*

Again, the choice of an appropriate criterion variable involves mainly non-statistical considerations. If the criterion measure chosen does not accurately reflect the trait we are measuring, then the correlation we obtain will be meaningless. The choice of a criterion variable must be defensible on logical and theoretical grounds.

There is one statistical caution which should be observed, however. If the criterion measure is made on only a segment of the relevant population, the obtained validity coefficient will be too low. If, in our test for predicting success in college, we base our criterion measure only on people who have completed college, ignoring those who dropped out, we will have done what is referred to as *restricting the spread of talent* on the test, and calculations made with such a restriction will systematically underestimate the magnitude of a true correlation. There is a correction available for such a restriction and it should be used whenever this problem is encountered.

How large should a validity coefficient be in order for a test to be useful? Normally, if the validity coefficient falls in the .40's to .50's range, the test is considered to be a good one. A correlation of .50 might not *seem* very high, since with a correlation of this magnitude we are accounting for only 25% of the total variance in Y (our criterion measure) from knowledge of the value of X (our predictor measure) (see pp. 147–148). However, we *have* reduced the uncertainty of our estimates of values of Y by 25% over what we would have obtained without having any knowledge of X, and this degree of reduction in uncertainty could be very significant in many practical situations. The relative value of a validity coefficient of a given magnitude will depend on practical considerations rather than on arbitrarily assigned levels of statistical significance. (Keep in mind that many factors enter into determining complex behavior other than those which can be measured through performance on written tests.)

In reading a published research report, especially one in which rather complex measures are taken, you should be alert for demonstrations of the reliability and validity of the measures used. If a research worker has constructed a test of some aptitude or ability and has used it in a study, but has reported no data (or no reference to such data) on the reliability and validity of the measures he used, it is entirely appropriate to entertain some skepticism about his conclusions. To blindly accept conclusions based on measures that have not been tested for reliability or validity is asking to be misled. The research worker's confidence in his own ability to produce valid measures is an exceedingly poor substitute for empirical proof.[1]

MULTIPLE CORRELATION COEFFICIENT

Until now we have limited our discussion of measures of association to situations where only two measures are being examined. However, there are many circumstances, particularly in the areas of testing and personnel selection, in which it is desirable to know the correlation between one measure and *several* others. The statistic used for this purpose is the *coefficient of multiple correlation* (R).

Suppose that we wished to predict performance in college. We have such measures as high school grades, intelligence test scores, socio-economic status of parents, and education of parents. Any one of these measures would provide some degree of predictability, since all of them correlate positively with performance in college. By using all of them, however, we may substantially increase the accuracy of the prediction. Quite powerful prediction equations can be developed with multiple R procedures, and the accuracy of prediction is much greater than when just one measure is used. However, this advantage is gained at considerable cost. For one thing, to arrive at a stable prediction equation with several variables, extremely large samples are needed. Multiple R's produced on samples of 50 to 100 subjects will not be very stable.

Stepwise Multiple Regression.   A variation on the standard multiple R procedure is a technique known as stepwise multiple regression. In this procedure variables are added one at a time to a multiple correlation and an analysis of variance F test is used to determine whether or not adding the new variable has significantly improved the prediction. With this process, variables can be continually added (or removed if no contribution is made by the addition of the variable) until the prediction has reached a maximum value. The calculations are such that the procedure is impossible without a high-speed digital computer. Use of the powerful analysis of variance techniques in conjunction with the multiple R greatly increases the stability of the obtained prediction equation. The stringent requirements on sample size can be relaxed somewhat with this technique as compared to the regular multiple R, but fairly large samples are still needed.

A more detailed discussion of the stepwise multiple regression technique is given in Chapter 11 (Multivariate Analysis).

AN EXAMPLE OF CORRELATIONAL RESEARCH

To see how correlational techniques are used in research work, you are asked to read the following study, which utilizes Pearson correlational methods and multiple correlation techniques to develop predictors of first grade performance.

Tests Built From Piaget's and Gesell's Tasks as Predictors of First-Grade Achievement

ALAN S. KAUFMAN, The Psychological Corporation

NADEEN L. KAUFMAN, Teachers College, Columbia University

80 children who were tested in kindergarten on the Gesell School Readiness Tests, a battery built from Piaget's tasks and the Lorge-Thorndike Intelligence Tests, were given the Stanford Achievement Test at the end of first grade. The tests were found to be excellent predictors of achievement: the Piaget and Gesell batteries each correlated .64 with SAT Composite; Lorge-Thorndike MA correlated .58. A measure of kindergarten teething level proved to be a poor predictor of achievement. The results offer empirical support to Ilg and Ames's claim that the Gesell battery is an excellent predictor of school readiness.

The main purpose of the present study is to compare the effectiveness of tests built from tasks devised by Gesell and Piaget as predictors of first-grade achievement. In a recent study, Kaufman (1971) explored the relationships between the theoretical frameworks of Gesell and Piaget by performing psychometric analyses of tests built from their tasks. The results of a correlational analysis showed the Piaget test and the Gesell School Readiness Tests to correlate about equally well with Lorge-Thorndike mental age and IQ, teething level, chronological age, and Warner's revised scale of fathers' occupations. A comparison of the predictive validities of the Gesell and Piaget tests afford another opportunity to relate their theories on the basis of empirical data.

Evidence for the predictive validity of the Piaget test is of practical importance because Piaget's theory and methods have become widely incorporated into American educational techniques (Athey & Rubadeau 1970; Bloom, Hastings, & Madaus 1971; Frost 1968). Yet, these validity data are of even more pressing importance for the Gesell School Readiness Tests since this battery has been claimed to be an excellent predictor of school readiness (Ilg & Ames 1965) despite a lack of empirical evidence and has been used to make crucial educational decisions for several years.

> *The opening section of the paper reviews the rationale and the need for such studies as that reported here.*

Ilg and Ames: A Point of View

For about a decade, Frances Ilg and Louise Ames of the Gesell Institute have been advocating the use of their developmental tests, along with teething level, as predictors of school readiness. In their book *School Readiness,* Ilg and Ames (1965) state: "A mere intelligence test does not and cannot attempt to measure a child's level of maturity. A child may be of clearly superior intelligence but may at the same time be behind others of his age in either physical or behavioral maturity. . . . What we really need to know in determining readiness for school entrance is a child's developmental level. We need to know at what age he is behaving as a total organism. . . . The child's behavioral level may, of course, be at, above, or below the level of his chronological age. But it is his behavioral level rather than his age in years which we consider to be the correct clue to good grade placement'' (pp. 17–18). Furthermore, they claim that the Gesell School Readiness Tests assess a child's developmental level or behavioral maturity and therefore should be used to determine his school placement. In *School Readiness* and elsewhere (Ames 1967, 1968; Ames & Ilg 1964) Ilg and Ames have outlined their theory and approach concerning the use of their tests in the school setting.

Basically, they feel that children at each chronological age are characterized by a particular set of behavioral patterns which can be evaluated by their tests. If, for example, a child of 6 is found to possess the patterns of a typical 5-year-old, Ames and Ilg feel that he should be placed in a school grade with others of his developmental level. Based on their clinical observations and research studies, Gesell Institute researchers have concluded that possibly as many as two-thirds of all kindergarten children are not ready for first grade by the following September. They feel that these children would benefit most by either repeating kindergarten or being placed in a transitional class (depending upon their developmental level) instead of being "overplaced" in first grade (Ilg & Ames 1965). One of the principal adjunct measures that Ilg and Ames recommend for use along with their developmental tests for assessing readiness is a child's teething level. They place much stock in the number of permanent teeth a child has as an indicator of his readiness for school, and Ames (1967) has stated that very slow teething by a child in the first or second grade "is indeed a sign that such a child needs to go slowly in school" (p. 54).

Thus, teething level and a battery of developmental tasks have been proclaimed as excellent predictors of school readiness. According to Dr. Ames (personal communication, 1971) about 2,500 people have received training in workshops during the past few years to learn the theory and methods propounded by the Gesell Institute and to understand the subtleties of interpreting the developmental placement tests. She indicated further that over 150 cities in 12 states are using the Gesell tests in some type of developmental program.

Unfortunately, there has been virtually no empirical evidence to show that the Gesell School Readiness Tests and teething level are, in fact, good predictors of school achievement. Ames and Ilg (1964) reported a .74 correlation between test scores in kindergarten and grade placement 6 years later, but this correlation may be spuriously high since the grade placement of children in a school closely affiliated with the Gesell Institute may well have been influenced by developmental test scores. Similarly, Ilg and Ames (1965, pp. 238–240) cite a study that shows advanced teething to be positively associated with teachers' ratings of achievement. However, the results of this study are dubious because no control group was used; achievement ratings were subjectively obtained; and 80% of the advanced teethers were female, suggesting that sex, rather than teething, may have been the crucial variable.

In view of the widespread use of the Gesell School Readiness Tests and teething level as predictors of readiness, coupled with the lack of evidence of their effectiveness, it seems clear that an objective study to evaluate their predictive validities — particularly in comparison with other measures — is a necessity. Therefore, the data were collected in order to determine: (1) how well tests built from Piaget's and Gesell's tasks, administered in kindergarten, predict first-grade achievement in reading skills, spelling, and arithmetic; (2) how the Piaget and Gesell tests compare with a conventional group intelligence test for the prediction of school achievement; (3) how well the Gesell, Piaget, and conventional intelligence tests correlate with school achievement when used as joint predictors; and (4) how well a measure of a child's teething level, obtained in kindergarten, predicts first-grade achievement.

METHOD

Subjects

The sample consisted of 80 Caucasian first-grade children (49 girls and 31 boys) attending the only elementary school in a Suffolk County, Long Island, New York school district. During the previous year, most of the kindergarten children in the school were administered the three predictor tests ($N = 103$). The 80 children in the present study are those in the group of 103 who were promoted and were still attending the same school 1 year later. Of the remaining 23, three remained in kindergarten on the basis of teacher recommendations, and 20 either moved away or entered parochial school.

The 80 children had a mean chronological age of 66.8 months ($SD = 3.7$) as of January 1 of their kindergarten school year, and were 16 months older when tested again in May of first grade. Their Lorge-Thorndike IQs ranged from 75 to 145 (mean $= 108.0$; $SD = 13.1$). In addition, Warner's revised scale of fathers' occupations (Warner, Meeker, & Eells 1960) was used for classification, and it was clear that the Ss tended to come from above-average socioeconomic backgrounds.

> *Note that the sample description is brief, but conveys the information necessary to acquaint the reader with the type of sample selected for study.*

Description of Measures

Gesell School Readiness Tests (predictor 1)—These tests are predominantly perceptual-motor and are described in detail in *School Readiness* (Ilg & Ames 1965). The subtests of interest in this 20-minute individually administered test battery are: (1) Initial Interview. Child is asked his age and birthday, the names and ages of his siblings, and the nature of his father's occupation. (2) Writing. Child tries to write his first and last names and numbers from 1 to 20. (3) Copy Forms. Child is asked to copy a circle, cross, square, equilateral triangle, diamond, and "divided rectangle" (a horizontal rectangle with two lines connecting the four corners and two lines connecting the midpoint of each side). (4) Incomplete Man. Child tries to complete the facial and body parts of a partially drawn man, and is asked questions about the man (e.g., "How does he feel inside?"). (5) Animals. Child is asked to name as many animals as he can and is allowed 1 minute.

Other tasks of the battery were not administered to the sample because of their difficulty for kindergarten children (e.g., the Monroe Visual Tests) or because they were not conducive to objective scoring (e.g., Home and School Preferences).

The unsystematic clinical method used to score the Gesell School Readiness Tests (GSRT) was not suitable for a rigorous psychometric analysis, so an objective scoring system was devised. The five subtests were divided into a total of 11 tasks, and each task was scored 0 through 9 where low scores indicated less-mature behavior and high scores were given to more-mature responses. Each score was designed to be equivalent to a different developmental age (DA), as shown below.

Task score............................0	1	2	3	4	5	6	7	8	9
Corresponding DA 4	4–4½	4½	4½–5	5	5–5½	5½	5½–6	6	6–7

The norms tables and narrative descriptions presented in *School Readiness* (Ilg & Ames 1965) formed the basis of the scoring system.

The Initial Interview and Animals subtests each consisted of only one task, so the task score was also the subtest score. For Writing, Copy Forms, and Incomplete Man, which each contained two to four tasks, subtest scores were obtained by summing the scores on the tasks constituting each subtest.

Total scores on the GSRT were computed by summing the 11 task scores, resulting in a maximum possible score of 99. A more complete description of the tasks and the scoring system has appeared elsewhere (Kaufman 1970, 1971).

The measures used in the study are described very briefly, since a full description has been published elsewhere.

The reliability (coefficient α) of the GSRT was found to be .84 for 103 kindergarten children, and the GSRT was shown to correlate substantially with Lorge-Thorndike IQ (.50) and MA (.61) for the same group of kindergarten children (Kaufman 1971).

Where relevant, data on the reliability of measures is provided.

Piaget battery (predictor 2). — This 20–25-minute individually administered battery was constructed from several of Piaget's tasks. In particular, the Piaget battery (PB) includes items from the areas of number (Piaget 1965), logic (Inhelder & Piaget 1969), space (Piaget & Inhelder 1967), and geometry (Piaget, Inhelder, & Szeminska 1964). Whenever possible, tasks requiring performance rather than verbalization were chosen. In addition, tasks were selected that had been investigated in at least one carefully planned major replication study.

The subtests in the PB are summarized below.

1. Length. Child has to compare the lengths of a straight and a curved piece of Play-Doh, matched on end points, and explain his reasoning.

2. Conservation of Number. Child is asked to demonstrate rudimentary knowledge of adding and subtracting. Then he tries to show evidence of identity conservation (i.e., evaluating whether the number of candies stays the same when poured from a plate to a glass) and equivalence conservation (i.e., explaining whether two equal rows of objects remain equal after one row undergoes shape transformation).

3. Ordination and Cardination. Child tries to make "staircases" out of first five and then nine slats, where the slats range from 2 to 6 inches. Then he is asked to insert two additional slats — which were "accidentally" left out — into the larger staircase. Finally, he is asked to count the steps and state the number of steps a small doll is shown to climb.

4. Straight Line. Child is asked to distinguish between pictures of straight and curved lines. He also tries to construct three different straight lines using match sticks in clay bases when the end points are provided.

5. Logical Classification. Child tries to sort a group of blocks that vary in color and shape. Then he is asked to demonstrate his knowledge of "some" and "all" (e.g., when shown four red squares, two red triangles, and two blue triangles, he is asked, "Are all the triangles blue?"). Finally, he tries to demonstrate his knowledge that an object can belong to more than one class (e.g., when shown a plate filled with red things and a set of blocks containing four red squares, he is asked, "Do the squares belong on the plate with the red things? Why?").

An objective scoring system was devised to score the PB. The five subtests were divided into a total of 13 tasks, and each task was scored 0 through 7. In general, higher scores were indicative of responses corresponding to Piaget's Stages IIb and III, while lower scores signified behavior characteristic of earlier developmental stages.

The Length subtest contained only one task, so the task score was also the subtest score. For the other four subtests, which each contained two to four tasks, subtest scores were obtained by summing the scores on the tasks included in each subtest.

Total scores on the PB were obtained by summing scores on the 13 tasks; thus, perfect performance (i.e., a score of 7 on each task) would result in a score of 91. More detailed information about the scoring of the tasks, and about the tasks themselves, can be found elsewhere (Kaufman 1970, 1971).

Similarly to the GSRT, the PB was found to be a reasonably reliable instrument when used with kindergarten children (coefficient $\alpha = .80$; $N = 103$), and also correlated rather highly with Lorge-Thorndike IQ (.55) and MA (.62) (Kaufman 1971).

Lorge-Thorndike Intelligence Tests, Level 1, Form A (predictor 3).—This group-administered conventional intelligence test contains 65 pictorial items which make up its three subtests: Oral Vocabulary, Pictorial Classification, and Pictorial Pairing. Each Lorge-Thorndike (L-T) subtest takes about 7–8 minutes to administer.

Teething level (predictor 4).—The aim of this measure is to assess the degree to which a child has lost his primary teeth and has gained his permanent teeth. The developmental examiner looked into each child's mouth and recorded the pertinent teething information. A 10-point scale was devised to measure a child's teething level: 0 = no teeth loose, none missing; 1 = no teeth missing, but one or more loose; 2 = no permanent teeth in, but one or more primary teeth out by natural causes; 3 = one tooth partially in (half in or less); 4 = two teeth partially in or one tooth completely in (more than half in); 5 = more than one but less than two teeth in (two teeth partially in count as one tooth completely in); 6 = two to two and one-half teeth in; 7 = three to three and one-half teeth in; 8 = four to four and one-half teeth in; 9 = five to five and one-half teeth in. In this scoring system, 6-year molars, incisors, cuspids, and bicuspids were all given equal weight in determining the number of permanent teeth that had come in.

Stanford Achievement Test (criterion).—This battery consists of six subtests at the Primary I level: Arithmetic, Spelling, Word Knowledge, Paragraph Meaning, Word Study Skills, and Vocabulary. For the present study the following *Stanford Achievement Test* (SAT) criteria were used:

1. Arithmetic—grade equivalent on Arithmetic subtest;
2. Spelling—grade equivalent on Spelling subtest;
3. Reading—median of the grade equivalents on Word Knowledge, Paragraph Meaning, Word Study Skills, and Vocabulary subtests;
4. Composite—median grade equivalent on all six subtests.

Procedure

The predictor tests were all administered in 1968–1969, while the Ss were in kindergarten. The GSRT was administered by a specially trained developmental examiner (the district psychologist) between mid-October 1968 and early February 1969. In addition, the developmental examiner recorded the status of each child's primary and permanent teeth at the end of each GSRT testing session. The PB was administered during a 3-week period in late January and early February 1969 and the L-T was given within a 1-week period during the middle of May 1969.

The criterion test, the SAT, was administered during May 1970, as the Ss were nearing completion of first grade.

Treatment of Data, Results, and Discussion

Table 1 presents means and standard deviations of all variables used as predictors in the present study. One of these variables is L-T Total Score; since the total or level on the L-T is essentially the same as mental age (MA), this variable is referred to as MA throughout the paper.

Table 1 also indicates means and SDs of the predictor variables for the sample of 103 that was tested in kindergarten. Only the GSRT total became appreciably restricted in

TABLE 1. Means and Standard Deviations of Predictor Variables

PREDICTOR VARIABLE	MAXIMUM POSSIBLE SCORE	PRESENT GROUP (N = 80)		ORIGINAL GROUP (N = 103)	
		Mean	*SD*	*Mean*	*SD*
Gesell School Readiness Tests ...	99	46.8	12.6	46.1	13.5
Piaget battery	91	55.4	14.1	54.8	13.9
Lorge-Thorndike Total Score	65	43.7	8.1	43.4	8.1
Lorge-Thorndike IQ	...	108.0	13.1	107.6	12.7
Teething level............................	9	1.7	2.8	1.6	2.7

range as the SD decreased from 13.5 to 12.6. This restriction may be traced primarily to the three students who remained in the school and were left back. Although none of the predictor tests were used to determine promotion to first grade, these three children were among the four lowest-scoring students on the GSRT (for $N = 103$). They also performed below average on the PB and L-T, but their performance on these tests was not sufficiently poor to produce range restriction. As a result of the restriction in range of GSRT scores, correlation coefficients involving this variable (presented below) would tend to be slight underestimates for the entire sample.

Table 2 shows correlations of the GSRT, PB, L-T, and teething level with Stanford Achievement Test criteria. Each of the three batteries correlated about the same with the composite score: for the Piaget and Gesell tests, this was a substantial .64; for the L-T, MA correlated .58 and IQ .57. Teething level, however, correlated poorly with SAT Composite ($r = .07$), and also did not correlate significantly with the other SAT criteria. Clearly, teething was a poor predictor of first-grade achievement.

TABLE 2. Correlations of Piaget, Gesell, and Lorge-Thorndike Tests, Taken Singly and Jointly, with Stanford Achievement Test Criteria (N = 80)

PREDICTORS	STANFORD ACHIEVEMENT TEST CRITERIA			
	Arithmetic	*Spelling*	*Reading*	*Composite*
Single:				
Gesell School Readiness Tests (GSRT)............	.61	.56	.63	.64
Piaget battery (PB)	.60	.53	.58	.64
Lorge-Thorndike mental age (L-T MA)	.58	.54	.51	.58
Lorge-Thorndike IQ (L-T IQ)...........................	.61	.50	.48	.57
Teething level	.07	.01	.11	.07
Multiple:				
GSRT · PB	.68	.61	.68	.72
GSRT · L-T (MA)	.67	.62	.66	.69
PB · L-T (MA)	.67	.60	.62	.69
GSRT · PB · L-T (MA)...................................	.71	.64	.69	.73
	Grade Equivalent			
Mean	2.1	2.2	2.2	2.2
SD..	0.6	0.9	0.8	0.6

Note.— The tests used as multiple predictors correlated as follows: GSRT × PB = .60; GSRT × L-T (MA) = .56; PB × L-T (MA) = .57. In addition, the subscores obtained from SAT correlated as follows: Arithmetic × Spelling = .72; Arithmetic × Reading = .79; Spelling × Reading = .87.

A brief discussion of multiple correlation is given on pages 156–157. The intercorrelations between the tests used to arrive at the multiple R are given in the footnote to Table 2. These additional data will help readers to evaluate the meaning of the multiple correlation. In selecting variables for a multiple correlation, the highest multiple R will be obtained under conditions where each individual variable correlates highly with the variable to be predicted and has a low correlation with all other variables used in the multiple R. If this seems puzzling at first, review the discussion on interpreting correlations (p. 148). Remember that the higher the correlation between two variables, the more variation in one variable can be explained by variation in the other. Since we are interested in explaining as much of the variation as possible in the variable to be predicted, we should select variables that have the highest correlation with the variable to be predicted. If two variables correlate highly with the criterion, and also with each other, much of the variation they account for is in common. Two variables that have a high correlation with the criterion and a low correlation with each other obviously explain different sources of variation.

When used as multiple predictors, the GSRT, PB, and L-T (MA) correlated .73 with SAT Composite, a substantial improvement over the effectiveness of any battery used alone. Interestingly, when L-T (MA)—a score obtained from a conventional intelligence test—is deleted as a predictor, the multiple correlation with SAT Composite is reduced only negligibly (see table 2). That is, the prediction obtained by using the Piaget and Gesell tests, each derived from a systematic developmental theory, is about as good as the prediction obtained from the three batteries together. However, it can be seen in table 2 that the elimination of either the PB or GSRT as one of the multiple predictors results in a more substantial decrease in the correlation with SAT Composite.

Table 2 also shows that the three predictor tests are about equally effective when the criterion is Arithmetic or Spelling. For the prediction of Reading, however, the data suggest that the GSRT may be the best of the three predictor tests. In particular, it correlated substantially higher with SAT than did L-T (MA) or L-T (IQ). In addition, for the present sample the multiple correlation with Reading was about the same when the GSRT and PB were used together (.68), as when all three predictor tests were considered (.69).

An evaluation of the PB and GSRT subtests as predictors of achievement (see table 3) showed that Writing, in the Gesell battery, correlated highest with SAT Composite (r = .61), followed by the PB subtest Ordination and Cardination (r = .59). These two subtests were also the best predictors of Arithmetic, Spelling, and Reading achievement for the present sample. When Writing and Ordination and Cardination are used as multiple predictors, a correlation of .68 is obtained with SAT Composite; If Conservation of Number is added as a third predictor, a multiple correlation of .71 results. It should be noted that computing multiple correlations in this fashion takes advantage of positive chance errors. Nevertheless, it is likely that excellent prediction of first-grade achievement may be obtained by using selected subtests from each battery.

Of course, cross-validation studies should be performed to help determine the best subtests from each battery and, in fact, to verify that the results obtained in the present study are also found when other samples are used. In particular, it would be interesting to see if the results of cross-validation studies support the present finding that scores on a conventional intelligence test add little to the prediction of overall first-grade achievement obtained by using Piaget and Gesell total test scores.

TABLE 3. Correlations of Gesell School Readiness Tests and Piaget Battery Subtests with Scores on the Stanford Achievement Test (N = 80)

VARIABLE	MAXIMUM SCORE	MEAN	SD	STANFORD ACHIEVEMENT TEST SCORES			
				Arithmetic	Spelling	Reading	Composite
GSRT subtests:							
1. Initial Interview..............	9	5.2	1.4	.46	.47	.43	.47
2. Writing.......................	18	7.1	4.0	.60	.58	.60	.61
3. Copy Forms	36	15.4	5.7	.45	.42	.48	.48
4. Incomplete Man	27	13.7	3.5	.40	.37	.48	.47
5. Animals	9	5.3	2.5	.24	.16	.20	.22
PB subtests:							
1. Length	7	3.0	1.7	.29	.28	.30	.32
2. Conservation of Number	21	12.9	4.4	.47	.43	.44	.51
3. Ordination and Cardination ...	28	19.3	5.9	.56	.48	.55	.59
4. Straight Line.................	14	7.9	3.1	.39	.34	.34	.41
5. Logical Classification.........	21	12.1	4.1	.34	.30	.35	.37

See pages 156–157 for a discussion of the limitations in the use of multiple R's.

Further Analysis of the Gesell School Readiness Tests and Teething Level

Since the GSRT and teething level are used in numerous school systems to place children in kindergarten, first grade, or transitional classes, more detailed analyses are presented in tables 4 and 5 to show how children classified at different developmental levels performed in first grade. To construct table 4, each child was placed in one of three developmental-age groupings (below age 5; age 5; above age 5) on the basis of GSRT performance. It was shown above in the description of the GSRT scoring system that each possible task score between 0 and 9 corresponded to a different developmental age (DA). For example, a score of 0 corresponded to a DA of 4; a score of 2 corresponded to a DA of 4½; etc. Thus, each child with an average score on the 11 tasks of about 4 (i.e., DA = 5) was placed in the middle group; those with an average score of 1–3 were placed in the lowest group (DA < 5); and those with average scores of 5 and above were categorized in the most mature group (DA > 5). Gesell Institute researchers score the GSRT on the basis of global DAs, and they then place each child in one of three categories: ready for first grade; questionably ready; and unready. The three developmental age groups described above and shown in table 4 seem to correspond rather well to their readiness categories based both on maturity level of test performance and on the percentage of children in each DA group (see Ilg & Ames 1965, pp. 22–23).

In table 4, one can see how well the children in each DA group achieved in first grade. Those with DAs greater than 5 in kindergarten (i.e., the ones presumably "ready" for first grade) all scored in the upper three-quarters of the sample on the SAT in first grade. At the other extreme, two-thirds of the group with DAs less than 5 (those presumably unready) were in the lowest quarter of the sample on first-grade achievement and *none* scored in the upper quarter. Clearly, a child's level on the GSRT in kindergarten can be used to predict his achievement in first grade rather accurately.

It should be noted that the three children who repeated kindergarten on the basis of teacher recommendations (*not* GSRT scores) were included in the analysis summarized

TABLE 4. Expectancy Table Showing Percentages of Children at Three Gesell Developmental Ages in Kindergarten Performing at Different Levels of First-Grade Achievement

DEVELOPMENTAL AGE ON GSRT	N	PERCENTAGE SCORING AT DIFFERENT LEVELS ON CRITERION (SAT)		
		Lower Quarter of Sample (GE 1.55 and Under)[a]	Middle Half of Sample (GE 1.60–2.55)	Upper Quarter of Sample (GE 2.60 and Above)
Greater than 5 (total score 50 and above)	29	0	45	55
Equal to 5 (total score 39–49)	33	21	67	12
Less than 5 (total score 38 and below)	21	67	33	0

Note.—An example of how to read the table is as follows: Of the 29 children with developmental ages greater than 5, none scored in the lower quarter on the SAT; 45% scored in the middle half; and 55% scored in the upper quarter. GE = grade equivalent.
[a] Includes three children who repeated kindergarten.

TABLE 5   Expectancy Table Showing Percentages of Children in Two Kindergarten Teething Categories Performing at Different Levels of First-Grade Achievement

TEETHING CATEGORY	N	PERCENTAGE SCORING AT DIFFERENT LEVELS ON CRITERION (SAT)		
		Lower Quarter of Sample (GE 1.55 and Under) a	Middle Half of Sample (GE 1.60–2.55)	Upper Quarter of Sample (GE 2.60 and Above)
Some permanent teeth (teething level scores 3–9).........	24	21	50	29
No permanent teeth (teething level scores 0–2).........	59	27	51	22
a Includes three children who repeated kindergarten. GE = grade equivalent.				

in table 4. They were categorized in the lower quarter of the sample on first-grade achievement, which seems like a reasonable assumption (particularly since two of the three were placed back in kindergarten after spending about half a year in first grade). All of the three repeaters had DAs well below 5.

> *In Table 4, a different kind of analysis is presented. The authors divide the subjects into groups performing at different levels of achievement and show that the Gesell tests can produce a similar grouping—evidence of the test's ability to predict achievement levels.*

Table 5 is similar to table 4 as it shows the relationship of teething level to first-grade achievement. Again, the ineffectiveness of teething as a predictor of school achievement is revealed. Of the 24 children who had some permanent teeth in kindergarten, 29% scored in the upper quarter on the SAT; this was not substantially larger than the 22% of the group with no permanent teeth that scored in the upper quarter. Although the relationship of teething level with first-grade achievement was attenuated due to a restriction of range in the teeth scores (two-thirds of the children had ratings of zero), it is apparent that there was virtually no tendency for advanced teethers to perform better in first grade than those less physiologically mature.

Correspondence with Previous Research

It is well known that conventional intelligence tests have been found useful for the prediction of school achievement. The present study has shown that tests built from Piaget's and Gesell's tasks may also be quite effective as predictors of school achievement. Some other Piaget-based tests have been shown to be good predictors of arithmetic achievement (Dodwell 1961; Freyberg 1966) and of achievement in a variety of school subjects (Almy, Chittenden, & Miller 1966; Goldschmid & Bentler 1968; Miller, Stephens, & McLaughlin 1969). However, most previous studies either evaluated a Piagetian test of limited coverage or use criteria of achievement that were not at the same levels of psychometric excellence and broad curricular coverage as a major achievement battery such as SAT.

One notable exception is a longitudinal study carried out by Dudek, Lester, Goldberg, and Dyer (1969). They administered nine of Pinard and Laurendeau's (1964) 27 tests to

100 kindergarten children to obtain a broad base of evaluation on Piagetian concepts. Total score on these tests correlated .63 with composite achievement on the California Achievement Test in first grade, proving to be the best of four predictors (including two intelligence tests). This substantial correlation, together with the virtually identical correlation of the PB with the SAT found in the present study, gives strong evidence that tests built from Piaget's tasks may be very effective for the prediction of achievement in traditional school subjects. Clearly, tests based on Piaget's theory would seem to be useful for conventional curriculums and need not be restricted to those curriculums with a specific Piagetian orientation.

The results of the present study also offer strong empirical support of the effectiveness of the GSRT as a predictor of school achievement. Although Ilg and Ames have been espousing this position with fervor based on their vast clinical experience (Ames 1967; Ilg & Ames 1965), it is obvious that the empirical justification is both necessary and long overdue. However, Ilg and Ames's claim that teething level is an effective predictor of school readiness was not borne out.

The findings of the present study concerning the GSRT and teething level agree generally with the results of other investigations. Although a good objective predictive study involving the GSRT has not been carried out previously, similar kinds of perceptual-motor tasks have been shown to correlate well with school achievement. For example, the Bender-Gestalt as a single predictor or in combination with other tests has been found to be quite effective (De Hirsch, Jansky, & Langford 1966; Hammer 1967; Koppitz, Mardis, & Stephens 1961; Koppitz, Sullivan, Blyth, & Shelton 1959). Also in accord with the present study was the finding by Chase (1970) that teething level was a poor predictor of school success. Some other investigators have evaluated carpal development as a predictor of school achievement. Raymond (1967) found that this variable was not a useful predictor of children's readiness for first grade, and Karlin (1957) found carpal development to correlate significantly with reading achievement in a statistical, but not in a practical, sense (i.e., skeletal age accounted for less than 10% of the variation in reading scores).

In this section of the paper, other research studies with similar findings are reviewed.

Practical Implications of Results

Based on the present findings, it seems clear that the GSRT ought to continue being used as a predictor of school readiness. However, Gesell Institute researchers and others who follow their system would be wise to use information about children's teething level with extreme caution. The results of the present investigation, and of Chase's (1970) work, suggest that teething level may not be a useful predictor of school readiness, but they are not definitive. Those interested in the relationship of physiological maturity to school achievement would be wise to conduct additional objective studies to determine the nature of such a relationship if, indeed, it does exist.

Although the present results clearly show the GSRT to be closely associated with performance in first grade, these results should not be construed as offering complete support for Ilg and Ames's theory and educational practices. The fact that the GSRT is an excellent predictor of achievement does not imply that a bulk of the low-scoring children should be placed back into kindergarten or into transitional classes. The design of the present study was not equipped to handle that question and, in fact, it is a difficult question to study objectively. In order to show that children with low DAs would benefit by not entering first grade on schedule, two groups of low-scoring children would have to be compared; a group that was placed in special pre-first-grade classes and a group that was placed in first grade despite being behaviorally immature. If the former group could be shown to benefit more than the latter group due to their grade placement — which would be very difficult to demonstrate experimentally — then Ilg and Ames's techniques would be supported.

The present investigators would suggest that the GSRT be used to assess how well kindergarten children might achieve in first grade, and perhaps to use the GSRT results as an aid to grouping within first grade, if this is desired. However, the investigators also would urge that test users who employ the test for grade placement do so cautiously until further objective research has been done with the Gesell battery.

Theoretical Implications of Results

The close similarity of the Piaget and Gesell tests as predictors of first-grade achievement accords well with previous findings that the two tests have much in common (Kaufman 1970, 1971). This similarity might suggest that the theories from which these tests were developed also have much in common.

In recent years, many psychologists have emphasized the disparity between the maturationist theory of Gesell and the interactionist theory of Piaget (e.g., Gagne 1968; Hunt 1969; Stott & Ball 1965). Nevertheless, the results of empirical comparisons of tasks built from their theories suggest that the differences in viewpoint may be of more semantic than practical interest.

From Ames's point of view, the closeness of the two tests as predictors of achievement, "confirms our belief that there is great correspondence between our own feelings and findings and methods and those of Piaget. People who like to promote controversy are in some instances trying to show that there is a conflict between the Gesell and Piaget points of view. Actually, they complement each other rather than conflict" (Ames 1970, personal communication).

REFERENCES

Almy, M., Chittenden, E., & Miller, P. *Young children's thinking.* New York: Teachers College Press, 1966.

Ames, L. B. *Is your child in the wrong grade?* New York: Harper & Row, 1967.

Ames, L. B. Strictly for parents: learning disabilities often result from sheer immaturity. *Journal of Learning Disabilities,* 1968, **1,** 54–59.

Ames, L. B., & Ilg, F. L. Gesell behavior tests as predictive of later grade placement. *Perceptual and Motor Skills,* 1964, **19,** 719–722.

Athey, I. J., & Rubadeau, D. O. (Eds.) *Educational implications of Piaget's theory.* Waltham, Mass.: Ginn-Blaisdell, 1970.

Bloom, B. S., Hastings, J. T., & Madaus, G. F. *Handbook on formative and summative evaluation of student learning.* New York: McGraw-Hill, 1971.

Chase, J. A. Differential behavioral characteristics of non-promoted children. Unpublished doctoral dissertation, University of Maine, 1970.

De Hirsch, K., Jansky, J. J., & Langford, W. S. *Predicting reading failure.* New York: Harper & Row, 1966.

Dodwell, P. C. Children's understanding of number concepts: characteristics of an individual and of a group test. *Canadian Journal of Psychology,* 1961, **15,** 29–36.

Dudek, S. Z., Lester, E. P., Goldberg, J. S., & Dyer, G. B. Relationship of Piaget measures to standard intelligence and motor scales. *Perceptual and Motor Skills,* 1969, **28,** 351–362.

Freyberg, P. S. Concept development in Piagetian terms in relation to school attainment. *Journal of Educational Psychology,* 1966, **57,** 164–168.

Frost, J. L. (Ed.) *Early childhood education rediscovered (readings).* New York: Holt, Rinehart & Winston, 1968.

Gagne, R. M. Contributions of learning to human development. *Psychological Review,* 1968, **75,** 177–191.

Goldschmid, M. L., & Bentler, P. M. The dimensions and measurement of conservation. *Child Development,* 1968, **39,** 787–802.

Hammer, G. T. *The group Bender Gestalt Test as a predictor of academic potential in first grade, with attention of environmental effects.* (Doctoral dissertation, University of California, Los Angeles.) Ann Arbor, Mich.: University Microfilms, 1967. No. 67-11,269.

Hunt, J. McV. The impact and limitations of the giant of developmental psychology. In David Elkind and John H. Flavell (Eds.), *Studies in cognitive development.* New York: Oxford University Press, 1969. Pp. 3–66.

Ilg, F. L., & Ames, L. B. *School readiness.* New York: Harper & Row, 1965.

Inhelder, B., & Piaget, J. *The early growth of logic in the child.* New York: Norton, 1969.

Karlin, R. Physical growth and success in undertaking beginning reading. *Journal of Educational Research,* 1957, **51,** 191–202.

Kaufman, A. S. Comparison of tests built from Piaget's and Gesell's tasks: an analysis of their psychometric properties and psychological meaning. Unpublished doctoral dissertation, Teachers College, Columbia University, 1970.

Kaufman, A. S. Piaget and Gesell: a psychometric analysis of tests built from their tasks. *Child Development,* 1971, **42,** 1341–1360.

Koppitz, E. M., Mardis, V., & Stephens, T. A note on screening school beginners with the Bender Gestalt Test. *Journal of Educational Psychology,* 1961, **52,** 80–81.

Koppitz, E. M., Sullivan, J., Blyth, D. D., and Shelton, J. Prediction of first grade school achievement with the Bender Gestalt Test and human figure drawings. *Journal of Clinical Psychology,* 1959, **15,** 164–168.

Miller, C. K., Stephens, W. B., & McLaughlin, J. A. The relationship between Piaget's conservation tasks and selected psycho-educational measures. Paper presented at the annual convention of the Eastern Psychological Association, Philadelphia, April 1969.

Piaget, J. *The child's conception of number.* New York: Norton, 1965.

Piaget, J., & Inhelder, B. *The child's conception of space.* New York: Norton, 1967.

Piaget, J., Inhelder, B., & Szeminska, A. *The child's conception of geometry.* New York: Harper & Row, 1964.

Pinard, A., & Laurendeau, M. A scale of mental development based on the theory of Jean Piaget: description of a project. *Journal of Research in Science Teaching,* 1964, **2,** 253–260.

Raymond, R. J., Jr. *Skeletal age as a predictor of school readiness in "project head start" children.* (Doctoral dissertation, University of Oklahoma.) Ann Arbor, Mich: University Microfilms, 1967. No. 67-9494.

Stott, L. H., & Ball, R. S. Infant and preschool mental tests: review and evaluation. *Monographs of the Society for Research in Child Development,* 1965, **30** (101, Serial No. 3), 33–35.

Warner, W. L., Meeker, M., & Eells, K. *Social class in America.* New York: Harper & Bros., 1960.

A study such as the one you have just finished reading illustrates very nicely the uses, advantages, and limitations of the correlational approach in research. A careful selection of techniques to represent different approaches to the prediction of school achievement permitted the investigators to establish a set of relationships from measures that were developed from research based on different theories of child development.

Research such as this has many practical benefits. The information gained from such studies as the one by Kaufman and Kaufman can aid educators interested in improving the methods by which they evaluate performance in school. However, it should be remembered that correlations are subject to a number of restrictions on the form of the data, the shape of the relationships, and the nature of the underlying distributions, and they need to be evaluated very carefully to insure that no conditions exist which might produce falsely high correlations, or indicate a relationship where none exists. Also, to obtain stable prediction equations with multiple R's it is necessary to have large samples. One must also cross-validate—carry out the study on a second sample and see how well the equations from the first sample will predict the relationships in the second.

NON-PARAMETRIC MEASURES OF CORRELATION

In a strict sense, two non-parametric measures have already been discussed. Both the contingency coefficient and the Spearman rank-difference coefficient are non-parametric in the sense that they are not dependent on the assumptions of a normal distribution. However, they are not usually thought of as non-parametric, whereas the following two measures are:

1. *Kendall rank-correlation coefficient*, symbolized by the letter tau, (τ), is a method of determining the relationship between two sets of ranks.

2. *Kendall coefficient of concordance*, (W), is a measure to determine the degree of association among several sets of ranks simultaneously.

A FEW REMARKS ABOUT TESTS (PSYCHOLOGICAL AND OTHERWISE)

Strictly speaking, the topic of tests and their construction is outside the scope of this book. However, understanding how tests are developed and constructed may be fundamental to evaluating the worth of research work. If a research study bases its conclusions either all or in part on a test that is inappropriate, out of date, or of dubious validity, the research, even if properly conducted, will have conclusions that are suspect.

It is also quite possible that individuals using this book may have occasion to investigate the possibility of using tests as part of their own professional work. Under such circumstances, knowing how to evaluate a test is of considerable importance. The appropriate test, used in the proper circumstances, can result in considerable improvement in the selection of people for particular tasks or for particular aptitudes or abilities. A test that is inappropriate or invalid for the purposes for which it is used may result in the serious misplacement or miscategorization of individuals for particular tasks or abilities.

Types of Tests

The following selected list indicates some of the areas for which tests have been constructed and published.

Intelligence	Spatial ability
Special aptitudes	Mechanical comprehension
College admission	Complex performance
Vocational Interest	Creativity
Personality measurement	Artistic ability

Any individual seeking specific information about tests should consult such works as Anastasi, A., *Differential Psychology*, 3rd ed., New York, Macmillan, 1958, or Cronbach, L. J., *Essentials of Psychological Testing*, 3rd ed., New York, Harper & Row, 1970. An excellent account is also given in Helmstader, G. C., *Principles of Psychological Measurement*, New York, Appleton-Century-Crofts, 1964. Books such as these not only offer information about types of tests and their characteristics but also provide a good general background on the techniques of developing tests, the problems involved in their use, and the criteria that a test should meet to be considered valid. A comprehensive listing of tests along with critical reviews can be found in Buros, O. K. (Ed.), *The Mental Measurements Yearbooks*, Highland Park, N.J., Gryphon Press, 1941–1965 (irregular).

Considerations in Evaluating a Test

1. Purpose of the Test. It seems foolishly obvious to say that a test should be appropriate for the purpose for which it is going to be used. However, the relevance or irrelevance of a particular test may not be immediately obvious. There is no shortage of research articles containing such statements as: "As a measure of emotional control, the Birdbatth test of Response to Authority was given to 34 subjects..." If, upon reading this, you accept uncritically that the Birdbatth test is an adequate measure of emotional control, you have then placed a considerable constraint on how much you will question any results that are reported. If you go and look up the Birdbatth test and find that Birdbatth designed his test as a measure of submissiveness to authority, you might well question how this test came to be construed as a "measure of emotional control." Redefining a test does not make it automatically valid for the new purpose for which it was redefined.

2. Tests As Commercial Products. There seems to be a tolerance for published tests that far exceeds the tolerance that would be allowed in evaluating other kinds of products. Individuals interested in selecting a test to measure a particular quality often choose tests indiscriminately, with the apparent attitude that the person who constructed a given test should be rewarded by an unqualified acceptance of his work, with no question as to whether his test actually means what he says it means. There is also the attitude that a given test seems "pretty good," and even though it may not be exactly what is wanted, it is probably close enough.

A much more appropriate attitude would be to consider a test the way you would any other commercial product. The authors and publishers of a test are offering it for sale and are claiming that the test will measure certain qualities or aptitudes. Since the test is offered for sale as a way of making money for the author and publisher, it should be evaluated on its merits and not simply on the basis of the claims of the publisher as to what it will accomplish.[2] The author and publisher should be prepared to offer some solid and definitive evidence that the test offered is actually valid for the purpose claimed.

3. Types of Validity. There are several categorizations of validity in testing, each with its particular advantages and drawbacks.

FACE VALIDITY. Perhaps the simplest form of validity is what is known as face validity. Face validity means that the test is judged by the very nature of the items in it to be valid for the purposes for which it is to be used. For example, a test item such as "I am over 6 feet tall. True_____ False_____" is valid by definition for the purpose of determining whether or not an individual is over 6 feet tall, as long as you assume that he answers it truthfully.

While that particular example may seem somewhat fanciful, it is easy to see how test items could be constructed that would seem valid for a particular purpose simply because of the way in which they were worded. In general, face valid tests can be considered worthless. The opinion of an individual, no matter how well qualified, as to what a test measures, is simply not a very good basis for determining the validity of a test (see p. 156).

CRITERION VALIDITY. In establishing the criterion validity of a test, some level of proficiency or skill is usually established. For example, it is possible to establish definite criteria for certain types of skills, such as flying an airplane. Validating a test against a criterion basically consists of establishing the fact that persons meeting or surpassing the criterion do considerably better on the test than persons who do not meet the criterion. In some cases, it must be demonstrated that persons reaching differing levels of ability on the criterion are similarly differentiated on the test.

In general, validation against a criterion can be a quite satisfactory method of establishing validity. However, it should be remembered that criteria are not permanent and everlasting. The sorts of skills that enabled a person to fly an airplane in 1930 may still be valid, but today a great many more skills are needed in addition. Many professions change so drastically within a 5- or 10-year period that criteria established prior to that time may be almost useless. Evaluating a test validated against a criterion requires that the time of validation and the changes that may have taken place also be considered. It is equally true that a test validated against a particular criterion can be considered in terms of that criterion *only*; it is inappropriate to generalize the usefulness or validity of the test beyond the specific criterion, unless additional validation data is collected.

CONSTRUCT VALIDITY. Construct validity is a considerably more complex process than the other types of validity discussed to this point. To develop the validity of a construct, the first step is to postulate that a certain test measures a certain characteristic of individuals. The next step is to postulate that individuals possessing this characteristic should show a certain kind of behavior as opposed to individuals not possessing such characteristics. Data must then be collected to see if this postulated relationship does in fact occur. Other kinds of postulates must be put forth and again tested by experiments to see if the relationships hold true.

As an example, take a construct such as "socialization." Socialization is an abstraction which must be defined in detail to be useful. The person testing for it can specify that behaviors represented by socialization would include such things as respect for and approval of law and order, concern for the rights and privileges of others, and attitudes of honesty and directness in transactions. He can then go on to develop some measures that he believes will measure this construct in people. Having developed his measure, he must then, to carry out construct validation, be prepared to state that people scoring high on his test will show certain specific patterns of behavior that are not true for people who have low scores. For example, he can postulate that people who score high on his measure, if put in an experimental situation where it is possible to cheat in order to win more money, will cheat much less often than people who have low scores. He must then carry out such an experiment to demonstrate that such differences in behavior actually exist between people scoring high and low on his measure.

This represents the first step in validating a test by the method of construct validity. As is evident, this is considerably more difficult and more demanding than validation by the other methods described. Basically, the process is the same as that used to validate scientific theories. In terms of knowing much more precisely what behaviors a test relates to, construct validation, although much more demanding, certainly provides a much better measure than any other method of validation.

VALIDATION AGAINST ANOTHER TEST (CONGRUENT VALIDITY). The process of validating one test in terms of another is quite common, particularly for developing a new test to measure particular abilities that is less time consuming than an existing test. However, the validity of the new test is then a direct function of the validity of the test it is validated against. If a new measure is validated against a test of doubtful validity, it can be no better than the original measure and may well be worse, depending on the reliability of the original measure.

THE VALIDITY OF SUBTESTS. This topic is not concerned with the direct validation of a test per se, but it should be mentioned in any discussion of validity. Many tests contain subtests that are supposed to measure different aspects of a particular ability (such as the subjects that make up many of the individually administered intelligence tests). In such a test it is always tempting to speculate what differences between subtests may mean. Without going into the mathematical reasons, let it be said that the reliability of the differences between two tests can be no greater than the reliability of the tests themselves. Unless the test has an extremely high reliability, the chances of the subject differences being reliable are near zero.

4. Other Considerations

TEST SCORING. There are many ways of scoring tests, some requiring considerable statistical sophistication to understand. However, it is the obligation of the test author and publisher to furnish clear documentation on the methods of scoring and the reasons for choosing the approach that was taken.

DOCUMENTATION. It is also the responsibility of the author and publisher to provide full and complete documentation of the validity and reliability of the test, the methods used to determine the validity and reliability, the subjects on whom the test was developed and on whom it was standardized, and all other information that is relevant to the use of the test. As an illustration of what should be provided, see the publication of the American Psychological Association, "Technical Recommendations for Psychological Tests and Diagnostic Techniques."[3] Admittedly, the standards set by this association are difficult to meet, but tests that do meet their criteria will seldom provide incorrect or misleading information.

FOOTNOTES

[1]*Nostra culpa.* We (the authors) once wrote a simple, multiple-choice exam to be used as one of the outcome measures in research we were conducting. Since we had reasonable confidence in our ability to write examination questions on material read, we did not bother to carry out any validation studies. Initial results were confusing, and as part of the process of clarifying our procedure we gave the examination to two samples of subjects similar to those used in the experiment. One sample of subjects

read the material for which the exam was written and the other sample answered the examination without reading the material. To our embarrassment, 8 out of the 20 questions were found to be more likely to be answered correctly when the subjects had *not* read the material. New items were prepared and a considerable amount of time was spent insuring that the revised examination really did discriminate between subjects who had and had not read the selection in question.

[2]An all too common practice among test developers is to attach the name of a university to a test, thus attempting to link the prestige of the University to the test. The fact that a test is called "The Stanford Apathy Test" or the "Michigan Malpractice and Perjury Inventory" usually means nothing more than that one of the developers of the test was at a particular University at the time this test was developed. There is no indication whatever by this practice that a university is associated with or endorses a particular test.

[3]Supplement to the *Psychological Bulletin*, 1954, **51**(2):2. Published by The American Psychological Association, Inc., 1700 Seventeenth Street, N.W., Washington, D.C., 1967.

chapter ten

factor and cluster analysis

The statistical methods known as factor analysis and cluster analysis are methods of great complexity, and for this reason we have chosen to discuss them in a separate chapter. Factor and cluster analysis will be treated as basically the same procedures, since they differ primarily in refinements in calculational procedures and not in interpretation. The actual processes and calculations undertaken in factor and cluster analysis are a mystery even to many competent research workers, principally because of the advanced mathematical background required to understand the computational process. Because of this, these techniques are often accorded more respect and veneration than perhaps they deserve.

The majority of factor and cluster analyses begin with a table of scores. From these scores a table of correlations is computed and arranged so that the Pearson r between all possible pairs of measures is known. For example, all possible correlations between five measures would be arranged in the following manner:

		MEASURES				
		1	2	3	4	5
MEASURES	1	(—)	.73	.26	.51	−.04
	2		(—)	.10	.85	.31
	3			(—)	.22	−.67
	4				(—)	.66
	5					(—)

By examining the correlations in the body of the table, we can see the relation of each measure to the others. For example, measure 1 has quite a high correlation with measure 2, a low correlation with measure 3, a fairly high correlation with measure 4, and practically no correlation with measure 5. Measure 2 has almost no correlation with measure 3, but a high correlation with measure 4, and a moderately low correlation with measure 5.

As you can seen, with a small set of measures such as this, it is possible to trace out the relationships just by inspecting the table. We would probably conclude that measures 1, 2 and 4, because of their high degree of inter-correlation, all have something in common. If these three measures were all measures of verbal skills, for example, we would expect fairly high positive relationships. If measure 1 were the score on a vocabulary test, measure 2 the score on a test of knowledge of antonyms of a set of words, and measure 4 the score on a test of ability to identify synonyms, we would not be surprised to find that a person who did very well on one measure also did well on the others. If measures 3 and 5 were based on a different kind of skill, such as the ability to grasp spatial relationships or to perform fine motor coordinations, we would not be too surprised if they showed low relationships with the verbal measures.

What we have done by inspecting this table and concluding that meas-ures 1, 2, and 4 are all indicators of the same common ability is similar to what the mathematical procedures of factor analysis accomplish. For five measures, it is relatively easy to inspect a table and to conclude what it is that certain measures have in common. This task soon becomes impossible as the number of measures increases. For example, the number of intercorrelations between 30 measures is 435. Clearly, it is virtually impossible to trace patterns of asso-ciation within that many intercorrelations. The methods of factor and cluster analysis have been developed to accomplish just such a task.

Before proceeding, you might wish to review part of Chapter 9, specifi-cally pages 146–150 on the limitations of the correlation coefficient and the conditions that data must meet for the Pearson r to be valid. A factor analysis can be carried out just as easily on invalid and meaningless correlations as on perfectly valid data, and there is nothing about the mathematical procedure which will indicate this, with the possible exception of difficulty in interpret-ing the results.

No attempt will be made here to describe any of the processes of calcula-tion, since understanding such calculation methods requires a moderately good background in calculus and matrix algebra.[1] It is sufficient to note that, through a series of calculations so extensive in nature as to be impractical without a large electronic computer, a series of factors are extracted from the table of intercorrelations. These factors are groupings of measures that are as-sociated with one another.

It is at this point in the analysis that the calculation techniques are of no further use and the judgment of the research worker takes over. A factor analy-sis does not *per se* come out with a result that says: "These measures go together and this group of measures goes together, and this measure does not group with anything else." When we perform a factor analysis we obtain a set of what are called *factor loadings*. A table of factor loadings for the five-measure example shown earlier might look something like the following:

MEASURES	Factors		
	I	II	III
1	.84	−.09	.11
2	.73	.01	.00
3	.21	.94	−.05
4	.71	−.21	.20
5	.00	.85	.13

The factor loadings are the numbers in the body of the table. The magnitude of the number is the indication of how much a given measure is associated with a given factor. For our purposes we can consider factor loadings to vary from 0.00 (no association) to plus or minus 1.00 (perfect relationship). According to the table, the calculation indicates that three factors are present. In Factor I, Measure 1 has a loading of .84, measure 2 a loading of .73, measure 3 a loading of .21, and so forth. The interpretation of factor loadings is similar to the interpretation of correlation coefficients (and with the same reservations): the higher the magnitude of the loading, the more that measure is associated with that factor. For this example, high factor loadings are present on Factor I for Measures 1, 2, and 4, and high factor loadings are present on Factor II for Measures 3 and 5.

Factor III is somewhat different. There are no loadings of any size present on Factor III, and we would probably dismiss it as not being a meaningful factor, limiting our interpretations to Factors I and II.

The process as described to this point is basically what a research worker who has carried out a factor analysis goes through in interpreting his data. Now let us re-examine some of the events:

1. The majority of factor analysis techniques can produce as many factors as there are measures, unless the calculation is stopped after a certain number of factors have been found. The criterion that is used to decide when enough factors have been found is arbitrary and is a decision that must be made by the research worker; factors can be extracted completely beyond meaning. For a problem with 35 measures, a reasonable guess would be that perhaps 5 to 8 meaningful factors would be found. Under unusual circumstances, this number might increase, but it is rather difficult to think of a set of data where 35 measures might result in as many as 20 meaningful factors. Factor analysis has as a goal the determination of common factors among a set of measures, and if the measures do not show very high correlations with each other, there is no point in doing the analysis.

2. The interpretation of the meaningfulness of the factors is entirely up to the research worker. There is nothing intrinsic about factor or cluster analytic methods that requires the measure grouped together to assume a sensible pattern to the researcher. For example, suppose a set of correlations of measures are obtained for college students and that these correlations are based on psychological test data, physical and physiological measures, political attitudes, and some information about the parents of the students. A factor analysis is performed and the first factor has the largest factor loadings on the following measures:

1. Intelligence
2. Weight
3. Age of mother at marriage

4. Blood pressure

5. Political affiliation of father

It would take a rather ingenious investigator to come up with an explanation that would encompass such a grouping. However, such groupings can happen, particularly under conditions where data of dubious reliability and validity are intercorrelated and little or no check is made on the validity of the correlations. There is nothing about a factor analysis that will resurrect or rehabilitate poor data—a factor analysis, like any other statistical technique, is no better than the data on which it is calculated.

3. The interpretation of a set of factor loadings is arbitrarily determined by the research worker. The point at which a factor loading is not thought to be meaningful is also an arbitrary decision made by the researcher. There are some constraints on this process; for example, a research worker who places great emphasis on a factor loading of .21 being present for a particular measure is in a position analogous to someone talking about the amazingly high relationship indicated by a correlation of .21! Nevertheless, it is the research worker who decides that he will include only those measures with loadings above .70 in his interpretation of the meaning of a given factor. If the cut-off point were to be lowered, and all measures with a factor loading of .50 were included, the interpretation of the factor, given the measures now included, might be radically different. The point is that a great deal of arbitrary judgment enters into factor and cluster analysis—a fact which is frequently overlooked. You do not have to accept either the interpretation given or the groupings as such.

4. In published research reports of factor analyses, you will frequently find such statements as "rotation to simple structure was done" or "a Varimax rotation was done." The rotation of factors is an additional calculation that often helps reduce ambiguity present in the initial analysis. The process of interpretation, as described earlier, is made easier, but the essential process is not changed by the use of rotation methods.

5. In factor analysis, as in other statistical methods, the number of subjects is an important consideration in evaluating the results. An elaborate factor analysis carried out on 10 subjects is probably not worth much because of the limited sample of individuals. Another consideration to keep in mind is that, for the analysis to be meaningful, the number of subjects should be considerably greater than the number of measures; the closer the number of measures to the number of subjects, the less confidence we can have in the meaningfulness of the entire analysis.

To illustrate how a factor analysis is reported and interpreted, we have reprinted one of our own research articles, in which this technique was employed.

The data were based on an extensive investigation of the effects of therapeutic brain lesions on the behavior of Parkinson patients. Parkinsonism is a disease occurring in individuals of advanced middle age and is characterized by weakness in the lower limbs, inability to make coordinated body movements, and tremors ranging from a mild trembling to shaking movements so extreme that the person is unable to carry out most acts requiring the use of the arms and hands. It is accompanied by a shuffling gait and a masklike facial expression. Surgical techniques have been developed that have been quite successful in either eliminating these symptoms or greatly reducing their severity. The research was an attempt to evaluate the effectiveness of the surgery by comparing the motor and speech performance of the patient before surgery with the performance three months after surgery.

To investigate this problem, two separate factor analyses were carried out. The first analysis was an examination of the factors and patterns of factor loadings for a group of 40 patients prior to surgery for Parkinsonism. The second factor analysis was done on the same 40 patients three months after surgery, and this analysis was then compared with the first analysis.

Unlike the earlier articles we have presented, this article will carry no accompanying commentary. It was originally written for a medical journal whose readers would not have very much familiarity with factor analysis as a method of analyzing data, and consequently, the report contains more explanatory material about the process of factor analysis and its interpretation than such studies usually provide.

Behavioral Changes in Parkinson Patients Following Surgery*

A FACTOR ANALYTIC STUDY

LEWIS PETRINOVICH and CURTIS HARDYCK

The medical literature on the effectiveness of therapeutic procedures in altering symptom patterns leaves one with a feeling of dissatisfaction. Too often the evaluation of therapeutic effectiveness is highly subjective—a state of affairs which makes it difficult for one clinician to communicate his procedures to another. This state of affairs also makes it difficult to evaluate the relative effectiveness of one therapeutic technique as compared with another.

If the clinical evaluation of medical procedures is to be on a scientific basis the data on which such evaluations are based must be as objective as possible, minimizing the clinician's subjective biases.

The problem of obtaining objective evaluations is quite evident in the treatment of Parkinsonism. The usual evaluative techniques involves the clinician's subjective evaluation of the change in efficiency of motor performance along some coarse, global continuum such as excellent results, good results, bad results. It is obvious that this is not satisfactory since the basis for the clinician's judgement is often not easy to discern. It is also clear to anyone who has examined Parkinsonian patients that the symptom pattern is quite different for different patients with the same diagnosis. It is impossible to determine in what area improvement has occurred when global ratings are used and it is just as impos-

*This research was supported by Grant ≠RD 554, Office of Vocational Rehabilitation.

This article originally appeared in *J. chron. Dis.* 1964, Vol. 17, pp. 225–233, and is reprinted with permission from Pergamon Press Ltd.

sible to know the clinician's subjective weighting of equal amounts of change in the several different motor dimensions involved.

Arthur A. Ward, Jr. expressed this same point of view, ". . . (There is) a major clinical problem that must be faced by anybody dealing with the problem of Parkinsonism; namely, the objective description and quantification of the disabilities. Objective data obviously are urgently needed if judgements are to be made regarding the efficiency of therapy, either surgical or medical" [1].

The purpose of this report is to present an objective method for evaluating the efficiency of motor function. An analysis will then be made of the pattern of motor symptoms associated with Parkinsonism. "Patients with Parkinsonism have a very complex type of disability and it is certainly very difficult to obtain objective data that are completely satisfactory" [1]. Obviously, if the disability is complex, a single global rating cannot adequately represent the many significant changes that might occur.

The method of evaluation to be presented uses sound motion pictures of patients performing a routine series of tasks. This paper presents the data for 40 patients preoperatively and for 30 patients three months postoperatively.

The preoperative ratings have been factor analyzed, the principal factors have been identified, and each patient has been assigned a score for each factor. This procedure is an objective, empirical description of the symptom pattern. The postoperative ratings were then factor analyzed, and the differences in the factor structure for the two analyses examined.

METHOD

Subjects

The subjects are 40 patients with a diagnosis of Parkinsonism. They are an unselected series and can be considered to represent a cross-section of the population treated at the Mt. Zion Institute. The mean age of the group at the time of the surgery is 57, ranging between 36 and 73 years. There were 25 males and 15 females. Of the 40 patients, 26 were followed 3 months postoperatively. In addition to these 26 patients, 4 patients were included in the 3-month postoperative group for whom preoperative movies were not available. The mean age of these 30 patients at the time of surgery was 55, ranging between 36 and 71 years; 18 were males and 12 were females.

Surgical Procedure

The surgical procedure has been described in detail elsewhere [1, 2]. It involves two steps: (1) a first stage, under general anesthetic, in which the target areas are localized and trephination is done; (2) a second stage, under local anesthetic, in which the therapeutic lesion is produced by heating the tissue at the tip of an electrode which contains a thermister bead. The targets are points within the ventrolateral nucleus of the thalamus and the globus pallidus.

Rating Procedure

The rating method has been described in detail elsewhere [1]. Briefly, a sound motion picture is taken of each patient performing a routine series of tasks. Their performance is rated by a panel of judges working independently. These ratings are made of movies taken before surgical treatment, 3 months following surgery, 1 year following surgery, and at one year intervals thereafter. The movies were rated in random sequence and the judges were given no information concerning the status of the patient at the time, i.e., preoperative or postoperative.

The following variables were rated (1) walking; (2) arm swing right; (3) arm swing left; (4) turning right; (5) turning left; (6) standing posture; (7) rising; (8) sitting; (9) general gross motor skill; (10) ability to grasp a glass of water and drink it with the right hand; (11) identical with (10) for the left hand; (12) ability to draw a circle, a triangle, and a spiral with the right hand; (13) identical with (12) for the left hand; (14) ability to write the phrase 'How are you' with the right hand; (15) ability to move the fingers independently up and down rhythmically 'as though playing a piano' with the right hand; (16) identical with (15) for the left hand; ability to round (17) and to spread (18) the lips several times as fast as possible, as though saying 'ooo - - - eee'; (19) ability to move the protruded tongue from side to side as rapidly as possible several times (lateral tongue movement); (20) facial expression right; (21) facial expression left; (22) speech intelligibility; (23) general efficiency rating; (24) face tremor; (25) upper limb tremor right; (26) upper limb tremor left; (27) lower limb tremor right; (28) lower limb tremor left.

Each variable was rated on a 9-point scale. The extremes of the scale are defined as 1 — incapacitated; unable to perform test even with assistance: 9 — superior performance; a performance that is superior for a 'normal' person of that age. The midpoint of the scale is defined as follows: 5 — moderate involvement; fair performance; a functional performance but accomplished slowly and with some difficulty. The complete definition of the rating numbers is given by Levin et al. [1]. The mean rating of the 9 judges is obtained for each of the 28 items in the movie scenario.

To determine the intra-judge reliabilities of the movie ratings 8 movies were rated twice by all judges. The mean of the 28 items was obtained and a correlational analysis was made. The average intra-judge reliability for these ratings is +0.87. The judges, therefore; are highly reliable in their ratings of the same movie.

To establish whether or not the judges were rating the same thing each judge's ratings were correlated with those of every other judge for the same 8 movies. The average inter-judge reliability is +0.80. This indicates that there was a high degree of agreement between different judges rating the same thing.

It is apparent, therefore, that the movies provide a highly reliable, objective method of assessing motor proficiency. Another advantage of this rating method is that the movies furnish a permanent record to which one can refer at a later time if any questions arise concerning a patient.

Statistical Procedure

Perhaps a brief statement outlining the logic of factor analysis will be of benefit here. To the extent that a set of variables intercorrelates, the variables can be said to share certain elements in common. For example, various measures of motor skills may possess in common the attributes of speed, accuracy, steadiness, etc. Factor analysis is a mathematical method of isolating these characteristics from a set of variables and grouping them together. A factor then, is a grouping of variables that have a certain characteristic in common. It accomplishes mathematically what can be done by inspection for a small group of variables but becomes too Herculean and confusing a task for large numbers of variables. The *loading* of a variable on a factor is a measure of the extent to which a given factor is present in a given variable. Factor loadings can reach a maximum of 1.00.

Rotation of factors is another mathematical technique which reduces the ambiguity often present in the preliminary analysis. It is best regarded as a mathematical method for deciding which factor a given variable is primarily associated with.

The composited ratings for 40 patients were first intercorrelated and the resulting matrix examined for first-order relationships. The variables are less highly related than would be expected on an intuitive basis. Out of a total of 378 intercorrelations, only 41 reach a

Intercorrelation Matrix Showing Relationships Among the 28 Variables Defined on Page 183

	1	2	3	4	5	6	7	8	9	10	11	12	13	14	15	16	17	18	19	20	21	22	23	24	25	26	27	28
1		.59	.58	.91	.92	.82	.82	.86	.92	.42	.42	.48	.34	.40	.53	.40	.28	.33	-.09	.60	.60	.16	.80	.01	.03	.11	.33	.23
2			.27	.60	.60	.60	.54	.53	.61	.51	.09	.60	.09	.49	.54	.02	.24	.25	-.18	.47	.34	.06	.59	.23	.38	-.03	.42	.21
3				.62	.61	.58	.56	.58	.63	.20	.52	.21	.49	.14	.20	.52	.21	.24	.02	.36	.44	.14	.55	-.06	-.10	.28	.28	.36
4					.95	.87	.86	.89	.95	.39	.44	.48	.36	.38	.52	.44	.32	.37	-.05	.64	.64	.20	.83	.02	.02	.09	.39	.28
5						.86	.86	.89	.95	.39	.47	.48	.37	.38	.51	.43	.33	.37	-.06	.63	.63	.20	.82	.02	.01	.09	.38	.28
6							.86	.89	.89	.47	.44	.55	.45	.43	.54	.46	.45	.49	.03	.68	.67	.27	.85	.17	.15	.19	.41	.30
7								.78	.84	.36	.47	.43	.33	.34	.16	.39	.26	.32	-.06	.56	.56	.17	.74	.00	.01	.07	.34	.26
8									.81	.26	.41	.43	.32	.34	.47	.39	.20	.27	-.11	.54	.56	.12	.74	.12	.17	.07	.34	.22
9										.66	.42	.42	.32	.34	.58	.50	.41	.47	-.01	.71	.69	.25	.89	.28	.06	.02	.28	.22
10											.51	.55	.45	.44	.63	.10	.36	.37	-.15	.45	.35	.18	.61	.28	.46	-.01	.16	.07
11												.22	.28	.13	.19	.66	.39	.20	-.01	.53	.53	.26	.54	.04	-.14	.37	.06	.07
12													.20	.69	.77	.10	.38	.43	.20	.56	.44	.13	.55	.49	.51	.48	.22	.05
13														.66	.13	.10	.36	.37	.26	.40	.52	.30	.62	.01	.13	.01	.22	.29
14															.17	.67	.48	.46	-.11	.46	.75	.10	.70	.30	-.14	.37	.12	-.01
15																.04	.40	.48	-.11	.60	.50	.20	.71	.49	.02	.41	.13	-.08
16																	.45	.48	.04	.43	.60	.37	.66	.04	.48	.37	.11	.21
17																		.87	.52	.73	.59	.37	.52	.53	.24	.31	.05	-.05
18																			.51	.76	.73	.61	.62	.48	.20	.29	.03	-.08
19																				.31	.77	.61	.66	.29	-.10	.26	-.12	-.14
20																					.75	.48	.79	.11	.19	.15	.17	-.01
21																						.50	.78	.29	.02	.22	.07	-.01
22																							.54	.26	.01	.22	-.01	-.10
23																								.36	.22	.21	.29	.19
24																									.43	.21	.27	.07
25																										.04	.31	.14
26																											.27	.38
27																												.57

value greater than +0.70. This high degree of independence within the matrix, in conjunction with the obtained reliability of +0.80 offers convincing evidence for the validity of the ratings.

Following the initial examination of the intercorrelations, a principal-components [3] factor analysis was computed. This was done at the Computer Center on the Berkeley campus of the University of California. The Multivariate Statistical Package System was used to perform the computations.

The initial estimates of the communalities were made by selecting the highest correlation of the variable with any other variable.

The original intercorrelation matrix for the first factor analysis, which was not printed in the original article, is reprinted here as an aid to understanding the discussion at the end of the article.

RESULTS

Analysis I

Five factors with latent roots greater than 1.00 were identified and subject to varimax rotation (see Table 1 for the rotated loadings).

Examination of the rotated factors yielded several clearly defined functional groupings of variables.

Factor I contains extremely high loadings on the variables of walking, turning right, turning left, arm swing left, arm swing right, standing, rising, sitting, general gross motor skill, and general efficiency rating. Smaller loadings are also present on the variables facial expression right and facial expression left. This factor best defines general *gross motor efficiency*.

Factor II contains high loadings on the variables of lips rounded, lips spread, lateral tongue movement, facial expression right, facial expression left, face tremor, and speech intelligibility. This factor would best seem to represent *speech and facial motor characteristics*.

Factor III has the largest loadings on the variables of arm swing right, drinking right, drawing right, fingers right, writing right, and upper limb tremor right. There seems to be little question here that this factor clearly represents *right side function*.

Factor IV contains only two loadings of significant size; lower limb tremor left and lower limb tremor right. It is highly questionable as to whether this is a meaningful factor, containing as it does, only two variables. It is possible that lower limb tremor, being rather difficult to rate is more subject to judge error and unreliability than many of our other variables. In our original intercorrelation matrix, these variables correlate highly with each other and not significantly with any other variables. This indicates that there may be a halo effect in rating.

Factor V contains the largest loadings on the variables of drinking left, drawing left, finger movement left, and upper limb tremor left. As in the loadings with Factor III, Factor V is easily identifiable as a *left side factor*.

In summarizing the results of the preoperative factor analysis, the factor patterns suggest an interesting and highly functional grouping of the motor behavior characteristic of Parkinsonism.

Analysis II

For the second analysis, the technique and method of procedure was identical with that of the first and five factors were again extracted from the second intercorrelation matrix. (See Table 2 for the rotated loadings.)

TABLE 1. Rotated Factor Loadings for Analysis I (Pre-operative)

VARIABLE NO.	I	II	III	IV	V	h²
1	0.90	0.04	0.22	0.05	0.14	0.89
2	0.54	0.03	0.50	0.26	0.16	0.64
3	0.57	0.02	-0.02	0.16	0.46	0.57
4	0.94	0.10	0.17	0.12	0.14	0.97
5	0.95	0.09	0.17	0.06	0.12	0.96
6	0.79	0.22	0.29	0.20	0.22	0.86
7	0.85	0.06	0.15	0.10	0.14	0.78
8	0.90	-0.02	0.14	0.00	0.15	0.86
9	0.91	0.16	0.26	0.07	0.23	0.98
10	0.25	0.02	0.80	0.00	0.15	0.74
11	-0.35	0.18	0.03	0.04	0.70	0.65
12	-0.33	0.12	0.84	0.04	0.06	0.85
13	0.21	0.26	0.13	0.09	0.77	0.74
14	0.27	0.09	0.71	0.04	0.00	0.59
15	0.43	0.21	0.66	0.12	0.04	0.69
16	0.35	0.34	-0.12	0.02	0.68	0.72
17	0.15	0.82	0.34	0.02	0.24	0.88
18	0.22	0.81	0.33	0.05	0.25	0.90
19	-0.11	0.69	-0.20	0.06	0.17	0.56
20	0.54	0.61	0.36	0.02	0.11	0.82
21	0.55	0.62	0.20	0.12	0.30	0.84
22	-0.13	0.68	0.00	0.04	0.13	0.50
23	-0.70	0.34	0.48	0.06	0.32	0.95
24	-0.12	0.56	0.32	0.38	0.13	0.40
25	-0.12	0.09	0.64	0.37	0.17	0.61
26	-0.05	0.26	-0.08	0.41	0.52	0.52
27	0.30	-0.03	0.11	0.76	0.02	0.68
28	0.19	-0.20	-0.03	0.68	0.32	0.65

Factor I remains essentially unchanged from the first analysis. Factor I again has the highest loadings on walking, sitting, turning right, turning left, standing, rising, general gross motor skill, and general efficiency. This factor remains, as before, an indicator of general *gross motor efficiency.*

Factor II also remains essentially unchanged from the first analysis. The largest loadings are on speech intelligibility, lips rounded, lips spread, facial expression right, facial expression left and lateral tongue. This factor remains an unambiguous *speech and facial motor factor.*

Factor III in our second analysis has departed considerably from the right side factor identified in the first analysis. Only three loadings are of a size sufficient to warrant attention, these loadings appearing on drawing right, drawing left, and writing right. The pattern present here is one of *fine motor skills* and we have labeled this factor as such.

Factor IV again represents a departure from the results of the first analysis, the significant loadings now appearing on face tremor, upper limb tremor left, upper limb tremor right, and lower limb tremor right. This factor is easily identifiable as a *tremor factor.* This factor bears some resemblance to Factor IV of the first analysis, but is now of much greater generality than in Analysis I.

Factor V in this analysis is in a somewhat similar position to Factor IV in the first analysis; it is perhaps best identified as an artifact. The only loadings in this factor are those of fingers right and fingers left; two variables of low correlation with all other variables except each other.

TABLE 2. Rotated Factor Loadings for Analysis II (Post-operative)

VARIABLE NO.	I	II	III	IV	V	h²
1	0.85	0.35	0.23	−0.02	−0.19	0.95
2	0.75	0.22	0.03	−0.17	−0.03	0.65
3	0.65	0.20	−0.00	−0.10	−0.30	0.57
4	0.85	0.35	0.19	0.00	−0.15	0.93
5	0.84	0.35	0.22	−0.05	−0.18	0.93
6	0.72	0.45	0.34	−0.06	−0.30	0.94
7	0.83	0.35	0.24	−0.16	−0.13	0.93
8	0.88	0.27	0.20	−0.20	−0.15	0.96
9	0.84	0.39	0.26	−0.07	−0.20	0.98
10	0.22	0.38	0.22	−0.03	−0.14	0.27
11	0.66	0.17	0.33	0.04	−0.37	0.72
12	0.14	0.17	0.93	−0.11	0.01	0.94
13	0.34	0.11	0.80	−0.00	−0.05	0.78
14	0.19	0.13	0.93	−0.08	−0.00	0.93
15	0.27	0.09	−0.00	−0.10	−0.75	0.66
16	0.33	0.09	0.02	−0.08	−0.85	0.85
17	0.30	0.81	0.00	−0.17	0.09	0.78
18	0.42	0.74	−0.05	−0.15	0.00	0.75
19	0.32	0.62	−0.18	−0.38	−0.12	0.68
20	0.34	0.80	0.24	−0.11	−0.09	0.84
21	0.35	0.77	0.28	−0.09	−0.25	0.88
22	0.12	0.84	0.27	−0.09	−0.08	0.82
23	0.68	0.56	0.30	−0.03	−0.30	0.96
24	0.31	0.28	0.13	−0.68	0.00	0.67
25	0.09	0.12	−0.05	−0.64	0.14	0.46
26	0.01	0.21	0.07	−0.67	−0.22	0.56
27	0.49	−0.13	−0.09	−0.38	0.17	0.44
28	−0.02	0.00	0.12	−0.61	−0.19	0.43

DISCUSSION

At this point, having presented the results of our analyses and the changes that occur in the factorial structure, it now remains to deal with the interpretation of this change. The communalities for both analyses indicate a high degree of generality for the variables across the obtained factors, accounting as they do for a large percentage of the variance in all variables.

The communality of a variable in a factor analysis is a measure of the extent to which that variable is accounted for by the factors. As can be seen in Tables 1 and 2, the communalities (h²), which can reach a maximum of 1.00 are all quite large.

Do the changes in the obtained factor structure represent real changes in behavior? Evidence from several sources can be marshalled for the affirmative.

The most interesting aspect of the changes in factor structure is the shift from factors representing gross motor behavior to factors representing fine motor behavior. In the first analysis, factors were found representing right and left side activity. These factors are replaced in the second analysis by factors representing fine motor skills and tremor, respectively. This could mean that improvement in gross motor skills has occurred to sufficient degree that variables which were previously masked by gross motor impairment are now more easily identified.

This finding could also be interpreted to mean that before operation there was a disparity in amount of involvement between the two sides. Improvement in the contralateral fine skills may have eliminated the sidedness component so that fine skills appeared as a separate factor.

TABLE 3.   Mean Values of Behavioral Ratings, Analyses I and II

VARIABLE NO.	I	II
1	4.62	5.51
2	2.64	4.08
3	2.65	4.04
4	4.65	5.53
5	4.64	5.42
6	5.01	5.80
7	5.21	6.26
8	4.92	6.00
9	4.58	5.57
10	5.23	6.04
11	4.18	5.87
12	5.15	5.59
13	4.60	4.97
14	4.43	5.34
15	3.95	4.92
16	3.86	4.94
17	5.26	6.22
18	5.12	6.05
19	5.10	5.91
20	4.84	5.56
21	4.87	5.47
22	5.38	6.22
23	4.64	5.60
24	7.32	7.70
25	5.66	6.60
26	5.72	6.71
27	7.01	7.84
28	7.25	7.48

Evidence for the former position is given by a comparison of the mean values for all variables, pre-and-post surgery. Examination of the mean values in Table 3 indicates that (1) improvement was present on all variables from pre-to post-surgery; (2) the mean improvement in gross motor skills (variables 1–9 and 23) was 1.06 whereas improvement in fine motor skills (variables 10–22 and 24–28) was 0.75. While this could represent a differential change that has occurred, it is also possible that this represents increased attention on the part of the judges to fine motor skills which were masked in the initial rating by the severity of the defect in gross motor performance.

As an illustration of the meaningfulness of the factor analysis, data on two of the patients will be presented in some detail.

Patient #10 improved markedly after surgery and patient #47 showed some drop in functioning following surgery. Table 4 presents the mean values on each variable for these patients.

Patient #10 showed marked improvement on all but two of the 28 variables and no drop in function on the remaining two (note that the two variables remaining unchanged were rated as normal initially). Patient #47 improved in respect of 11 of the variables, remained constant in two variables and showed a deterioration of function in the remaining 15 variables. The relationship of the factor structure to the change in performance is shown by the factor scores.

As part of each factor analysis, factor scores were obtained for each patient on the five rotated factors. A patient's factor score can be regarded as the result of a multiple regression equation of the variables on the factor, with the factor loading serving as the regression coefficient. By use of this technique, those variables with the highest loadings on a factor will contribute most to the determination of the final score. The score itself

TABLE 4. Mean Values of Behavioral Ratings, Pre-operative and Post-operative, for Two Patients

| VARIABLE NO. | PATIENT ≠ 10 | | PATIENT ≠ 47 | |
	Pre	Post	Pre	Post
1	4.11	6.77	3.88	3.11
2	2.55	5.00	1.22	2.11
3	4.33	7.00	1.44	2.00
4	5.00	7.33	4.44	2.77
5	5.22	7.11	4.44	2.77
6	5.11	7.33	5.22	3.88
7	4.33	7.11	4.22	3.66
8	4.44	7.33	4.55	3.66
9	4.55	7.11	4.11	3.44
10	4.88	7.44	3.22	5.22
11	6.33	7.55	4.88	4.11
12	4.77	7.33	3.66	4.55
13	5.00	7.00	4.11	3.88
14	3.33	6.77	3.44	3.88
15	4.11	7.33	3.22	4.22
16	5.66	7.66	4.66	4.44
17	6.00	7.88	5.00	5.44
18	5.22	7.88	4.22	4.33
19	6.44	7.44	4.55	4.55
20	3.44	6.66	4.55	4.55
21	4.22	6.55	5.11	4.55
22	6.55	7.44	6.22	6.00
23	4.66	7.11	4.00	4.66
24	7.66	8.00	7.22	6.77
25	3.22	5.66	3.88	6.77
26	7.66	8.00	5.33	4.22
27	8.00	8.00	5.33	7.11
28	8.00	8.00	7.55	4.66

can be interpreted as measurement of the amount of the factor for a particular patient. Thus, patients can be ordered with respect to their scores on factors.

The factor scores for our analyses are set with a mean score of 10.00 and a standard deviation of 1.00. Comparison cannot be made on more than the first two factors because of the change in factor structure. Patient #10 initially had factor scores of 10.00 (Factor I) and 9.90 (Factor II) while patient #47 had factor scores of 10.16 and 10.10. In the post-operative analysis, patient #10 now receives scores of 11.03 and 10.35 while patient #47 has scores of 7.97 and 9.99.

As can be seen by comparing these changes in factor scores with the values given in Table 4 these scores closely reflect the changes in the variables grouped within Factors I and II.

CONCLUSIONS

The following suggestions are offered regarding the procedures used here:

1. The high reliability and marked differentiation among variables in the original rating procedure presents strong evidence for the validity of movie ratings in assessing change.

2. Advanced statistical techniques such as factor analysis allow for a precise and efficient solution to the complex problem of evaluating the multivariate changes in behavior

that frequently occur as a result of neurosurgical procedures. This is not meant to imply that this is the only solution; other precise models of evaluation are also available. However, the factor analytic method does possess the advantage of specifying the pattern of change and the shift in importance of motor variables as is illustrated by our findings.

3. Approaches to evaluation such as the one used in this paper allow the development and investigation of further hypotheses concerning the differential effects of various lesion sites, the development of predictive equations concerning suitability of a given surgical procedure and the evaluation of social and psychological variables in relation to the motor ratings.

4. Statistical models allow the examination and testing of the validity of rational groupings of variables. For example, the emergence of tremor and fine motor skill factors in the second analysis is a result which would not necessarily have been identified by a rational classification of our motor ratings.

SUMMARY

Factor analytic procedures were applied to ratings of motor performance of two groups of patients with a diagnosis of Parkinsonism. The first analysis, prior to surgery, revealed the presence of five principal factors: general gross motor efficiency, speech, right side activity, lower limb tremor, and left side activity. The second analysis, following surgery, also revealed the factors of general gross motor efficiency and speech. In the second analysis there were three new factors: tremor, fine motor skills, and finger movement. A comparison of patients' factor scores with the changes present in the original ratings indicates a high degree of validity for this approach to the evaluation of behavioral change as the result of surgery.

REFERENCES

Levin, G., Feinstein, B., Kreul, E. J., Alberts, W. W., and Wright, E. W., Jr.: Stereotaxic surgery for parkinsonism: a method of evaluation and clinical results, *J. Neurosurg.* **18,** 210, 1961.
Feinstein, B., Alberts, W. W., Wright, E. W., Jr., and Levin, G.: A stereotaxic technique in man allowing multiple spatial and temporal approaches to intracranial targets, *J. Neurosurg.* **17,** 708, 1960.
Harman, H. H.: *Modern Factor Analysis,* University of Chicago Press, 1960.

What sort of commentary can be made about these results? First of all, note that much of the interpretation is arbitrary. In evaluating the meaningfulness of our results, we made some arbitrary decisions as to when a factor loading was of sufficient size to be considered meaningful. Another research worker familiar with this area of research might well examine our data and conclude that some of our emphases and interpretations are unwarranted. Selecting a different level at which a factor loading is considered as meaningful could change some of our interpretations considerably. Similarly, another researcher could examine our interpretation of Factor IV and conclude that our explanation does not fit with his view of the data. Factors, as is true of any statistical quantity, do not interpret themselves, nor do they define their own meaningfulness. The interpretation is the task and the responsibility of the research worker.

On the other hand, use of factor analysis allowed us to reduce drastically the number of entities we had to keep in mind in interpreting our data. It was suggested earlier that you try to interpret the relationships using the original set of intercorrelations. A few minutes of such effort should convince you that this is not a very efficient way to proceed and that making conceptual sense out of the data would be much easier if there were fewer quantities to deal with. The most important consideration is that the groupings arrived at by the analysis make both psychological and medical sense in terms of our knowledge and opinions as to what functions should group together. The factors extracted here make sense in terms of some of the patterns of loss of function that characterize Parkinsonism.

There is probably a temptation at this point to conclude that we have not learned anything from the factor analysis that we did not know earlier. This is not true. Although we may have suspected such groupings before the analysis, the process of factor analysis did serve as an independent check on our groupings and helped to define functional relationships. In short, it did what statistical techniques are meant to do—provide information about the correctness or incorrectness of a research hypothesis.

FOOTNOTES

[1]Further discussion of these methods can be found in R. Gorsuch, *Factor analysis*, Philadelphia: W. B. Saunders Company, 1973; H. Harman, *Modern factor analysis*, Chicago: University of Chicago Press, 1960; P. Horst, *Factor analysis of data matrices*, New York: Holt, Rinehart & Winston, 1965; and R. C. Tryon and D. E. Bailey, *Cluster analysis*, New York: McGraw-Hill, 1970.

chapter eleven

multivariate statistical methods

"Oh, you press the button down.
The data goes 'round and around,
Whoa-ho-ho-ho-ho-ho,
And it comes out here."

Many research workers in the social sciences are still unfamiliar with multivariate statistical methods. This is regrettable, because the development of these methods signals a considerable advance in knowledge over the majority of the methods we have discussed in this book. Unfortunately, in order to understand multivariate methods a knowledge of matrix algebra is necessary, and to carry out calculations without the aid of a large high-speed digital computer is almost impossible. For these and other reasons, many research workers in the social and behavioral sciences have avoided multivariate analyses.

Complexity notwithstanding, it is clear to us that multivariate statistical methods will dominate social science research in the future. The reason is quite simple: Studying one variable at a time, especially in the social sciences, almost always creates an artificial situation in which the research worker is forced to ignore other variables that may affect the phenomenon he is studying and base his conclusions on a restricted view of the data.

Multivariate methods, on the other hand, allow the researcher not only to consider multiple measures when studying a particular problem but also to see how these variables change in relation to one another. This provides a more complete and realistic picture of the phenomenon under study. The additional information gained represents an immense increase in the power of the methods used to understand a problem. Since we are seldom interested in just one aspect of a problem, multivariate methods allow us to study phenomena under conditions more nearly approaching their natural complexity.

Multivariate analysis, as we define it here, refers to any situation in which more than one variable at a time is studied under controlled conditions. We have already examined some multivariate methods in our discussion of the analysis of variance with more than one variable (see Chapter 8, pp. 124–128), and the article by Rohwer and Lynch); in the discussion of multiple correlation (see Chapter 9, pp. 156–157, and the article by Kaufman and Kaufman); and in the discussion of factor analysis (Chapter 10 and the accompanying article). These are all circumstances where multiple variables are examined and their interrelationships studied. In general, the techniques we will discuss in this chapter are extensions of such techniques as analysis of variance and multiple correlation.

Our presentation of multivariate methods will differ somewhat from our presentation of the univariate (single variable) methods. There will be no extended discussion of sampling distributions, assumptions for use, and many of the other considerations which occupied us in earlier chapters. To some extent this is because multivariate methods are still relatively new and some of their properties are not as yet known. However, the majority of the methods represent extensions of existing methods, and the requirements and limitations for the multivariate methods are similar to those for univariate methods.

There will also be no working out of examples. As mentioned earlier, understanding multivariate methods requires a knowledge of matrix algebra. Also, the calculations are of such complexity that showing an example would only create a great amount of confusion. Since calculation is not practical without access to a large digital computer, much of our discussion will refer to particular computer routines used to produce the results.

We must emphasize that you will find these methods more difficult than much of the preceding material. However, any understanding that is gained will be repaid with a heightened appreciation of the conceptual complexity that can be attained using these statistical procedures. With these methods, we can study the relationships among variables truly scientifically, as there is no need to distort reality by artificially isolating the variables from their meaningful contexts.

A total of four multivariate methods will be discussed: *two-group discriminant function analysis; multiple group discriminant function analysis; stepwise multiple regression analysis;* and *multivariate analysis of variance.*

These methods will be presented through the discussion of various examples we have encountered in research settings. Since a computer is necessary to carry out these methods, we will in the course of our discussion present some printed results generated by a computer, discuss the elements involved, and interpret some of the material shown. Hopefully this will give you a clearer picture of what can be accomplished using multivariate statistical methods.

PREPARING DATA FOR A DIGITAL COMPUTER

Before proceeding with the statistical example, a few words about how such analyses are prepared may be helpful. The observations are punched on cards such as the one shown in Figure 11–1, usually referred to as IBM cards. This type of card, which was developed by International Business Machines, is used by all the different types of computers.

For the computing system used by the authors (a Control Data Corpora-

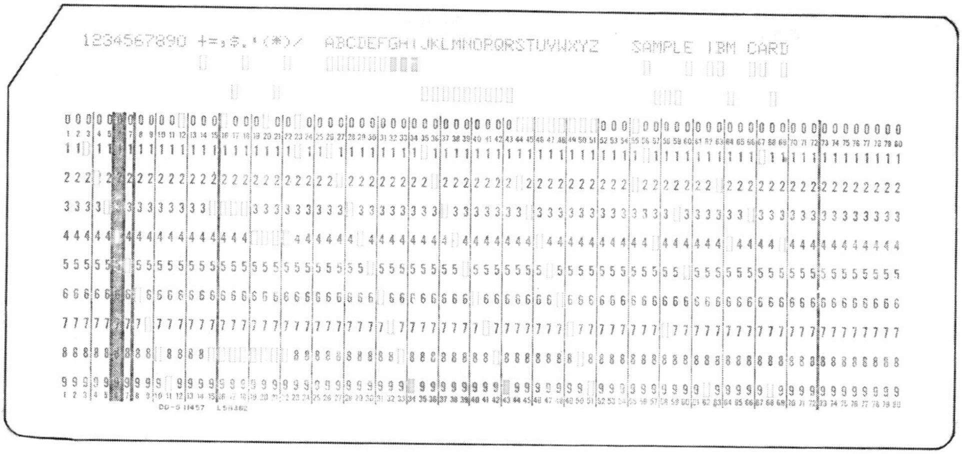

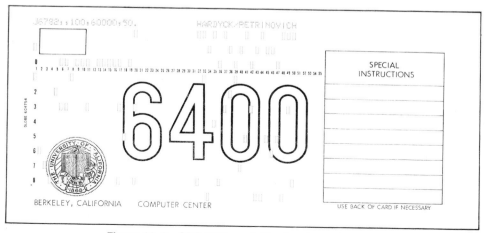

Figure 11–1 Punched IBM card.

tion CDC 6400 computer at the University of California at Berkeley), a computer run would be prepared as follows (see Figure 11–2).

The set of numbers on the 6400 card shown in Figure 11–2 is interpreted as follows:

J6782: This is the account number to which the cost of the computing will be charged.

,___,: If a magnetic tape were to be used in the computations to follow, the number "1" would have been punched between the commas. Since no tape is needed, this space is left blank.

100: This is an estimate of the time needed to do the calculations. The units of time are specialized for the computer and will not be dealt with here, other than to comment that 100 is equal to about 1 minute. In other words, you are estimating that your computing will take less than 1 minute of computer

Figure 11–2 CDC 6400 card. (See text for explanation.)

time. (Note: the actual time needed to do these calculations was 3.74 seconds.)

60000: This is an estimate of the amount of memory needed in the computer to carry out the computing.

50.: This is an estimate of the number of pages to be printed. Note that a period follows this number, indicating that no more information is contained on this card, other than the name of the person requesting the computing.[1]

TWO-GROUP DISCRIMINANT FUNCTION ANALYSIS

To illustrate how multivariate techniques work, we will examine a problem, first by univariate methods and then by the more appropriate multivariate technique. Suppose that a manufacturing firm has been accused of discriminatory practices in the hiring of women. The claim is made that women are paid less than men for the same work, even when women employees are better educated and have worked more years for the company.

The firm denies this and agrees that an analysis should be made of their payroll department as a test case. The variables that are to be examined are:

1. Number of years employed by the company.
2. Number of years of education.
3. Months of appropriate professional experience prior to being employed by the current company.
4. Job classification.
5. Pay.
6. Percentage of midpoint pay (This refers to the salary ranges for a given job classification. For example, a job classified as level 5 might have a salary range from $1000 to $2500 per month. The midpoint of this range is $1750. The percentage of midpoint pay is an individual's salary in relation to this midpoint. An individual earning $1000 would be earning 57% of the midpoint pay. An individual at the same job level earning $2000 per month is earning 114% of the midpoint pay.)

In our problem, the payroll department of the manufacturing firm has 73 employees—24 women and 49 men. Six of the women employees (25%) have college degrees and 41 of the men (84%) have college degrees. There are 18 women (75%) with no college degree and 8 men (16%) with no college degree. The ratios of men and women with degrees are clearly quite different, but such a difference between ratios is not sufficient to argue that the firm discriminates against women.

A univariate analysis of this problem could be done by dividing employees into men and women and calculating a *t* statistic (Chapter 8) for each of the above variables to see if the groups differ. This would be a total of 6 *t* tests, which must then be interpreted to provide an overall answer. Rather than take this approach, a computer may be used to perform a two-group discriminant function analysis. In this analysis, the two groups of men and women without college degrees are identified, and a procedure is carried out which produces the optimal linear combination of measures that will predict group membership.

The process of predicting group membership is conceptually similar to the procedure carried out in the ordinary prediction equations discussed in Chapter 9, pp. 150–151. In the prediction example discussed in Chapter 9, the problem is solved for one variable with a straight line equation of the form $Y' = a + bX$ (see p. 151 for examples). This allows us to predict an individual's Y score from his score on the X variable. In a discriminant function analysis, the task is to predict into which of two groups an individual should be classified. A discriminant function analysis can be done with as few as two variables or with an extremely large number of variables; the computing routine determines the maximum amount of variation that can be associated with differences between the defined groups, and develops the prediction equations that will predict this difference.

In our example—the problem of sex discrimination in employment—we assume the statistical hypothesis that it is impossible to predict sex on the basis of the measures of professional experience, years employed, pay, and so on. In other words, if there are no systematic differences on the measures, classification into groups by means of the discriminant function technique should be no better than we would obtain by tossing a coin and deciding on the basis of heads or tails whether a person is female or male.

The computer routine used to carry out these particular calculations (such routines are called *computer programs*) was developed by the Health Sciences Computing Facility at the University of California at Los Angeles and is one of a series known collectively as BMD, standing for Biological-Medical computing routines. The program used for the discriminant function is known as BMD 04M. The instruction card for the discriminant function (usually known as the control card or cards) is reproduced in Figure 11–3. In this analysis, we will compare the men and women who do not have college degrees on the 6 measures listed earlier.

The results of the calculations produced by the computer are reproduced in Figure 11–4, page 199. Initially, the program computes the arithmetic means for the defined groups on each variable and lists the difference be-

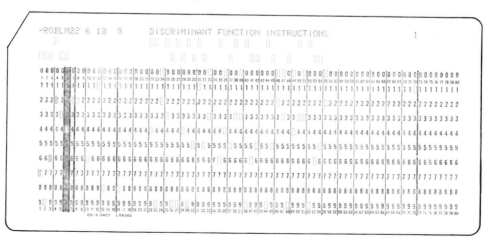

Figure 11–3 Discriminant function card.

tween means. The numbers listed under Mean 1 are the means for women on the 6 variables listed on page 196. The 6-letter code preceding each variable is an identifying code.

1. YRSCOMP = number of years employed by the company
2. YRSED = number of years of education
3. MOPROX = months of professional experience prior to current employment
4. JOBCL = job classification
5. PAY = pay
6. %MDPAY = percentage of midpoint pay

The next items of interest are the "discriminant function coefficients," which are listed in order for each of the 6 variables. These coefficients are the values used in predicting group membership and are an extension of the type of linear prediction discussed in Chapter 9. When only one variable is used to predict Y from X, we use the equation $Y' = a + bX$. Similarly, the discriminant function coefficients predict group membership from multiple measures. For any given individual, the prediction is made by multiplying the coefficients by the score on each of the 6 variables. The actual equation would be of the following form:

$$.01595\text{YRSCOMP} + .13681\text{YRSED} + .00040\text{MOPROX}$$
$$+ .03771\text{JOBCL} + (-.0061\text{PAY}) + (-.01408\%\text{MDPAY})$$
$$= \text{prediction of group membership}$$

After solving this equation, the computing routine then makes a probability judgment of group membership (based on the relationship of the predicted score to the means of the two groups) and assigns membership accordingly.

The statistic computed for this type of analysis is known as the Mahalanobis D^2 and is a measure of the distance between the two groups over all variables when the measurement units are equalized. The Mahalanobis D^2 is evaluated by means of an F statistic (see Chapter 8, pp. 123–126). The F statistic is used to evaluate the significance of the amount of variation associated with differences between groups. For this example, the tabled value of the F statistic at the .001 level is 6.18. Since our calculated value is 6.58, we conclude that there is a significant amount of variation in the measures used and that this variation can predict group membership—in this example, sex.

Even more striking differences are shown in the columns headed First Group (rank of women) and Second Group (rank of men). In our example, the first 18 ranks are composed entirely of the women employees. In other words, the ability to predict sex from the measures used is perfect—no member of any group is misclassified.

To appreciate this, consider what would happen if the groups were classified on the basis of chance. Since there are 8 men and 18 women in this sample, the probability of selecting a woman for Group 1 by chance is equal to 18 divided by 26, which equals .6923077. The probability that all 18 women would be placed in Group I by chance is equal to $(.6923077)^{18}$ or .00133470.

```
BMD04M - DISCRIMINANT ANALYSIS-TWO GROUPS - VERSION OF MAY  26, 1964
HEALTH SCIENCES COMPUTING FACILITY, UCLA

PROBLEM NO.  03
NUMBER OF VARIABLES    6

VARIABLE MEANS BY GROUP AND DIFFERENCE IN MEANS
VARIABLE        MEAN 1          MEAN 2          DIFFERENCE
YRSCOMP  1       5.61111         5.87500          -.26389
YRSED    2      13.05556        12.25000           .80556
MOPROX   3      93.16667       167.25000         -74.08333
JOBCL    4       6.27778         7.37500          -1.09722
PAY      5    1036.38889      1310.00000        -273.61111
%MDPAY   6      81.12778        93.50000         -12.37222
```

```
SUM OF PRODUCTS OF DEV. FROM MEANS
    655.16276     -20.36111    1739.41667      137.31944    17072.72222       243.39444
    -20.36111      12.44444     508.33333       -2.02778      434.61111        30.97222
   1739.41667     508.33333  284364.00000     3648.41667   505859.83333      7658.31667
    137.31944      -2.02778    3648.41667      187.48611    18201.05556        34.26111
  17072.72222     434.61111  505859.83333    18201.05556  2057628.27778     17352.30556
    243.39444      30.97222    7658.31667       34.26111    17352.30556      1016.75611
```

```
INVERSE OF SUM OF PRODUCTS OF DEV. FROM MEANS
     .00258       .00526        .00005         .00307       -.00006       -.00025
     .00526       .10480       -.00007         .01955       -.00021       -.00094
     .00005      -.00007        .00001         .00035       -.00001        .00000
     .00307       .01955        .00035         .11514       -.00125        .01344
    -.00006      -.00021       -.00001        -.00125        .00001       -.00014
    -.00025      -.00094        .00000         .01344       -.00014        .00303
```

```
DISCRIMINANT FUNCTION COEFFICIENTS
     .01595       .13681        .00040         .03771       -.00061       -.01408

MAHALANOBIS DSQUARE=        9.00911

F( 6, 19)=         5.58358
```

```
POP. NO.     SAMPLE SIZE       MEAN Z          VARIANCE Z        STD. DEV. Z
   1             18             .37729           .01797             .13404
   2              8             .00191           .00999             .09995
```

```
         FIRST GROUP      SECOND GROUP     FIRST GROUP   SECOND GROUP
RANK       VALUES           VALUES          ITEM NO.      ITEM NO.
  1         .74807                             14
  2         .54311                             14
  3         .54246                              3
  4         .45936                              2
  5         .42982                              4
  6         .41915                             18
  7         .40070                             16
  8         .39358                             11
  9         .33604                             13
 10         .32707                             10
 11         .32578                             17
 12         .31428                              1
                                                7
```

```
 13         .29077                                            12
 14         .28167                                             9
 15         .27888                                            15
 16         .26531                                             6
 17         .23252                                             8
 18         .20281                                             5
 19                          .13846                                         3
 20                          .02530                                         2
 21                          .04555                                         7
 22                          .04317                                         5
 23                          .02291                                         4
 24                         -.03157                                         8
 25                         -.08438                                         6
 26                         -.18423                                         1
```

Figure 11–4 Computer output for two-group discriminant function analysis.

What can we conclude from this analysis? We have shown that it is possible to predict perfectly group membership on the basis of the measures used. In relation to this, examination of the means for each of the measures shows that the women have worked longer for the company, have slightly more education, have much less professional experience, are paid less, have lower job classifications, and earn a lower percentage of midpoint pay. Unless a substantial argument can be made that the months of professional experience (the only variable on which men have the higher value) justifies the other differences, we would conclude that there is a good deal of evidence for discriminatory hiring practices against women.

If we now wish to check our results on a second sample of employees, we could select another department within the company, perhaps another office department, take the same 6 measures that were used in the first study, and apply the equations to all individuals under the condition that we do not know which are men and which are women. If we are still able to separate the sexes on a second sample, we would conclude that the hiring practices of the entire company are characterized by sexual discrimination.

DISCRIMINANT FUNCTION ANALYSIS OF MULTIPLE GROUPS

The two-group discriminant function analysis just discussed can be generalized to allow classification of multiple groups. As an example, let us use some data from a study of problem-solving ability in children growing up in three different environmental settings, and attempt to predict the environmental settings in which the children live. In our example, a total of 9 measures of problem-solving ability were taken on 271 children: 91 living in an isolated farm area where they do not see other children (other than siblings) until they begin school; 91 living in a small village; and 89 living in a medium sized city.

An analysis of variance of the three groups (see Chapter 8) indicates that there is a significant amount of variation associated with differences in environmental setting as compared to differences present within the various groups. However, we would like to know more than the fact that significant differences are present for all the tests given (note that this requires 9 separate univariate analyses of variance; one for each measure). We would like to know if there is some combination of measures that will allow us to predict membership in the three groups.

To calculate this, we again use a BMD computing routine—for this problem, the routine known as BMD 05M *(discriminant analysis for multiple groups).* (See Figure 11–5.)

The computing instructions will not be shown here since the process is quite similar to that shown for the two-group example. The groups are identified and the computing routine again calculates the optimal combination of measures to identify group membership. The first part of the computer print (known as *computer output*) again lists the means for each group on each measure. The statistic is again a version of the Mahalanobis D^2, which is referred to in the output as the "generalized Mahalanobis D^2." The value of D^2 is 105.80835, and can be interpreted with reference to a different type of statistical table from that of the previous example—the statistic known as chi-square (see Chapter 8, p. 139 for a discussion of chi-square). For 18 degrees of freedom, the tabled value of chi-square at the .001 level is equal to 42.31. There is clearly a significant amount of variation in the measures, which is associated with differences between environmental groups, since our obtained value of 105.80835 far exceeds the tabled value of 42.31.

The coefficients for the 9 measures for each group are then printed. The process of solving the equation is similar to that described for the two-group example and will not be repeated here. The next section, entitled "evaluation of classification functions for each case," indicates how each person is classified. The prediction equations are solved for each person and the probability of that person's being a member of Group 1, 2, or 3 is calculated. The person is then assigned to the group on the basis of this probability. For the first subject (case #1) the largest probability is .55848 for Group 1 and the subject is accordingly classified as a member of Group 1—children from the isolated farm area. The classifications and probabilities are shown only for the first 20 subjects, since there is little purpose here in printing out the full table for all 271 children. The "classification matrix" at the end provides us with a summary of the overall accuracy of group membership classification. For this example, the number of subjects in each group is sufficiently close to make unnecessary the computing of probabilities of assignment by chance. A chance level of classification would be 33%. Examining the frequencies for Group 1, we find that 49 out of 91 persons were accurately classified, a gain of 21% over chance. For Group 2, the accuracy is poor: only 35 out of 91, or 6% over chance. For Group 3, the accuracy is best of all: 60 out of 89, or 35% improvement over chance. We can conclude that although our ability to predict membership is far from the phenomenal result found for our first example, in which prediction was perfect, our ability to identify environmental groups on the basis of the tests used *is* a great improvement over chance alone.

The accuracy of the predictions obtained here is not as phenomenal as that for the predictions in the two-group problem. However, the analysis serves to sharpen our focus in continuing research on problems such as this one. From this analysis, we have learned that there are characteristics of the measures used that help to identify differences between groups. We can now continue research and attempt to determine what specific characteristics of the measures used are most effective in detecting differences between the groups. In doing this, we hope to understand the characteristics that differentiate the groups and to determine the implications of these findings for theories of children's learning, problem-solving ability, and thinking. The multiple discriminant function analysis was useful here in that it enabled us to determine those variables that were most important in discriminating between the groups. Clearly there would be no point in simply identifying the groups, since we already know which children belong in which group. However, use of the discrimination function techniques allows us to find exactly which measures are most effective in determining differences between the groups, thus providing direction for future studies.

STEPWISE MULTIPLE REGRESSION

In Chapter 9, the concepts of regression and correlation were discussed at some length, and the technique of multiple correlation was discussed in the text and used in the accompanying article by Kaufman and Kaufman. The technique of stepwise multiple regression combines the multiple regression method with an F test to produce a powerful method of estimating the accuracy with which a set of measures can be used in combination to predict another measure.

To appreciate the relationship of correlation and analysis of variance, it is useful to think of a correlation as an index of the amount of variation in one variable that is associated with variation in another variable. To the extent that two sets of variation are associated, one set can then be predicted from the other. In the analysis of variance, the total variation present in a set of measurements is separated into two components: variation within groups and variation between groups (review Chapter 8, if necessary). In multiple correlation and regression, the variation present in a set of scores (which we will call variable Y) can be broken into several components: (1) variation that can be predicted from several other measures; (2) A, B, C, X, etc.; and (3) variation that cannot be predicted from any combination of these other measures. The ratio of variation that *can* be predicted to variation that *cannot* be predicted is analogous to the ratio of variation *between* groups to the variation *within* groups in the analysis of variance. Since the variation that can be predicted relative to the variation that cannot be predicted is analogous to the situation found in analysis of variance, this ratio can be tested with the F statistic just as the ratio of variation between groups to within groups is tested in the analysis of variance for independent groups.

To illustrate, we will begin with a univariate example. In the correlation and prediction example in Chapter 9, we predicted the height of a younger

```
BMD05M - DISCRIMINANT ANALYSIS-SEVERAL GROUPS - VERSION OF MAY 27, 1964
HEALTH SCIENCES COMPUTING FACILITY, UCLA

PROBLEM NO.   AG
NUMBER OF VARIABLES    9


GROUP              1              2              3         TOTAL

SAMPLE            91             91             89           271

MEAN SCORES
   1   CLSINC    2.51648        2.82418        3.40449
   2   MULCLS    2.48352        2.73626        2.94382
   3   MULREL    2.19780        2.28571        2.75034
   4   CONVOL    2.28571        2.81319        3.08989
   5   CINTVL    2.42857        2.74725        2.86517
   6   COCCVL    2.39560        2.57143        2.59551
   7   PERSPC    3.38462        3.47253        3.24719
   8   VEREGO    2.47253        2.84615        3.14607
   9   ROLTAK    2.73626        2.86813        3.28090



THE VALUE  105.80835 CAN BE USED AS CHI-SQUARE WITH 18
DEGREES OF FREEDOM TO TEST THE HYPOTHESIS THAT THE MEAN
VALUES ARE THE SAME IN ALL THE   3 GROUPS FOR THESE  9
VARIABLES.




FUNCTION          1              2              3
```

Figure 11–5 Computer output for discriminant function analysis of multiple groups.

Figure 11–5 *continued on opposite page.*

sister from the height of an older sister by means of the equation $Y' = a + bX$, where X is the height of the older sister, Y' is the predicted height of the younger sister, and a and b are constants which determine a reference point and the rate at which X changes relative to Y, respectively. We also commented that the correlation coefficient, r, was best interpreted by squaring it to obtain r^2, which can be interpreted as the proportion of variation in Y associated with variation in X. It is also possible to calculate an F statistic to determine whether or not the amount of variation in Y predicted by variation in X is statistically significant. If the correlation between X and Y is known, the calculation of the F statistic is quite simple, being given by

$$\frac{r}{(1 - r^2)/(N - 2)}$$

If we substitute the values from the example in Chapter 9, where the correlation between the heights of siblings is equal to .87 for 13 pairs of siblings, we obtain the equation shown at the top of the next page.

COEFFICIENT

	1	2	3
1	2.61755	2.86609	3.50126
2	2.03249	2.26058	2.20874
3	1.28670	1.07587	1.60653
4	-1.77915	-1.56419	-1.57442
5	1.80262	1.97155	2.02432
6	4.35221	4.38790	4.21389
7	5.83221	5.91744	5.43301
8	1.15194	1.48195	1.72069
9	3.47033	3.55462	4.09992

CONSTANT   -28.55571   -31.99963   -35.59365

EVALUATION OF CLASSIFICATION FUNCTIONS FOR EACH CASE

FUNCTION	1	2	3	LARGEST PROBABILITY	FUNC.NO.FOR LARGEST PROBABILITY
GROUP 1					
CASE					
1	.55848	.37705	.06446	.55848	1
2	.10877	.17686	.71436	.71436	3
3	.44463	.50010	.05536	.50000	2
4	.45611	.40104	.14286	.45611	1
5	.43759	.23447	.32794	.43759	1
6	.29050	.45745	.24505	.45745	2
7	.52400	.36725	.10675	.52400	1
8	.73625	.21085	.05290	.73625	1
9	.24933	.38772	.36245	.38772	2
10	.28443	.46954	.24604	.46954	2
11	.23242	.46551	.30107	.46551	2
12	.73459	.22576	.03965	.73459	1
13	.82846	.16484	.00670	.82846	1
14	.21623	.21926	.56450	.56450	3
15	.57447	.35163	.07390	.57447	1
16	.34579	.34605	.30816	.34605	2
17	.27975	.31702	.40323	.40323	3
18	.59493	.35347	.05161	.59493	1
19	.43410	.31140	.25450	.43410	1
20	.33361	.35939	.30680	.35939	2

CLASSIFICATION MATRIX

FUNCTION	1	2	3	TOTAL
GROUP				
1	49	23	19	91
2	26	35	30	91
3	13	16	60	89

Figure 11–5 *continued.*

$$F = \frac{(.87)^2}{(1 - .87^2)/(13 - 2)} = \frac{.7569}{.2431/11} = \frac{.7569}{.0221} = 34.2489$$

The tabled value of the F statistic for 1 and 2 degrees of freedom at the .01 level is 9.65. Therefore, we can conclude that a significant amount of variation in Y is predicted by corresponding variation in X.

When we use stepwise regression analysis, we are doing exactly the same thing except that we now use several variables to predict a single Y variable. Just as we use the F statistic to evaluate whether or not a single variable produces a significant effect, we use the F statistic to evaluate the degree of improvement in prediction as we add each of several variables to the prediction equation.

The logic of the method for multiple variables is exactly the same as that for a single variable. However, the computational complexity changes drastically. Computing a prediction equation for one predictor variable is a moderately easy task; computing the prediction equations with multiple predictor variables (as we have seen in the equation shown for the discriminant function analysis) is practically impossible without a computer.

To illustrate the use of stepwise multiple regression methods, we will use the data of the last example, in which there were 9 measures of problem-solving ability. In addition to these 9 measures, we have developed a new measure of verbal problem-solving ability and administered it to the 134 children on whom we obtained the other 9 measures. In developing a new test, there is always the possibility that you have only found another way to measure something already measured completely by your existing tests. Therefore, we would like to know to what extent the new verbal skills measure overlaps with the other tests of problem-solving ability. One way to do this is to attempt to predict the scores on the new measure by combinations of the other tests. If we can perfectly predict the scores on the new test from some combination of the previous tests, then we can conclude that the new test does not measure anything not already measured by the existing tests. We again use one of the BMD computing routines, BMD 02R (Fig. 11–7).

The means and standard deviations for all variables are printed at the beginning of the computer output. The 6-letter codes preceding each variable are, as before, identifying descriptions. The variable to be predicted is the last one. PRNOUN. The next step is the calculation of the correlation coefficients between all the variables. Once these are calculated, the solution of the prediction equation can begin.

In examining the correlation matrix, we can see that the highest correlation with variable 10 is variable 8. The computing routine selects this as the first predictor variable. The "multiple R" is actually only the correlation between variables 8 and 10 at this first step, and the value of .262 is identical to the univariate r between variables 8 and 10.

The significance of this relationship can be tested by the F statistic, as shown in the next two lines of print. The F statistic of 38.913 is clearly significant since it exceeds the tabled F value of 6.81 for 1 and 132 degrees of freedom by a considerable margin. This means that a significant amount of variation in variable 10 can be predicted from variation in variable 8.

The columns on the right list the variables not included in the equation.

The column headed "partial correlations" is of particular interest here. If you examine the original intercorrelation matrix, you can see that the variable having the next to the highest correlation with variable 10 (after variable 8) is variable 1, with an r of .249. If we now look at the column for variable 8, which is already in the prediction equation, we see that variables 1 and 8 intercorrelate only .119, which is less than they correlate with variable 10. However, variables 1 and 8 do have some variation in common, as indicated by the r of .119. The value of .21980 in the "partial correlations" column is the correlation of variable 1 with variable 10, minus the effects of the correlation between variables 1 and 8. The net effect is to reduce the correlation of 1 with 10 from .249 to .21980. The other partial correlations in the column are interpreted in the same manner. The general rule is that the more the two measures have the same variation in common, the more they will be reduced in size by the subtraction process. For example, variable 9 (which correlated .265 with variable 8, and .155 with variable 10) has been reduced to .03354 by the subtraction of the variation that variables 8 and 9 have in common.

In Step 2 of the analysis, the computing routine selects variable 1, since it has the next highest correlation (.2198) with number 10 after the subtraction of common variation is completed. The effect on the multiple R is to raise it from .4772 to .5148, and the amount of variation predicted (given by R^2) from .23 to .26. The F statistic is again calculated and found to be 23.615, which is significant. This means that a statistically significant amount of variation over that already accounted for has been predicted by the addition of variable 1 to the prediction equation.

The computing routine continues in this manner, entering new variables and testing to determine whether or not a significant amount of variation is accounted for by the addition of each new variable in turn.

Note, however, that the multiple R increases very slowly after the first few variables have been entered. The correlation between the first variable

```
BMD02D - STEPWISE REGRESSION
HEALTH SCIENCES COMP. FAC., UCLA VERSION 4/13/65
FSU - CAL VERSION 8/18/71
(IF ALTERNATE INPUT TAPE IS USED, SPECIFY TAPE3 ON
BOTH THE CDC REQUEST CARD AND THE BMD PROBLM CARD.)


PROBLEM CODE                        HUNPRN
NUMBER OF CASES                       134
NUMBER OF ORIGINAL VARIABLES           10
NUMBER OF VARIABLES ADDED              -0
TOTAL NUMBER OF VARIABLES              10
NUMBER OF SUB-PROBLEMS                  1
```

VARIABLE		MEAN	STANDARD DEVIATION
CLSINC	1	3.00000	.91766
MULCLS	2	2.81343	.79631
MULREL	3	2.39552	1.02612
CONVOL	4	2.78358	1.11963
CINTVL	5	2.82090	1.06093
CCCCVL	6	2.58209	.64071
PERSPC	7	3.41791	.76874
VEREGO	8	2.85821	.89403
ROLTAK	9	2.82836	.81827
PRNOUN	10	2.54478	.92269

Figure 11–6 Computer output for stepwise multiple regression.

Figure 11–6 continued on following page.

Text continued on page 212.

CORRELATION MATRIX

VARIABLE NUMBER	1	2	3	4	5	6	7	8	9	10
1	1.000									
2	.247	1.000								
3	.256	.404	1.000							
4	.351	.384	.350	1.000						
5	.154	.227	.342	.558	1.000					
6	.205	.259	.253	.387	.398	1.000				
7	-.021	-.019	-.011	-.027	-.073	-.052	1.000			
8	.119	.026	.012	.172	.044	.132	.262	1.000		
9	.110	.089	.010	.156	-.062	-.023	.079	.265	1.000	
10	.249	-.017	-.007	.173	-.030	-.045	-.122	.477	.155	1.000

SUB-PROBLEM 1

DEPENDENT VARIABLE	10
MAXIMUM NUMBER OF STEPS	20
F-LEVEL FOR INCLUSION	.010000
F-LEVEL FOR DELETION	.005000
TOLERANCE LEVEL	.001000

STEP NUMBER   1
VARIABLE ENTERED   8

MULTIPLE R   .4772
STD. ERROR OF EST. .8139

ANALYSIS OF VARIANCE

	DF	SUM OF SQUARES	MEAN SQUARE	F RATIO
REGRESSION	1	25.780	25.780	38.913
RESIDUAL	132	87.451	.663	

VARIABLES IN EQUATION

VARIABLE	COEFFICIENT	STD. ERROR	F TO REMOVE
(CONSTANT	1.13724)		
VEREGO 8	.49245	.07894	38.9132

VARIABLES NOT IN EQUATION

VARIABLE		PARTIAL CORR.	TOLERANCE	F TO ENTER
CLSINC	1	.21980	.9858	6.6502
MULCLS	2	.00478	.9993	.0030
MULREL	3	-.01463	.9998	.0281
CONVOL	4	.10531	.9704	1.4692
CINTVL	5	-.05845	.9980	.4491
COCCVL	6	-.02112	.9826	.0585
PERSPC	7	-.00371	.9314	.0018
ROLTAK	9	.03354	.9300	.1476

Figure 11-6 *continued on opposite page.*

STEP NUMBER 2
VARIABLE ENTERED 1

MULTIPLE R   .5148
STD. ERROR OF EST. .7971

ANALYSIS OF VARIANCE

	DF	SUM OF SQUARES	MEAN SQUARE	F RATIO
REGRESSION	2	30.005	15.003	23.615
RESIDUAL	131	83.226	.635	

VARIABLES IN EQUATION

VARIABLE	COEFFICIENT	STD. ERROR	F TO REMOVE
(CONSTANT	.61876)		
CLSINC 1	.19562	.07586	6.6502
VEREGO 8	.46853	.07784	36.2109

VARIABLES NOT IN EQUATION

VARIABLE	PARTIAL CORR.	TOLERANCE	F TO ENTER
MULCLS 2	-.05205	.9390	.3532
MULREL 3	-.07515	.9344	.7384
CONVOL 4	.03375	.6595	.1482
CINTVL 5	-.09488	.9755	1.1810
COCCVL 6	-.06612	.9464	.5708
PERSPC 7	.00856	.9286	.0095
ROLTAK 9	.01594	.9237	.0330

STEP NUMBER 3
VARIABLE ENTERED 5

MULTIPLE R   .5212
STD. ERROR OF EST. .7965

ANALYSIS OF VARIANCE

	DF	SUM OF SQUARES	MEAN SQUARE	F RATIO
REGRESSION	3	30.755	10.252	16.158
RESIDUAL	130	82.477	.634	

Figure 11-6 *continued on following page.*

VARIABLES IN EQUATION					VARIABLES NOT IN EQUATION			
VARIABLE	COEFFICIENT	STD. ERROR	F TO REMOVE		VARIABLE	PARTIAL CORR.	TOLERANCE	F TO ENTER
(CONSTANT)	.77883				MULCLS 2	-.03413	.9024	.1504
CLSINC 1	.20815	.07668	7.3694		MULREL 3	-.04773	.8404	.2945
CINTVL 5	-.07163	.06591	1.1810		CONVOL 4	.10491	.5920	1.4355
VEREGO 8	.47077	.07783	36.5826		COCCVL 6	-.03280	.8110	.1389
					PFRSPC 7	.00087	.9225	.0001
					ROLTAK 9	-.00747	.9163	.0072

STEP NUMBER 4
VARIABLE ENTERED 4

MULTIPLE R .5288
STD. ERROR OF EST. .7952

ANALYSIS OF VARIANCE

	DF	SUM OF SQUARES	MEAN SQUARE	F RATIO
REGRESSION	4	31.662	7.916	12.518
RESIDUAL	129	81.569	.632	

VARIABLES IN EQUATION					VARIABLES NOT IN EQUATION			
VARIABLE	COEFFICIENT	STD. ERROR	F TO REMOVE		VARIABLE	PARTIAL CORR.	TOLERANCE	F TO ENTER
(CONSTANT)	.78990				MULCLS 2	-.06555	.8353	.5523
CLSINC 1	.17816	.08054	4.8937		MULREL 3	-.06425	.8221	.5305
CONVOL 4	.09593	.08004	1.4355		COCCVL 6	-.05040	.7905	.3259
CINTVL 5	-.12462	.07929	2.4706		PFRSPC 7	-.00487	.9198	.0030
VEREGO 8	.45653	.07860	33.7420		ROLTAK 9	-.01112	.8882	.0158

Figure 11–6 *continued on opposite page.*

STEP NUMBER 5
VARIABLE ENTERED 2

MULTIPLE R .5317
STD. ERROR OF EST. .7966

ANALYSIS OF VARIANCE

	DF	SUM OF SQUARES	MEAN SQUARE	F RATIO
REGRESSION	5	32.013	6.403	10.090
RESIDUAL	128	81.219	.635	

VARIABLES IN EQUATION

VARIABLE	COEFFICIENT	STD. ERROR	F TO REMOVE
(CONSTANT	.92321)		
CLSINC 1	.18623	.08140	5.2336
MULCLS 2	-.07053	.09490	.5523
CONVOL 4	-.11277	.08333	1.8314
CINTVL 5	-.12369	.07943	2.4245
VEREGO 8	.45354	.07884	33.0892

VARIABLES NOT IN EQUATION

VARIABLE	PARTIAL CORR.	TOLERANCE	F TO ENTER
MULREL 3	-.04694	.7491	.2804
COCCVL 6	-.04267	.7783	.2317
PERSFC 7	-.00574	.9196	.0042
ROLTAK 9	-.00842	.8867	.0090

STEP NUMBER 6
VARIABLE ENTERED 3

MULTIPLE R .5332
STD. ERROR OF EST. .7988

ANALYSIS OF VARIANCE

	DF	SUM OF SQUARES	MEAN SQUARE	F RATIO
REGRESSION	6	32.192	5.365	8.408
RESIDUAL	127	81.040	.638	

VARIABLES IN EQUATION

VARIABLE	COEFFICIENT	STD. ERROR	F TO REMOVE

VARIABLES NOT IN EQUATION

VARIABLE	PARTIAL CORR.	TOLERANCE	F TO ENTER

Figure 11-6 *continued on following page.*

```
(CONSTANT     .93272 )
CLSINC  1    .19238    .08238    5.4367          COCCVL  6   -.04026    .7760    .2045
MULCLS  2   -.06479    .09970     .3020          PERSPC  7   -.00464    .9191    .0027
MULREL  3   -.04130    .07799    2.2804          ROLTAK  9   -.00961    .8861    .0116
CONVOL  4   -.11566    .08375    1.9073
CINTVL  5   -.11517    .08127    2.0084
VEREGO  8    .45198    .07912   32.6320


STEP NUMBER  7
VARIABLE ENTERED  6


MULTIPLE R           .5343
STD. ERROR OF EST.   .8013

ANALYSIS OF VARIANCE
                DF   SUM OF SQUARES   MEAN SQUARE   F RATIO
REGRESSION       7       32.323          4.618       7.191
RESIDUAL       126       80.908           .642


          VARIABLES IN EQUATION                          VARIABLES NOT IN EQUATION

VARIABLE  COEFFICIENT  STD. ERROR  F TO REMOVE   VARIABLE  PARTIAL CORR.  TOLERANCE  F TO ENTER

(CONSTANT  1.00417 )
CLSINC  1    .19459    .08282    5.5200          PERSPC  7   -.00231    .9160    .0007
MULCLS  2   -.05010    .10055     .2482          ROLTAK  9   -.01300    .8801    .0211
MULREL  3   -.02940    .07835     .2529
CONVOL  4   -.12016    .08460    2.0175
CINTVL  5   -.10638    .08381    1.6113
COCCVL  6   -.05568    .12311     .2045
VEREGO  8    .45537    .07973   32.6247
```

Figure 11-6 continued on opposite page.

```
STEP NUMBER   8
VARIABLE ENTERED   9

MULTIPLE R           .5344
STD. ERROR OF EST.   .8045

ANALYSIS OF VARIANCE
                  DF    SUM OF SQUARES   MEAN SQUARE   F RATIO
REGRESSION         8        32.337         4.042        6.246
RESIDUAL         125        80.895          .647

         VARIABLES IN EQUATION                          VARIABLES NOT IN EQUATION
VARIABLE   COEFFICIENT  STD. ERROR  F TO REMOVE   VARIABLE   PARTIAL CORR.  TOLERANCE  F TO ENTER
(CONSTANT   1.03302 )
CLSINC 1      .19507      .08321      5.4955       PERSPC 7    -.00226        .9160      .0006
MBLCLS 2     -.04928      .17110       .2876
MURREL 3     -.03964      .07868       .2538
CRAVPL 4     -.12226      .08615      2.0140
CLSTVL 5     -.10815      .08501      1.6186
CDCCVL 6     -.05717      .12402       .2125
VEREGO 8      .45823      .08240     30.8612
RPLTAK 9     -.01320      .09087       .0211

F-LEVEL INSUFFICIENT FOR FURTHER COMPUTATION

FINISH CARD ENCOUNTERED
PROGRAM TERMINATED
```

Figure 11-6 continued.

(8) and variable 10 was .4772; with the next variable entered (1), it rose to .5148; with the third variable, .5212. By the time the last of 8 variables was entered into the equation, the multiple R was only .5344. There is relatively little gain, then, with the addition of each variable after the first one. If economy were a factor here, it would probably not pay to continue using any variables other than the first one to predict the value of variable 10.

The process of entering new variables is continued until the results of the F statistic computation indicate that no significant contribution is made by the addition of more variables. The final multiple R of .5344 (and R² of .2846) indicates that only .286 of the variation in variable 10 can be predicted from the combination of the 8 variables entered into the equation. If we are satisfied that our tests are reliable, then we are safe in concluding that variable 10 is a measure of abilities not predicted by our other 9 tests.

MULTIVARIATE ANALYSIS OF VARIANCE

Analysis of variance has already been dealt with at some length in Chapter 8 and, as we mentioned at the beginning of this chapter, the examples (and the article by Rohwer and Lynch) illustrate one way to deal with relationships between more than one variable.

In the multivariate analysis of variance, it is possible to study multiple measures as well as to consider the extent to which the various measures are interrelated.

To illustrate a multivariate analysis of variance, we will examine two comparisons, using the same set of data used earlier to demonstrate discriminant function analysis of multiple groups. The variables are measures of problem-solving ability and of social cognitive skills. The tests were given to children aged 7, 8, and 9, in three different environmental settings—isolated farms, a small village, and a medium sized town. The design can be graphically represented as shown in the diagram below.

We are interested in knowing whether there are significant differences associated with environmental settings and with age. In the univariate model, we could carry out 10 separate analyses of variance, one for each measure, and

AGE

	7	8	9
Isolated farm			
LOCATION Small village			
Medium sized town			

assess the significance of each measure separately—a cumbersome procedure, both in terms of the labor required and in the process of trying to interpret all the separate analyses.

The computer program used to carry out these computations is known as *multivariance.*[1]

For illustrative purposes, we will consider two of the possible comparisons for the location and age problem. The first hypothesis tested is that there are statistically significant differences associated with different environmental settings on the 10 measures administered. The computer output for multivariance (Fig. 11-7) indicates that the multivariate F is equal to 5.6885 for environmental setting, a value which is significant at less than the .0001 level. We conclude that there is a significant difference among the groups. Basically, the multivariate F statistic is obtained from a set of linear prediction equations similar to those encountered in discriminant function analysis and stepwise multiple regressions. These equations maximize the amount of variation associated with differences in location.

The columns below the multivariate F value list, from left to right, the names of the variables and the calculations for each measure independently. The column headed "Hypothesis Mean Square" contains the estimates of the variation associated with between group differences on a particular measure. The first value in the "Univariate F" column is the F statistic we would obtain if we carried out a univariate analysis of variance on variable 1, CLSINC. The next column indicates the probability, or statistical significance, of the univariate F.

The next column, "Step Down F," is a more complex measure. It is a measure of the significance of the F statistic when all variation from the preceding measure has been removed. As an illustration, suppose that two measures which had a correlation of .90 were given to groups of subjects. If a statistically significant difference were found between groups for the first measure, there would probably also be a statistically significant difference on the second measure since the two are so highly related. For the "Step Down F," the first value in the column is identical to the value in the "Univariate F" column. However, the next value down in the column decreases in size from the univariate value of 7.5977 to a step down value of 6.0892. This decrease is due to the removal of variation that measures 1 and 2 have in common. Thus, we learn not only that measure 2 is statistically significant but also that what it measures is essentially independent of measure 1. The results for measure 4 are quite different. Here, the univariate F of 5.6900 is significant at the .004 level. The stepwise F value shrinks to 1.2301 and the probability of .2959 fails to reach acceptable significance levels. The reason for this shrinkage is that the variation accounted for by measure 4 is largely accounted for by the first three measures. Thus, we learn not only which of our separate measures are making significant contributions to the measured differences between groups but also the extent of the independence of the contributions they make to those measurements.

If we now look at a second part of the analysis, we can examine the extent of the differences associated with ages 7, 8, and 9. For this comparison, the multivariate F is 4.6428, again significant at the .0001 level. Examination of the univariate F values for each measure indicates that all but measures 6 and 7 are also significant. However, when we examine the step down F values, we find that measures 5, 6, and 7 do not reach an acceptable level of significance

L01AAG
L02AAG

1,0, LOCATION ONE, ALL AGES VS L0 2 AND 3 ALL AGES
2,0, LOCATION TWO ALL AGES VS LOCATION 1 AND 3 ALL AGES

F-RATIO FOR MULTIVARIATE TEST OF EQUALITY OF MEAN VECTORS= 5.6885

D.F.= 20. AND 232.0000   P LESS THAN .0001

VARIABLE	HYPOTHESIS MEAN SQ	UNIVARIATE F	P LESS THAN	STEP DOWN F	P LESS THAN
1 CLSINC	2.0631	2.8332	.0627	2.8332	.0627
2 MULCLS	4.2346	7.5977	.0008	6.0892	.0031
3 MULREL	9.6143	11.7194	.0001	6.1415	.0029
4 CONVOL	5.4502	5.6900	.0044	1.2301	.2959
5 CINTVL	14.7957	16.7042	.0001	10.1666	.0001
6 COCCVL	2.1073	5.4822	.0053	.3229	.7247
7 PERSPC	1.9682	3.5114	.0329	3.3343	.0390
8 VEREGO	4.6463	7.2815	.0011	5.3415	.0061
9 ROLTAK	5.8714	10.8250	.0001	8.2089	.0005
10 PRNGUN	6.6479	11.0490	.0001	6.8547	.0016

DEGREES OF FREEDOM FOR HYPOTHESIS= 2
DEGREES OF FREEDOM FOR ERROR= 125.

Figure 11-7 Computer output for multivariate analysis of variance.

Figure 11-7 continued on opposite page.

```
0,1,    AGE 1 VS AGES 2 AND 3 ALL LOCATIONS             AG1-23
0,2,    AGES 2 VS AGES 1 AND 3 ALL LOCATIONS            AG2-13


F-RATIO FOR MULTIVARIATE TEST OF EQUALITY OF MEAN VECTORS=   4.6428

        D.F.=   20.  AND   232.0000    P LESS THAN  .0001
```

VARIABLE	HYPOTHESIS MEAN SQ	UNIVARIATE F	P LESS THAN	STEP DOWN F	P LESS THAN
1 CLSINC	7.5083	10.3109	.0001	10.3109	.0001
2 MULCLS	2.6988	4.8421	.0095	3.3322	.0390
3 MUCREL	6.6913	6.1564	.0005	4.3022	.0157
4 CONVOL	14.7673	15.4169	.0001	7.7794	.0007
5 CINTVL	4.2154	4.7591	.0132	.4371	.6470
6 COCCVL	.4423	1.1506	.3199	1.0294	.3604
7 PERSPC	.3779	.6741	.5115	.5070	.6037
8 VEREGO	5.9472	8.8501	.0003	4.8580	.0094
9 ROLTAK	4.0944	7.5488	.0009	2.5128	.0855
10 PRNOUN	10.0507	16.7047	.0001	7.8352	.0007

```
DEGREES OF FREEDOM FOR HYPOTHESIS=   2
DEGREES OF FREEDOM FOR ERROR=  125.
ERROR TERM IS ON PAGE   0
```

Figure 11–7 *continued.*

under the step down tests. We can conclude that although the differences attributable to differences in age are significant, they are not very powerful nor are they as effective over as many measures as are the differences attributable to differences in environmental setting.

In our opinion, the multivariate analysis of variance is an extraordinarily powerful tool, since multiple conditions can be studied using multiple measurements in a way in which the individual effects and interactions of conditions and measurements can be assessed directly. We know of no other measures that give the research worker in the behavioral sciences such a wide variety of flexible procedures to apply to the complex situations with which such scientists must contend.

EPILOGUE

The material presented in this chapter on multivariate analysis has been more difficult reading than the rest of this book. This is unfortunate but unavoidable, since multivariate techniques represent a step forward in the techniques available to study natural phenomena. In our opinion, multivariate analysis methods will predominate in the future and will result in drastic changes in the manner in which research workers think about problems and how they design their research. These methods make it possible to ask specific and precise questions of considerable complexity in natural settings. This makes it possible to conduct theoretically significant research and to evaluate the effects of naturally occurring parametric variations in the context in which they normally occur. In this way, the natural correlations among the manifold influences on behavior can be preserved and the separate effects of these influences can be studied statistically without causing atypical isolation of either individuals or variables.

Note that we mentioned *theoretically* significant research. Statistical techniques are useful only for answering questions that the research worker wants to ask; if he is confused, no statistical technique will help. One danger of multivariate techniques is the tendency of the research worker to hope that they will provide answers when he has no clear idea of the question he wishes to ask. There is all too often a tendency to hope that the computer will solve the confusions and ambiguities that are present and somehow make sense out of the relationships of many variables. This is a vain hope. Multivariate analysis will not clear up confusion about multiple variables any more than single variable statistics will clear up confusion about a single variable. When dealing with more powerful statistical methods, it is just as important that the reasoning behind the calculations is just as powerful as the statistical method. Statistical calculations are no substitute for thinking.

FOOTNOTE

[1]For additional information about the computer programs referred to in this chapter, consult the following sources. (Be advised, however, that the instruction manuals for these routines assume at least an intermediate level of knowledge about statistical methods.) Information about the BMD computing routines may be obtained from Biomedical Computer Programs, University of California Press, Berkeley, California, 94720. Information about the MULTIVARIANCE program may be obtained from National Educational Resources, Inc., 215 Kenwood Ave., Ann Arbor, Michigan, 48103.

appendix a:

statistical symbols

Statistical symbols and notation seem to provide one of the principal sources of trauma in introductory statistics courses. There is something about the combination of Greek letters and mathematical signs that produces unreasoning fear. We have avoided the use of statistical symbols in our calculations for just that reason. However, there are some benefits to knowing the symbols commonly used in statistics, and the most common ones are presented below. It should be mentioned that statistical notation is *not* standardized and that there is a good deal of variation among textbooks. We have tried here to select the most common usage.

English Letter Symbols

a	the symbol used to indicate the intersect constant in a regression equation
b	the symbol used to indicate the slope constant in a regression equation
c	any unspecified constant
C	symbol for the contingency coefficient
D	the difference between a set of paired measurements
$\bar{D}$	the arithmetic mean of the difference between a set of paired measurements
f	usually used to indicate the frequency of a set of scores
F	the symbol for the test statistic in analysis of variance and co-variance
H_0	a symbol sometimes used to stand for the null hypothesis
H_1	a symbol used to stand for the alternate hypothesis to H_0
H	the statistic used in the Kruskal-Wallis one-way analysis of variance by ranks
n	the number of cases in a subsample
N	the number of cases in a sample
p	probability

p	proportion
r	the Pearson product moment correlation coefficient
r_b	the biserial correlation coefficient
r_{pb}	the point biserial correlation coefficient
r_t	the tetrachoric correlation coefficient
r_s	the Spearman rank correlation coefficient
r_{xx}	symbol for the reliability coefficient
s	symbol for the standard deviation of a sample
$s_{\bar{x}}$	symbol for the standard error of a mean
t	the statistic used in the *t* test of the significance of a difference between two groups
U	the statistic in the Mann-Whitney test for the significance of the difference between two groups.
W	the statistic in the Kendall coefficient of concordance
X	any score
$\bar{X}$	symbol for the arithmetic mean of a set of scores
Y	any other score in relation to X. Pairs of scores as in correlations are usually referred to as X and Y scores.
z	value expressed in standard score form. Standard scores for a set of scores are produced by subtracting each score from the mean and dividing the difference by the standard deviation.

Greek Letter Symbols

χ^2	chi square, a statistic used in frequency comparisons (see Chapter 8, p. 139)
χ^2_r	the statistic used in the Friedman two-way analysis of variance by ranks
ϵ^2	epsilon square, a variation on the correlation ratio to correct for bias introduced by the number of columns in the table
μ	mu, symbol for the mean of a population
Σ	"the sum of." In statistical notation, the expression ΣX means to add up all the X's (scores).
σ	symbol for the standard deviation of a population
τ	tau, the symbol for the Kendall rank correlation coefficient (Chapter 9, p. 171)

Mathematical Instructions

$+$	add
$-$	subtract
$\times, \cdot, ()()$	multiply
$\div, /$	divide
$\bigcirc^2$	square
$\sqrt{}$	square root
$=$	equal to
$\neq$	not equal to
$<$	less than
$>$	greater than
$\geq$	equal to or greater than
$\leq$	equal to or less than
∞	infinity
$!$	factorial

index

5 14 182